A
BURGLAR'S
GUIDE TO
THE CITY

A BURGLAR'S GUIDE TO THE CITY

GEOFF MANAUGH

FARRAR, STRAUS AND GIROUX   NEW YORK

Farrar, Straus and Giroux
18 West 18th Street, New York 10011

Printed in the United States of America
First edition, 2016

Library of Congress Cataloging-in-Publication Data
Names: Manaugh, Geoff, author.
Title: A burglar's guide to the city / Geoff Manaugh.
Description: First edition. | New York : Farrar, Straus and Giroux,
    [2016]
Identifiers: LCCN 2015034638 | ISBN 9780374117269 (pbk.) |
    ISBN 9780374710286 (e-book)
Subjects: LCSH: Burglary. | Burglary—Planning. | Burglars—
    Psychology. | Crime prevention.
Classification: LCC HV6648 .M36 2016 | DDC 364.16/22—dc23
LC record available at http://lccn.loc.gov/2015034638

Designed by Jonathan D. Lippincott

Our books may be purchased in bulk for promotional, educational,
or business use. Please contact your local bookseller or the
Macmillan Corporate and Premium Sales Department at
1-800-221-7945, extension 5442, or by e-mail at
MacmillanSpecialMarkets@macmillan.com.

www.fsgbooks.com • www.fsgoriginals.com
www.twitter.com/fsgbooks • www.facebook.com/fsgbooks

10   9   8   7   6   5   4   3

Contents

A
BURGLAR'S
GUIDE TO
THE CITY

1

SPACE INVADERS

The Man Who Knew Too Much

George Leonidas Leslie moved to New York in 1869, the same year the Brooklyn Bridge began construction. The city was still reeling from the effects of the Civil War, which had come to a bloody end only four years earlier; displaced families and internal immigrants with battle-scarred bodies roamed the streets looking for work, and the army's impenetrable forts and armories still loomed over distant neighborhoods like castles. Away from all the shadows and poverty, in an ever-increasing blaze of artificial light, Manhattan was lurching forward into the so-called Gilded Age, as industrialists, financiers, and railroad barons brought with them a rising tide of brick and lime-stone mansions, with elaborate private gardens, art galleries, hidden vaults, and ballrooms. The disparities in wealth and privilege could not have been more noticeable—or more of an open dare, an irresistible challenge, for someone freshly arrived in the city intent on leapfrogging all the darkness and dirt, conning his way directly into the comfortable halls of the well-to-do.

At the time, New York was just reaching the delirious pace of acceleration that would make it the global capital of the twentieth century, an icon of American entrepreneurialism and a real-time test bed for what a modern city should be. New technologies were emerging and interacting with one another in ways that had not—indeed, could not have—been anticipated. No one knew what form the puzzle of the city would soon take. The invention of the elevator in 1853 would have urban effects beyond even the most optimistic forecasts, sending buildings soaring into the sky, while an experimental pneumatic underground transportation system prototyped beneath Broadway by inventor Alfred Ely Beach would, years later, inspire the great labyrinth of the New York City subway system.

Leslie had been trained as an architect at the University of Cincinnati, where he graduated with honors. Always with one eye on the buildings taking shape around him, he would stroll past the buzzing construction sites of Fifth Avenue—supermansions built using so much rock, they were more like mountains than houses—and go for long walks along the city's docks, watching the boroughs knit themselves together as the elegant and monumental spine of the Brooklyn Bridge took shape. He was charismatic, well connected, and could have worked for any of the wealthiest clients in the city, from private bankers to financiers.

But his first thoughts upon arrival were not about joining the parade of design and construction on display, still less about how his own remarkable architectural talents might help to beautify the city for those who could never afford to live like kings.

His first thoughts were that he could use his architectural skills to rob the place blind.

What followed would inaugurate one of the most spatially astonishing crime sprees in U.S. history. Nineteenth-century New York City police chief George Washington Walling estimated that Leslie and his gang were behind an incredible 80 percent of all bank robberies in the United States at the time, until Leslie's betrayal in the spring of 1878. This would include the great Manhattan Savings Institution heist of October 1878, which netted nearly $3 million from one of the most impregnable buildings in North America. Leslie had been planning the heist obsessively, continuously, down to the building's every architectural detail, for more than three years—but he would be murdered by a member of his own crew before he could participate.

Seduced by the lavish lifestyles of his potential clients and future colleagues, Leslie gave in to temptation and began to misuse his professional training. To his peers, he seemed to have a long and successful career ahead of him as a designer of private homes, banks, and offices. To Leslie, this was not nearly enough—and either way, it was far too slow. Leslie was debonair and ambitious, talking his way up the social hierarchy and seeking out the owners of businesses and financial institutions, including John A. Roebling, engineer of the Brooklyn Bridge, and Wall Street financier Jim Fisk.

Leslie would wheedle his way into private gatherings, not just for the cocktails and social camaraderie, but to case the place. *Oh,* he might say to a wealthy businessman or bank owner at a dinner party, as if he had just thought of something off the top of his head. *I'm an architect, you know—I'd love to see the blueprints for your new bank downtown. I'm working on one myself and I'm having trouble with the vault. If I could just take a quick look, I'd be most appreciative. Do you have the plans here?* Through good old-fashioned social engineering, Leslie would thus gain access to key documents or structural drawings of future targets—a backstage pass to the entire metropolis—the way a car aficionado might ask to take a peek under your hood. No one thought twice of it—why would they? Leslie dressed well, he had been trained as an architect, and his illicit spatial knowledge of the city only continued to grow.

At the same time, Leslie went to work cultivating contacts on the opposite end of the social ladder: tradesmen of a different kind, and experts in darker undertakings. Leslie's secret weapon here was a notorious fence of stolen goods, the Prussian-born Fredericka Mandelbaum, widely known as Marm. Her eye for trickery and subterfuge extended even to architecture: she had a dumbwaiter installed inside a false chamber in her home chimney, where she could stash sensitive items in a rush. Rather than opening or closing the flue, a small lever in the fireplace would lift her hot goods to safety. In her own way, Mandelbaum was a Dickensian supervillain, complete with a labyrinthine lair on Manhattan's Lower East Side. Her thieves' den there boasted multiple entrances, unmarked doors, armed guards, and even a disguised access point through a pub on Rivington Street. These all led into a goods yard where deals and trades could be made.

More important, for Leslie, Mandelbaum owned a cluster of warehouses over the river in Brooklyn where she would store, hide, and sell stolen merchandise. On the receiving end of her unpredictable generosity, Leslie was given free rein to use those warehouses as a kind of architectural training ground for future burglaries.

Here Leslie's spatial skills truly flourished: deep in the vast interiors of Mandelbaum's warehouses, with almost no risk of detection or exposure, feeling safely isolated from Manhattan by the still-unfinished Brooklyn Bridge, he built his duplicates and copies at full scale. If Leslie could not obtain a set of blueprints, he would simply draft his own, depositing some money in the bank he planned to rob, then using his time in the space to look around and study his surroundings. Beyond his training and charisma, Leslie was preternaturally gifted with an eye for easily missed architectural details. He was able to see blind spots and vulnerabilities where other people might not look at all. Leslie could sketch building interiors and the dimensions of private safes from memory, building up a burglar's library of architectural documents far more exciting than anything he had studied back in school. He and his gang would then use these bootleg plans to guide their construction of exact models, like stage sets on which the art of burglary could be rehearsed to perfection.

Arguably, Leslie's gang was responsible for establishing what would later become the well-worn Hollywood trope of the *duplicate vault*: a detailed replica of the eventual target, assembled in order to practice and implement sophisticated methods of entry. Think *Ocean's Eleven*, *The Italian Job*, or even *Inception*, with those films' warehouse scenes full of architecturally ambitious burglary crews tinkering amid models and floor plans. Leslie set the template for this technique way back in the 1870s, constructing life-size, 1:1 mock-ups of bank vaults, buying black-market copies of private safes, and installing them all like a burglar's showroom in an archipelago of gaslit warehouses scattered around the cobblestone streets of old Brooklyn. Leslie's obsession with specifics extended even down to pieces of furniture that might get in the way during his gangs' impending assaults. He would arrange chairs and sofas, work desks and cabinets, in their proper places, then coach his team in the darkness with a stopwatch to make sure they got the sequence exactly right, without bumping a single table.

In short, he robbed the banks of nineteenth-century America by making copies of them, declaring replicant architectural warfare on the moneyed classes of the East Coast.

Always casing something, either for himself or because other gangs had commissioned him to design their next heist, Leslie inhabited a city of spectacular raids and speculative break-ins yet to occur, a world where criminal opportunities were hidden in the very architecture of the metropolis, just a different way of using its streets and buildings. Lines of sight, potential hiding places, how shadows were cast at different times of day, routes into and out of a bank vault, even the specific order of streets that led to and away from a chosen target: these were the landmarks Leslie looked for and noted. He inhabited a parallel New York, a wire diagram of every potential entrance and connection.

Leslie was so dedicated to detail, so confident in his abilities, that he would often case the interiors of banks both during business hours and long after: before his gang robbed the Manhattan Savings Institution in October 1878, Leslie had already broken into the bank twice, stealing nothing, simply checking out the building for himself and verifying that he had the correct combination for the vault door. This gives Leslie the air of an addict, seemingly unable to resist the lure of an uninhabited architectural space emptied of its workers, unable to turn down the illicit thrill of a bank interior that temporarily belonged to him alone, having realized long ago that the best way to commune with an architectural space was by breaking into it.

Leslie's gang augmented their rigorous training with clever visual tricks and social camouflage. Upon arrival in Dexter, Maine, for a February 1878 bank heist, he and his crew members avoided each other on the streets and rented rooms in different hotels so they'd never be seen as a group. Leslie then equipped them all with costumes stolen from the New York opera, ensuring that they'd remain unrecognizable during the commission of the crime. He had done this before over the years, once forcing a gang member—the man who would later become Leslie's murderer—to dress like a woman and serve as a lookout while his team robbed the Ocean National Bank in Manhattan. In Maine, the group's disguises included new clothes, wigs, and fake beards; a black stage screen was unrolled and carefully held aloft to help hide their burglary from the street. This tendency for flair transformed Leslie's criminal actions and the loose gang of confidants with whom he burgled into a kind of avant-garde, wandering theatrical troupe, an ingenious production crew whose work combined stagecraft, architecture, and cosmetic subterfuge in their quest to find entrance into the closed spaces of the city.

The group's peculiar genius for burglary comes across in small but spectacular details, memorably described by Leslie's biographer J. North Conway in his book *King of Heists*. In January 1876, Conway explains, the gang made their way to Northampton, Massachusetts, to rob a bank there. Leslie had already taken several trips to Northampton before the actual heist to study the design and layout of the town itself, even walking a variety of potential getaway routes. He had learned years earlier that architectural expertise is nothing without urban expertise: if you don't know how to get away from a crime, you might as well not commit it.

Here in Northampton, Leslie's gang turned their attention from *space* to *time*. Before they hit the bank itself, they broke into the lodgings of the bank watchman, to incapacitate him during their crime. If he was tied up, the group reckoned straightforwardly enough, then he couldn't stop them or call the police. However, anticipating the watchman's future narrative of the heist, which would naturally include details of when the perpetrators arrived, how long they spent in the vault, and, most important, what time they fled into the shadows of the New England night, they also tampered with the watchman's clocks, stopping or breaking them. The watchman and his family thus sat, immobile and clueless about how much time had passed, as if forcibly removed from the present moment, left to wait in a criminal purgatory. It could have been twenty minutes or it could have been two hours, but by the time they were found and freed, Leslie's crew was long gone.

Pirates of space-time, dressed in opera costumes, picking bank locks and assembling duplicate vaults in abandoned Brooklyn warehouses, Leslie's gang and their astonishing success rate set a delirious precedent for future burglaries to come. Leslie thus became both burglary's patron saint and architecture's fallen superhero, its in-house

Lucifer of breaking and entering. His darkest accomplishment, however, was hardwiring crime into architectural history, making burglary a necessary theme in any complete discussion of the city. Burglary is the original sin of the metropolis. Indeed, you cannot tell the story of buildings without telling the story of the people who want to break into them: burglars are a necessary part of the tale, a deviant counternarrative as old as the built environment itself.

Today, security expert Bruce Schneier would call Leslie a *defector*: someone who has used his access, training, or skills against the very people those talents were meant to benefit. Think of the doctor who becomes a torturer, the IT expert who becomes a cybercriminal, the corrupt cop who becomes a dealer. Leslie, the architect-burglar, the great betrayer, called into question one of the most basic requirements of urban living and of cosmopolitanism itself: the ability to live alongside one another without descending into constant fear or worry. That requires trust. For Schneier, when we lack trust, we need security—in other words, if only we could have faith in one another's intentions, then we would not need all those door locks and burglar alarms. What is a society like ours left with, then, if the very architects who design our buildings become the people most likely to break into them?

George Leonidas Leslie, the greatest burglar of the nineteenth century, poses a fundamental, perhaps existential, threat to the urban social contract. He implies that none of us understand how buildings really work—how the city operates—and, worse, that someone else out there has a better idea and is fully prepared to use that knowledge against us. By turning his architectural knowledge into a tool not for increasing the public good but for breaking into the city, he became a trickster figure at the birth of the modern metropolis, installing crime in its very structure like a Trojan horse.

Today, nearly 150 years later, burglary and architecture still go hand in hand; if you look closely, from just the right angle, every city implies the crimes that will someday take place there. Burglary is designed into the city as surely as your morning commute.

Pros and Cons

In one sense, burglars seem to understand architecture better than the rest of us. They misuse it, pass through it, and ignore any limitations a building tries to impose. Burglars don't need doors; they'll punch holes through walls or slice down through ceilings instead. Burglars unpeel a building from the inside out to hide inside the drywall (or underneath the floorboards, or up in the trusses of an unlit crawl space). They are masters of architectural origami, demonstrating skills the rest of us only wish we had, dark wizards of cities and buildings, unlimited by laws that hold the rest of us in.

Burglars seem to exist in *Matrix* space, a world where— to paraphrase that film's own metaphysics—not only *is there no door*, but there are no walls, roofs, or ceilings.

Burglary, in this sense, is a world of dissolving walls and pop-up entryways through to other worlds (or, at least, through to other rooms and buildings). After all, if two rooms aren't connected now, they will be soon. If there is no route from one building to another, a burglar will find a way—even if it means digging a tunnel between the two using discarded mining equipment picked up for cheap in California. Burglars reveal with often eye-popping brutality how buildings can really be used—misused, abused, and turned against themselves—introducing perforations, holes, cuts, and other willful misconnections, as if sculpting a building in reverse, slicing open doorways and corridors where you and I would have seen only obstruction.

For the burglar, every building is infinite, endlessly weaving back into itself through meshed gears made of fire escapes and secondary stairways, window frames and screened-in porches, pet doors and ventilation shafts, everything interpenetrating, everything mixed together in a fantastic knot. Rooms and halls coil together like dragons inside of dragons or snakes eating their own tails, rooms opening onto every other room in the city. For the burglar, doors are everywhere. Where we see locks and alarms, they see M. C. Escher.

In another sense, however, burglars are idiots, incapable of using a door when cutting through drywall for twenty minutes will do the trick. But then they'll get stuck in the insulation, or they'll trip and plummet through the roof into the wrong grocery store, or they'll accidentally set fire to the very place they've been trying so hard to enter (it's happened).

You'd be excused for thinking burglars have absolutely no idea how to use the built environment. It's like a perceptual disorder in which certain people can no longer distinguish solid surface from open space, door from wall—so, lashing out against a world they don't fully understand, burglars knock holes in the sides of buildings, or they rappel through skylights using tactical mountaineering ropes, instead of just opening the front door. They could simply walk inside—but no.

Like someone who doesn't know how to program a VCR, burglars fumble, curse, and hit all the wrong buttons, mistaking doorknobs for something they're meant to avoid, breaking glass, crawling through doggie doors, and displaying incredible acts of spatial ignorance, as if they are somehow incapable of getting from one side of a room to the other without injuring themselves or others. But maybe it's not their fault. Maybe no one ever taught them how to use a building. Maybe it's just neurodiversity. We could call it *burglar's syndrome*, a spatial disease, something that compels you to misuse buildings.

But let's settle, instead, on a middle ground and say it's some combination of the two extremes: burglars are idiot masters of the built environment, drunk Jedis of architectural space.

🜚

Think of the guy who used to crawl through pet doors to get inside people's houses, slithering in through openings no wider than a dachshund to rob Kansas City families blind. He was only arrested after he "emerged" one night, in the words of the local police department, to find an undercover cop car sitting in the driveway. Perhaps someone had seen his legs slipping through the doggie door, like an octopus squeezing through a hole in the hull of a ship, or maybe the fuzz had been onto him all along. Either way, it was over. His architectural adventure was done.

Or consider the man whose ongoing spree of rare-book burglaries at a French monastery "seemed like the work of the devil." He had found an old map of the sprawling architectural structure in a local archive, noticing one key detail, a feature everyone else had forgotten: a secret passage that led from the monastery attic down to a cabinet in the monks' library. No one seems entirely sure why the hidden route was there in the first place—perhaps for eavesdropping on colleagues' private conversations. In nearly two years, this mischievous burglar stole an astonishing eleven hundred books. He was only caught when the local police, not fully convinced these crimes were the work of Satan, installed a hidden camera.

Unbeknownst to the man, he had a kindred soul on the other side of the world in the form of Stephen Blumberg, an obsessive book thief and library burglar who amassed a collection of stolen works that was at one point estimated to be worth nearly $20 million. His many targets included the special collections of the University of Southern California in Los Angeles—which he broke into by shimmying up the chutes of an old dumbwaiter system formerly used for accessing the library's closed stacks. Deactivated long ago, the shafts were still there, offering an alternative system of movement hidden within the walls of the library itself.

Of course, there was also the guy who pushed himself through the drop-off box of a dry cleaner in the middle of the night in Moultrie, Georgia, only to be caught by the shop's surveillance cameras. We see a man in his late teens slithering into the store, well past daily business hours, wearing what appears to be a camouflage hoodie. On the video, "bits and pieces of him start showing up inside the store," the police investigator later explained, as if a procession of disconnected body parts had magically begun appearing from nowhere—a possession, a haunting, a poltergeist.

Or just a burglar.

Think of the man in Dallas, Texas, who wasn't happy with what he found inside one building, so he broke through a wall of Sheetrock to rob the cash register next door. It became a regular thing for him, a reliable gig: he returned again and again to tunnel from one shop to the other, compulsively. The store's owners later complained to police that the same man had "broken through the same wall at the store four other times since the summer," stealing more than $20,000 from the shop in months. It was, from the burglar's perspective, easy money. At this rate, from one shop alone, he could pull in $60,000 a year. If the only thing standing between him and the middle class was a few pieces of Sheetrock, why not? What's the point of work when you can just pop through a wall at 3:00 a.m. to collect your pay?

Think of another burglar, back East in Cockeysville,

Maryland. Before he was captured, the man became known as the "drywall burglar," like some architectural bogeyman haunting the suburbs. He would slice his way through the drywall of home after home, once raiding an entire block of town houses without ever coming out for air. He didn't need to. He was the worm in the apple, eating from one unit to the next—and the next, and the next—carrying TVs, laptops, and cell phones back with him through this makeshift excavation, this aboveground nest of tunnels punched through the suburban world outside Baltimore, a whorled halo of negative space left behind him like a vortex through which household goods would disappear. When police finally arrested him, they found stolen remote controls shoved into his sweatpants pockets.

Then there was a guy in New York who nearly outdid them both. He would break into an apartment next to a restaurant, then chip away at the wall until he could slip through and grab whatever he came for—in one case, some chocolate soufflé cupcakes. And a pork belly. And some ribs and a bottle of sake. When I got in touch with the Manhattan District Attorney's Office to talk about the case, I got a wonderfully sarcastic e-mail back from their press officer, who, while asking me not to quote him directly, said something very close to the effect of, if you want to write a book about a guy who knocked a hole through drywall to steal a bottle of sake, then be my guest. He attached the case files, regardless.

Or perhaps we could talk about the guy who police found hiding inside the wall of a bookstore just before dawn in the corn-belt town of Clinton, Iowa; unsurprisingly, given his choice of hiding place and his delusional belief that a bookstore would have enough money to steal, he was also busted for possession of drug paraphernalia. There's actually another man who got trapped inside a wall, at a JCPenney in Rhode Island, where he'd been trying to hide from police. He had burrowed deeper and deeper into the building like a tick, first through a ceiling tile, then sideways into the wall, before finally getting stuck there; the local fire department had to be called to dig him out, like pulling a human splinter from the retail subconscious of the world, an archaeological excavation in which a living man was disinterred, extracted from the built environment. Or think of the guy out in Oregon— one of my all-time favorite stories—who dressed up in a ghillie suit, a tangled mass of fake vegetation woven into nets, originally meant to camouflage military snipers by making them indistinguishable from plant life. Disguised as a plant, he then slipped into his target, which, of all things—because you couldn't make this up, it would be impossible to take this seriously in a work of fiction—was a museum of rocks and minerals. He was after their gold and gemstones. Simulating one kind of landscape, he broke into a museum of another—where he was immediately seen and arrested. Perhaps he should have dressed up like quartz.

Think of the nude boy in Milwaukee, Wisconsin, who became disoriented and trapped inside the air duct of the veterinarian's office from which he'd been hoping to steal some tranquilizers. The poor kid had clearly been born unlucky: he was left "naked and trapped in an air vent for more than ten hours," the local newspaper reported. This clothing-optional burglar had apparently been so frantic to escape that "it looked like a squirrel had gotten in there," the manager later told police. The metal was dented and the boy's knuckles were rubbed raw. Unable to find a window to squeeze through, he had thought it would make more sense to enter from above, so he cut his way into the air vent from a hiding spot on the roof; he then removed all of his clothing and slipped, naked as the day he was born, down into the building with a flashlight in one hand and a hammer in the other, like some surreal nudist remake of *Die Hard*. Until he got stuck.

Such stories are not rare. Think of the guy wearing fake dreadlocks who then magically, almost shamanically, "escaped through the ceiling" of a suburban bank outside Chicago. Like a stage act: one minute he was there, the next he was a pair of feet disappearing through the ceiling tiles. Only he didn't escape, you see, because police later found him trapped there, at one o'clock in the morning, and they had to cut him free, dreadlocks and all. It's a fate so common as to be predictable. Consider a burglar down in New Zealand who managed to hide (for a while) by crawling up inside the ceiling like a creature from *Aliens*. He could've stayed there. He could've gotten away with it. But when the police arrived, one of the officers spotted "a toe poking out of ceiling insulation." He nearly missed it, but the toe was there, like some glitch in his peripheral vision. The game was up.

The parade of body parts continues: toes, wigs, legs,

arms, whole nude bodies, sticking out of places where they should never have been in the first place. Think of the man in Lyon, France, who was busted because of his ear—his earprint, more specifically, which he stupidly left on almost all the doors of the eighty or so student flats he broke into when he leaned in to hear if anyone was home. An ear here, a pair of shoes slipping through the ceiling there: all these detached human body parts moving around on the periphery of the world, passing through walls and architecture, appearing for an instant then gone, intersecting with our reality like visitors from another dimension.

But they're just burglars.

Someone walks into one building and comes out another, like some larcenous variation on a Victorian-era parlor trick. People cut into one room only to emerge from the one next door moments later—but they do so on all fours, using doors meant for animals, or they squirm through holes in the floor like worms, like serpents, as if shape-shifting back and forth between species, between minerals and plants, burrowing their way into buildings before disappearing again through the ceiling in ways that architects would never have imagined nor planned.

People usually focus on what burglars take, but it's how they move that's so consistently interesting. Burglars explore. They might not live in a city full of secret passages and trapdoors—but they make it look as if they do. They have their own tools and floor plans, their own ways to get from A to B. They'll curl up inside refrigerators, climb through ceilings, use garbage chutes and fall twenty-one floors straight into the emergency room when they could simply have taken the stairs. They'll slip through porch screens and stow themselves inside clothes dryers till the police come busting in to find them. They'll open the wrong doors, scamper up shipping pallets instead of ladders only to cut back down through a building's roof, and they'll break into one shop simply to get better access to the one next door. They flash in and out of the world like ghosts, like neutrinos, a phantasmagoria of body parts from nowhere, a whirl of unexpected visitors and uninvited guests.

The world, it seems, is infested with burglars. Slice open the city and you'll find a dozen tucked up inside, like some strange new diorama at the natural history museum. Attics, basements, walls, closets, and crawl spaces; alleys, parks, sewers, streets, and backyards: all of these margins and peripheries, subsidiary rooms and edge-spaces, are put to brilliantly unexpected use by people intent on stealing things. Like disembodied stagehands—removing objects from one scene and placing them down again in another, dismantling and reassembling their sets in different buildings and cities around the world—burglars watch our houses in silence, awaiting their cues, professional moving crews no one actually hired.

We could start with any one of these stories, then, but each of them would take us to the same place—so we might as well trademark the final takeaway: *Burglars use cities better.*™ Even if, in the end, almost all of them get caught.

Operation Stagehand

This kind of spatial expertise cuts both ways. As burglars have chipped and slithered away at their self-chosen jobs throughout the cities of the world, the FBI have become twenty-first-century break-in artists extraordinaire, controlling the scenography of intrusion to a degree that would stun even Hollywood concept artists. The FBI's present-day program tasked with making sure that state-sanctioned break-ins go off without a hitch is code-named, appropriately enough, Stagehand.

Picture G-men dressed as traffic cops, (mis)directing cars away from certain streets and intersections; parking buses in front of mob-operated shops to disguise the lock-picking operation going down on the other side; even carrying their own collections of dust around with them in envelopes and vials, in case they disturb any dust-covered objects (or floors or tables or any other flat surface) in a target's apartment. They sprinkle replacement dust as they walk backward out the door, and as if it were fairy tale, no one will ever know they were there.

They call the team Tactical Operations, or TacOps, a distributed crew of government-sanctioned burglars—in the best possible use of that word, masters of architecture, commanders of built space—who have, over decades, developed all-but-limitless techniques for obtaining covert entry into the built environment. They anesthetize dogs, feed cats, walk around on twelve-foot stilts to install bugs in someone's ceiling tiles, and buy the exact same make and model of, say, a desk lamp that a target might also own, to replace even the most mundane appliances with secretly miked federal surrogates. They're like rogue shoppers duplicating your every move.

Stagehand agents will hide behind fake bushes controlled with umbrella mechanisms—pop-up shrubbery, like something out of Monty Python. They make it look as if the local phone system needs to be fixed, flipping up manholes and sitting on the street near orange safety cones, all the while doing nothing but conducting a lookout. They pose as health inspectors. They make 3-D models of the insides of locks. They sell ice cream from mobile stalls while actually engaging in deep surveillance. They even send themselves to something called *elevator school* to learn how they might hijack vertical transport through architectural space for their own crime-fighting ends— sometimes standing atop an elevator car for hours at a time, waiting for office workers or building residents to disappear, before making their move on a suspect's office or home.

FBI special agents have started their own garbage-removal firms and perfected paint-matching algorithms for touch-up jobs in case they scratch walls or leave marks behind. They put tape down where a target's furniture currently stands so that they can slide it all back exactly in place when the operation is over. Some even carry rakes— tiny rakes like those you'd use for a desktop Zen garden— to pull their footprints out of a carpet, erasing every trace of themselves, thread by thread, as they exit.

They'll do whatever they can to avoid snowy nights— think of the footprints—but, if necessary, backup special agents will arrive with shovels and, pretending to be concerned neighbors, clear all the snow from the target location, like a governmentally financed act of God. In fact, why not, they'll even continue up the street, shoveling snow from driveways and sidewalks as if nothing in the world could be more natural.

Easily one of the more outlandish stories of surreptitious entry I came across while researching this book comes from a book by journalist Ronald Kessler purporting to reveal "the secrets of the FBI." While breaking into what is described only as a Soviet-bloc embassy, one of the participating agents promptly died of a heart attack. Right there, he collapsed onto the carpet, his heart giving out. Not only did the other agents on the case have to carry him out, but his body relaxed in its sudden death to the grotesque extent that "his bowels emptied on an oriental rug in the office," Kessler explains. Not only did the team have to remove the entire rug from the embassy in the middle of the night, but they had to find a twenty-four-hour dry cleaner to fix the stain. Then, because the carpet would still be partially wet the next morning, they decided to paint the ceiling above it to make it look as if a water pipe had ruptured in one of the rooms above. Then and only then—improvised narratives piling on top of outright lies, newly cleaned rugs drying below freshly painted ceilings—could the FBI effectively rid the target building of their traces. Go big or go home.

Even when not acting as part of a federally sanctioned burglary supercrew, FBI bank-crime investigators and other law enforcement professionals tasked with solving burglaries have developed their own interpretive expertise, their own unique insights into the built environment: a body of spatial knowledge cultivated for no other reason than to understand the city more thoroughly and more accurately than the criminals they are trying to track. They will analyze a work of architecture, for example, not for its aesthetics or for its history, but for its security flaws or for its ability to yield forensic evidence—dust patterns on windowsills, footprints in the carpet, a second-floor window left unlocked. This means that they are often astonishingly attuned to overlooked details and vulnerabilities in the design of buildings, whole neighborhoods, and, as we'll discuss in the next chapter, even the transportation infrastructure of a major American metropolis. As any FBI agent can tell you, Los Angeles became the bank robbery capital of the world in large part because of its freeways.

In genre literature, the curious police officer or the detective who pays obsessively close attention to the details of our everyday environment is a mainstay; examples can be found everywhere from Agatha Christie and Alain Robbe-Grillet to whatever thriller is currently topping the airport bestseller list. You see this attention to architectural nuance in nearly every heist film. No other genre gets away with showing characters hunched over floor plans, gesturing intensely at detailed maps of buildings, arguing over precise sequences of hallways and rooms, pointing with incredible drama at the tiniest spatial detail. Even the location of property lines implies high drama. The burglars will unroll a set of blueprints, draw plans on a chalkboard, or scrawl a building's outlines in the sand, dirt, or snow; and the police will do the same. They'll consult old maps and talk to building superintendents. There'll be a close-up of fingers pointing at plans. People will diagram things. Maybe someone will even build a scale model. Suddenly, architecture itself is deeply suspenseful. It's as if the heist genre had been invented for no other reason than to dramatize the unveiling of floor plans.

In the real-life world of architecture and urban planning, however, altogether too rarely is this point of view— how humans can take advantage of the built environment's spatial opportunities for crime—taken seriously as a critical perspective on urban form. As we'll discover time and again in the stories that make up this book, burglars and police officers—that is, cops and robbers, good guys and bad guys, bandits and detectives, that eternal yin and yang of the world, its black and white, its good and evil—pay at least as much attention to the patterns and particularities of built space as architects do, and for far more strategically urgent reasons.

Having reported on architecture and urban design for more than a decade now, as well as having taught design studios on two continents on opposite sides of the world, I've found that architects love to think they're the only ones truly concerned about the built environment. It is equal parts self-pity and arrogance, despair and pride. If architects are to be believed, no one but them pays any attention to the buildings around them. But what became increasingly clear during my research for this book is that some of the most interesting responses to a building, whether it's a high-rise apartment or an art museum, don't come from architects at all, but from the people who are hoping to rob it. The people who case its doors and windows, who slink down its halls looking for surveillance cameras, who wait at all odd hours of the day and night to find rhythms of vulnerability in the way a building is used or guarded. They might not quote Le Corbusier, and they probably don't know who Walter Benjamin is, but they certainly have something important to say about architecture.

One of the most perceptive things I've heard anyone say about the built environment came from a man using the pseudonym Jack Dakswin. A retired burglar based in Toronto, Dakswin amazed me with tales of his extensive, homeschooled expertise in the city's fire code, explaining how the city's own regulations can be read from the outside-in by astute burglars, turning Toronto's fire code into a kind of targeting system. Simply by looking at the regulated placement of fire escapes on the sides of residential high-rises, Dakswin could deduce which floors had fewer apartments (fewer would mean larger, more expensive apartments, more likely to be filled with luxury goods) and even where, on each floor, you might expect to find elevator shafts and apartment entrances. He could thus build up a surprisingly accurate mental map of a building's interior simply by looking at its fire escapes, a virtuoso act of anticipatory architectural interpretation that most architects today would be hard-pressed to replicate.

His spatial knowledge extended far beyond individual buildings. Dakswin spoke in surprisingly granular detail about the timing of postal delivery routes in greater Toronto, of hotel block-booking practices during rare-coin conferences (once a favorite target of his), and even of the minutiae of insurance companies, burglar alarms, and electrical warranties. If there is a true urban expert, Dakswin's testimony suggests, then it is not a professor at an Ivy League school or even a policy wonk slaving away in municipal government; it is an anonymous burglar so well versed in the legal and spatial marginalia of his or her city that it's as if every room, apartment, home, and private business there is an open book—or an open plan, one ripe for use when the time is right.

Yet learning to think like a burglar—or a police detective—is very much not the approach taught in architecture school, and it is nothing at all like what is imagined by the general public as "normal" architectural behavior. Venerable architecture critic Witold Rybczynski, for instance, suggests in his book *How Architecture Works: A Humanist's Toolkit* that "the first question you ask yourself approaching a building is: Where is the front door?" But this is by no means the first architectural question many among us will ask; it is altogether too straightforward a query for a segment of the population. Some of us deliberately and strategically seek out, say, an attic window within reach of a strong tree branch or an unlocked storm shelter leading down into someone's basement, even a badly fit screen door that looks easy to slip through around back. Perhaps you even did this yourself as a teenager, just looking for a new way to sneak out of the house past your bedtime or to avoid the all-seeing gaze of your girlfriend's parents.

If so, congrats: you were looking at a building the way a burglar would. There's a bit of George Leonidas Leslie in us all.

A Burglar's Guide to the City

As the FBI defines it, burglary is "the unlawful entry of a structure to commit a felony or theft." Burglary is thus an explicitly *spatial* crime: it requires a perpetrator to enter an architectural structure illegally, thus differentiating burglary from mere theft, pickpocketing, or robbery. Sensing there might still be some potential confusion here, the FBI quickly adds that their own "definition of 'structure' includes apartment, barn, house trailer or houseboat when used as a permanent dwelling, office, railroad car (but not automobile), stable, and vessel (i.e., ship)."

So much for the Bureau's reputation for being neat and tidy—such a list clearly risks being subject to constant, ever more detailed architectural updates. Is a shed technically a "barn"? Is a dog kennel just a different kind of "stable"? It depends on which lawyer you ask. Oddly enough, contemporary burglary law reveals that some of the most intense—certainly the most consequential— architectural arguments today are not occurring inside the hallowed halls of academia, but inside law offices looking to redefine what a building is. Even the way the

FBI tiptoes around its own attempt at definitions makes it clear that burglary involves a fluid yet confusingly specific definition of architectural space: a "house trailer or houseboat" can be subject to burglary, for example, but only if it is "used as a permanent dwelling."

Nevertheless, to commit burglary you must cross some imaginary border, or invisible plane, and enter another clearly defined architectural space—a volume of air, an enclosure—with the intention of committing a crime there. Without walls and thresholds—without doorways, floors, and window frames, or even roofs, awnings, and screened-in porches—burglary would not be legally possible. It is a spatial crime, one whose parameters are baked into the very elements of the built environment.

To put this another way, *burglary requires architecture*. Not infrequently, only because of some aspect of a building's design is burglary even possible. A blind spot, a vulnerability, a badly placed window, a shadowy alcove, an unlocked skylight, a useful proximity between one structure and the next—the burglar sees this opportunity and pounces. Solving certain burglaries thus often has the feel of an architectural analysis. How did the criminal enter? Can we deduce from the method of entry that a person was there to commit a crime? In many states you can be charged with burglary simply for unnecessarily using a side entrance or coming in through the garage rather than the front door: an indirect approach to the built environment is considered legally suspicious.

So I wanted to learn more about how burglars see the city—what a town, a street, a neighborhood, looks like through their eyes, as spaces of seemingly endless possibility. I wanted to learn from cops and robbers both what the built environment can really do, equally fascinated and horrified by the on-again, off-again brilliant stupidity of the burglar's approach to architecture, with its X-ray vision of secret passages, spatial agents, and the porous world they inhabit together, where everything architects take for granted can literally be undercut, punched through, knocked down, or simply sidestepped.

Burglars, it seemed to me, are uniquely ambitious in what they want from the buildings around them—to walk through walls, to enter through third-story windows rather than through front doors, and to pop up from below, emerging from the city's sewers like half-dreamed creatures of local folklore. They are as magical and otherworldly as they are so endearingly incompetent, so stupidly unprepared for a world of well-policed walls and ceilings.

Somewhere between absurdity and genius, I thought, there should be a new guide to the city: an idiot's guide, a guide for people who can't use floors and ceilings the right way, for people who don't understand doors or windows, who can't even let the ground itself rest untouched without trying to dig a tunnel through it.

There should be *a burglar's guide to the city.*

2

CRIME IS JUST ANOTHER WAY TO USE THE CITY

Y ou want to see *The Brady Bunch* house?" The helicopter radio was crackling and I wasn't sure I had heard the pilot correctly. Had there been a burglary there? I tried to adjust my headset.

"You mean the house from the TV show?" I asked, pulling the microphone closer to my mouth. I began imagining some bizarre fictional heist involving Mr. Brady's personal collection of blueprints. He had been an architect in the show, after all; he could have had plans for the entire neighborhood. He could have been another

George Leonidas Leslie. A more interesting version of *The Brady Bunch* started unfolding in my head.

The helicopter suddenly banked right and we shuddered northwest across Los Angeles. L.A. is the second-most-populous city in the United States, yet what we refer to as if it were one place with a single, clearly expressed identity is actually a diffuse network of much smaller cities and distinct neighborhoods so expansive that the outer limits of Los Angeles County frame an area nearly the size of Rhode Island. This not only reveals the fluidity of the concept of a city—where a suburban landscape on a large enough scale becomes urban—it also suggests that cities of this type require a different sort of policing, and that they produce different sorts of crime.

The physical design of a metropolis—its public transit and its street grid, its climate and its topography—can inadvertently result in weak spots that only become clear when criminals take advantage of them, whether that's to commit bank heists, burglaries, drive-by shootings, or murders. This means that, to a surprising extent, the way a city was built can catalyze or help inspire certain criminal acts.

The reverse is also true. The various parameters that define a city—including the most basic details, like its size and shape—affect how that city can be policed. This can be as obvious as a water-based city such as Stockholm or New York City requiring a more active harbor division, or it can be far more subtle. For example, the impenetrable, fingerprint-like density of London has, in part, helped to encourage the near-infinite proliferation of street-level surveillance cameras, whereas the wide-open sprawl of Greater Los Angeles has led to NASA-sanctioned police-helicopter patrols. These distinctive forms of policing, in turn, affect the kinds of crimes that are committed in each city.

If there is a general law of urban criminality here, it's that cities get the types of crime their design calls for.

I was riding along with the LAPD Air Support Division on a routine night flight. It would be two and a half hours in total airtime, the duration of all LAPD helicopter patrols, but we weren't finding a whole lot to do. This evening, for good or for bad, had almost no criminal activity for us to track. The radio was silent. Our moments of highest tension weren't new crimes being called in but high winds blowing in from the San Fernando Valley. Rather than a night of aerial adventure, we just hovered for a while near the towers downtown before almost exaggeratedly roaring off after whatever radio blips finally reached us—a reported holdup of a 7-Eleven near Glendale that was over long before we got there, a fight of some kind in a park near USC that we never witnessed. Nothing boiled over or lasted long enough for us to respond, leaving us with nothing to do but kill time above the city.

Nearly an hour went by like this before the pilot got an idea. Feeling the need to show me *something*—to give this night at least some redeeming value for the backseat passenger—and having already heard about my interest in architecture, the pilot and his tactical flight officer quickly cooked up a plan. L.A. is full of architecture, they must have thought; famous buildings are everywhere.

So—why not?—let's show this guy the city. At least until another crime was called in, they'd give me an architectural tour of Los Angeles at night, possibly the most surreal such tour in the city's history, a flyby sequence of greatest hits led by none other than the LAPD.

First up? *The Brady Bunch* house.

The Air Support Division of the Los Angeles Police Department operates out of a labyrinthine building on Ramirez Street in the city's downtown, near the concrete viaduct of the Los Angeles River. It appears to have no real façade, but is instead a looming mass of utilitarian architecture tucked immediately beside the 101 Freeway, across the street from a Denny's. Approached from the back, via Cesar Chavez Avenue, it resembles nothing but a gargantuan parking garage ringed with chain-link fence and barbed wire.

After you've been cleared for entry by a security guard stationed in a small building at street level, you're instructed to drive back into an alleyway between two warehouses, abruptly coming to a series of half-hidden concrete ramps that soar up to the right through the parking garage. Finally, leaving your car behind on this massive apron of concrete and walking toward a wall-size mural of a police helicopter, shining angelic under fluorescent lights, you climb a small flight of steps. There, you ring a buzzer on the door of the actual command center for the nation's largest municipal helicopter fleet—and you're in. It's a bit like climbing up into an airport control tower, and in some ways, that's exactly what you've done.

The building's landing deck is the size of an aircraft carrier: a vast meadow of painted concrete baking in the Southern California sun. This makes the Air Support Division's HQ a kind of beached warship in the heart of the city. The inner sanctum of this megastructure is a dense sequence of small corridors and stairways, and even this at times resembles the guts of a military ship. Helicopter timetables and safety-procedure posters are tacked up on the walls, and an erasable whiteboard keeps track of who is flying what and when. I have never seen the facility crowded, although there are an awful lot of chairs, as if waiting for some future gathering. A TV plays nonstop, showing the news, weather, or whatever else the officers might want to watch before going up on their next patrol. More often than not, it's just relaying news to an empty room.

Anyone's geographic understanding of a city can be profoundly improved when given access to an aerial view—when the city is laid out below you like a diagram—and this is all the more true when your job requires you to survey the city from above, imagining getaway routes and potential hideaways, possible next turns and preemptive roadblocks. The officers have uniquely unfettered access to a fundamentally different experience of the city, in which Los Angeles must constantly be reinterpreted from above with the intention of locating, tracking, or interrupting criminal activity. This perspective reveals not only overlooked connections between distant neighborhoods but distinct possibilities for committing—or preventing—crime on a city scale. Police helicopters also come with special optical technologies, often borrowed from the military, including dynamic-mapping software and forward-looking infrared (FLIR) cameras. Seeing the city through this literal new lens can be transformative.

From a civilian perspective, however, the police helicopter is not necessarily a welcome sight. That the police can track us from above, without a warrant or any probable cause, has justifiably inspired no end of Orwellian fears about a coming dystopia of unstoppable panoptic control. In *City of Quartz*, his apocalyptic portrait of mid-1990s Los Angeles, author Mike Davis portrays the LAPD as an invasive "space police," a darkly futuristic force of winged overlords buzz-bombing whole neighborhoods across the city and scanning the metropolis from above with their helicopters, military radios, and geostationary satellites. As I was to learn on my helicopter flights with the LAPD, surveillance missions often occur at heights of ten thousand feet or more, making those helicopters invisible to the naked eye, even while they meticulously track a single car or pedestrian for hours at a time.

One of the most memorable moments in Davis's book is when he describes how LAPD pilots navigate the city: "To facilitate ground-air synchronization, thousands of residential rooftops have been painted with identifying street numbers, transforming the aerial view of the city into a huge police grid." With this incredible image, Davis implies that the police have stealthily redesigned urban space to suit their own needs, even painting our addresses onto the roofs of our buildings without us noticing, all so that we can be more easily corralled. To Mike Davis, we are not civilians; we are sheep.

Seen from above, however, the situation is far less intimidating. Those police-branded rooftop numbers from *City of Quartz* are all but nonexistent, for example, and all of the pilots and tactical flight officers with whom I spoke agreed that it is precisely the lack of such numbers that presents one of the main barriers to doing their job most effectively. The LAPD's "Burglary Prevention" page specifically suggests that Angelenos should "mark your address with large, reflectorized numbers on the roof of your building for high visibility to police helicopter patrols," clearly implying that most buildings currently lack this identifying feature.

On another flight at the height of summer, things seemed to be winding down toward the end of our late-afternoon patrol. I was flying with a different tactical flight officer, a prickly, no-nonsense woman in her midthirties who didn't seem to appreciate having a civilian along for the ride. But then an urgent call came in for Air Support, and we raced off to the north, the farthest I would go on these flights, all the way nearly to the mountains that separate L.A. from the deserts beyond. We were at the northern fringe of the San Fernando Valley, flying over a part of the city known as Pacoima, where a woman had allegedly barricaded herself inside a house with a loaded 9 mm handgun. Why she had done this was not at all clear—and it would remain unexplained to us—but the police needed to set up a perimeter.

This was an ideal opportunity, I thought, to witness how the Air Support Division could put its unique perspective to work in establishing the outer spatial edge of an event such as this, identifying, assessing, and describing the streets, directions, and nearby properties where, if the woman fled, she was most likely to end up. This was the anticipatory geography of crime, where the helicopter crew's job was to preempt any possibility of escape: to guess where the suspect might go next and to have police officers there waiting. This looked like a particularly interesting case because the street grid here was "out of sync," in the tactical flight officer's words, with the rest of the city. On top of that, she pointed out, the immediate neighborhood was also punctuated by strange, L-shaped streets and culs-de-sac, not only presenting a unique geometric problem for the tactical flight officer but giving her a narrative challenge in relaying which bend in a certain street she wanted a patrol car to head toward. (Her directions would be misunderstood more than once, leading to audible frustration on both sides of the radio.)

The tactical flight officer kept coming back to the name of the woman who had barricaded herself inside the house; she seemed distracted by it. The name had reminded her of something, she said, but she couldn't quite figure out what it was; I began to imagine that we were circling over one of the LAPD's most wanted criminals. While radioing down to an ever-increasing number of patrol cars filling the streets below, carefully arranging them like chess pieces throughout the neighborhood, the tactical flight officer kept saying the woman's name out loud, like a mantra, again and again.

Then it struck her. "Isn't that the girl from *Where the Sidewalk Ends?*" I thought she was making some sort of cryptic comment about the nature of the city down below, where any demands for walkability had long ago ceded the landscape to a metastasis of parking lots and home-improvement warehouses, but she was simply recalling the classic Shel Silverstein book.

"'Sarah Cynthia Sylvia Stout,'" the officer said, almost singsong, "'would not take the garbage out,'" and then she and her pilot were back on the radio, lining up cops, organizing a perimeter two, three, four, even five streets away. I laughed, hearing in her voice an unexpected weariness, if not actual boredom, as police officers fanned out through the neighborhood below, slinking into backyards, occupying the spaces between buildings, even posting a sniper up on a residential carport across the street from the barricaded home. This wasn't high drama for the tactical flight officer, let alone an opportunity to catch one of L.A.'s most elusive outlaws. "Sarah Cynthia Sylvia Stout," she muttered again, looking down at the world beneath us. "I wonder if she's ever read Shel Silverstein." She was peering through binoculars as she said this, but actually appeared to be focusing on the mountain landscape to our immediate north. I got the impression this was the last thing in the world either she or the pilot wanted to be doing.

The feeling here—that armed home barricades and tactical police geometries coordinated from above in order to lock down an entire neighborhood were such run-of-the-mill activities that they inspired memories of a children's book by Shel Silverstein—only increased when the pilot suddenly widened his orbit. We had been flying in a nauseatingly tight circle over the suspect's barricaded home, and the change in pattern helped clear my head. The pilot called my attention to a huge Oakland Raiders logo extravagantly tiled into the bottom of someone's swimming pool. "Do you see that?" he deadpanned. "There's probably half a dozen of those around here. If we get out of here early enough, I'll show you some more. Some people must really like football." He didn't sound excited by this; he sounded bored.

Later, when we were back on the ground, I would learn he was a die-hard ice hockey fan and that, a year earlier, when the L.A. Kings had won the Stanley Cup, he'd flown the trophy around the city as a ride-along in his helicopter, strapped into the back with seat belts. He took the Stanley Cup all over Greater Los Angeles for two and a half hours, in a kind of aerial victory lap, all the while following suspicious vehicles, tracking suspects, and responding to calls. It sounded like one of those early-medieval paintings of knights shocked into conversion to the Church by divine visions of hovering chalices shining inexplicably in midair—a kind of Roman triumph at one thousand feet, as if blessing the city from above— only here it was a professional-sports trophy gleaming above the city like a religious vision brought to you by the LAPD.

My point is simply that, for all the tens of millions of dollars spent on helicopter patrols over Los Angeles each year, the possibly more disconcerting reality is that you probably *aren't* being watched. Those sinister government forces swirling around you like Valkyries are, as likely as not, flying with a headache over neighborhoods they've already seen so many times that they've been reduced to studying the tiles in someone's swimming pool, or even helplessly ticcing on riffs from children's books as nearly unbelievable suspect names come buzzing through on the police radio.

It's hard to know which is more dystopian: the idea that your every move is being studied by occasionally malign figures of anonymous government authority, or that everything you've done in the public sphere has for years now been secretly recorded for no particular reason, by people who would rather be doing almost anything else, in an apotheosis of archival bureaucracy that you yourself pay for through tax.

I was reminded of a study I'd once read about surveillance-camera operators in the U.K.; an anthropologist had gone to work in a CCTV control room for a season to see what life was like "behind the screens" (the title of the paper). While most Brits are convinced they're living through the rise of an all-pervasive surveillance state, being filmed from every conceivable angle at every time of day, the reality was far more diffuse and disorganized. In a particularly stark example, one security-room supervisor admitted that he would arrive at work each day and, first thing, train one of the cameras away from the building he was being paid to protect in order to watch his own car out in the parking lot. He would make himself a cup of tea, read the morning's sports pages, and spy on his car against possible break-ins.

Despite these reservations, the expense of patrolling

Los Angeles from above is easy enough to justify. The city is huge. Whole regions would otherwise never see a patrol—roadless ocean cliffs, mountain fire trails, desert parks, and meandering canyons, to name but a few. The Air Support Division ensures that a huge terrain can be protected and served by the LAPD.

This claim is supported by, of all people, NASA, who nearly fifty years ago commissioned a broad study on the aerial policing of Los Angeles. That NASA was involved suggests that L.A. was considered so alien both to police officers and to scientists that it resembled the landscape of another world. There is Mars, there is the moon, and there is Los Angeles.

The resulting report, called "Effectiveness Analysis of Helicopter Patrols," drawing on research by NASA's Pasadena-based Jet Propulsion Laboratory, was published in July 1970. The basic goal was to discover, through empirical testing, whether specific urban forms are more appropriately patrolled from above. Do certain types of cities require helicopter patrols—and if so, what are the inflection points that could push a metropolis over this limit, from ground-based policing to a need for light aircraft? Had Los Angeles crossed this threshold?

NASA's answer at the time was *yes*—albeit specifically in the fight against auto theft, and even more specifically limited to L.A.'s West Valley and University divisions. Nonetheless, NASA optimistically concluded not that helicopters should replace ground-based policing but that "the helicopter-car patrol team affects almost three times as many arrests as the city as a whole per reported offense."

A similar study has not since been undertaken, with the effect that evaluation of the performance of aerial police patrols, to a fairly large extent, relies even today on the good word of a crime study published in 1970. A May 2013 investigation by Los Angeles public radio station KPCC came to a slightly more damning conclusion: the Air Support Division "reviews its statistics every couple of months, but it never analyzes those numbers to determine the helicopters' effectiveness," instead leaving it up to the vagaries of self-assessment to say whether the division is still doing a good job.

Nevertheless, fast-forward half a century since the NASA study, and L.A. now has the largest police helicopter force in the world. Is there something about Los Angeles—how it was designed or the topography it covers—that leads to certain kinds of crimes, as well as to a particular method of policing? In the 1990s, for example, L.A. became the bank robbery capital of the world, as well as a city globally known for its televised car chases. Could there be a connection between the two?

Los Angeles as Police Utopia

My primary guide for understanding the Air Support Division was Tactical Flight Officer Cole Burdette, whom I unfortunately never had an opportunity to fly with. Burdette is originally from Michigan, though he is now thoroughly an Angeleno. He is observant, focused, and extremely detail oriented; he would frequently restart entire paragraphs of explanation about something until he got the exact narrative sequence correct, and only then would he move on to his next point or answer. Those answers were also astonishingly exact in their geographic references: he would bring up precise intersections and even business addresses somewhere out there in the sprawl of the city, and he never once referred to a map. Each pinpoint location would then serve a specific role in Burdette's ensuing explanations—sometimes even five or ten minutes later—as he attempted to make clear why a certain crime or event had unfolded in one way and not another.

It was obvious right away that Burdette had turned himself into a kind of one-man atlas of the city, possessing a vision of Los Angeles that rivals—in fact, exceeds—that of any urban geographer, city planner, or local architect. His knowledge of the terrain is both geographically extensive and highly granular, the product of thousands of hours of flight time, reconciling the constantly moving map of the city displayed on his helicopter's monitor with the actual streets tangled below. Dressed in his olive-green flight uniform and sporting a military-style haircut, Burdette walked me through the Air Support Division HQ on a quick tour, our final destination a classroom-like space lined with whiteboards where we could talk about burglary and the city.

Los Angeles is a fundamentally different kind of place, he explained, from New York or Chicago—or even San Francisco—with their skyscrapers and deep, canyon-like streets. Those dense clusters of high-rises and towers make thorough aerial patrols nearly impossible, as well as potentially dangerous and economically unnecessary. Out here in Los Angeles, however, you simply cannot see the whole city if you rely solely on ground patrols. Limiting yourself to roads—that is, thinking merely in two dimensions, like a driver—is clearly not going to work. As a cop trying to anticipate how burglars might use the city, you have to think three-dimensionally. Volumetrically. You have to think in a fundamentally different spatial way about the city laid out below, including how neighborhoods are actually connected and what the most efficient routes might be between them. After all, this is how criminals think, Burdette explained, and this is how they pioneer new geographic ways to escape from you.

I asked him, if he could redesign the city from the perspective of an LAPD tactical flight officer, what he would add or change to make his job easier. Burdette exhaled. What would be great, he finally said, would be a consistent application of the city's numbering system, from neighborhood to neighborhood, and then, as if channeling Mike Davis, to paint large identifying numbers on the roofs of building complexes, such as schools and hospitals. If those sorts of buildings could be numbered in a clockwise direction, starting with the entry building, he explained, then the job of a helicopter crew in directing officers to a specific structure deep in the sprawl of the city would be almost infinitely easier. When I asked what he meant when he said that a more consistent application of the city's grid would be useful, he told me about the rules of four.

The idea of studying the urban and architectural—
even numerical—visions of police is by no means new or
unique to my own research. Thomas More's *Utopia* is a
foundational text in the peculiar genre of describing the
ideal metropolis; it is equal parts political theory and moral
treatise, with a strong undercurrent of speculative design.
What is the perfect city? More asks. What would it look
like and how would it work? As it happens, one of the
book's earliest passages is a reflection on how to prevent
not just crime but specifically theft and robbery in a perfect society.

Prior to writing *Utopia*, Thomas More was under-
sheriff of London. He was a cop. It should come as no
surprise, then, to see that an LAPD tactical flight officer
or, for that matter, an FBI special agent might also dabble
in large-scale spatial thinking, where visionary law enforcement becomes its own strange form of architectural
or urban design. After all, they belong to a distinguished
lineage: More's *Utopia* shows that police visions of the
metropolis are integral to the Western literary tradition.
Indeed, the possibility that a twenty-first-century *Utopia*
might yet be written by a retired police helicopter pilot or
by an FBI bank-crime investigator is oddly compelling,
even if, as with More's own classic text, it is unlikely that
every aspect of their ideal city would appeal to everyone's
taste.

Using the rules of four, Burdette told me, he could
navigate to basically any building in Los Angeles. It was
as if some secret code had been found hidden within the
city's addressing system, an occult arithmetic uncovered

by police helicopter crews to cast a spell over the metropolis below. In reality, the rules of four fall somewhere between a rule of thumb and an algorithm, and they allow for nearly instantaneous yet accurate aerial navigation. Using them, Burdette explained, he and his pilot could fly from edge to edge of the entire metropolis, reading the streets below like the scanning arm of a hard drive—then swooping down into that shining grid wherever a crime had occurred.

"The way the parcels work in the city of Los Angeles," Burdette began, "is that Main Street and First Street are the hub of the city." This is also where the LAPD built its headquarters, a huge new building I was able to visit later for a meeting with detectives from the Burglary Special Section. The LAPD is thus literally at the very center of the metropolis, its numerological heart: it is the zero point from which everything else emanates, with Los Angeles a kind of giant mandala built by the police, airborne lords of the spiderweb.

Street numbers get bigger heading south from police headquarters, and it works arithmetically. "If it's the fourth house south of the corner on the west side of the street," Burdette explained, speaking very carefully and watching to be sure I was following him, "then the address is going to be an odd number. The rules of four mean that I can do four times four—it's the fourth house, times four—which is sixteen. But, because the numbers on that side of the street are odd, we know we're going to be looking at either fifteen or seventeen. So, if the address is south of Thirty-Eighth Street and it's the fourth house on the west side of the street, then it's going to be 3815 or 3817. It is going to be that address. If it's on the other side of the street, it's going to be even—it's going to be 3816 or 3818."

There are holes, however, gaps in the urban fabric where a certain street will disappear for several blocks before reappearing farther on. I remembered the other tactical flight officer mentioning that we had been flying over a part of the city that was out of sync with the city's grid, and now her comment actually made sense: the streets there were resistant to these street-counting techniques, as if falling outside the navigational wizardry of the police department. It's not just the city's grid or its transportation infrastructure that can affect burglars or the police who track them; something as immaterial as the mathematics of the city's street-numbering system can affect the ability of the police to interrupt crimes that might be occurring.

In a short essay called "Every Move Will Be Recorded," historian Grégoire Chamayou recounts a hypothetical system of urban surveillance devised by an eighteenth-century police officer named Jacques François Guillauté. In a book about police reform written for King Louis XV of France, Guillauté proposed thoroughly and rigorously updating the Parisian address system. This would require a behemoth piece of machinery that operated a bit like an oversize index-card file—or what Chamayou describes as a "huge archiving machine linked to a map in a central room"—and some arithmetical cartography.

"Paris was to be divided into distinct districts," Chamayou writes, "each receiving a letter, and each being subdivided into smaller sub-districts. In each sub-district each street had accordingly to receive a specific name. On each street, each house had to receive a number, engraved on the front of the house—which was not the case at the time. Each floor of each building was also to have a number engraved on the wall. On each floor, each door should be identified with a letter . . . In short, the whole city was to be reorganized according to the principles of a rationalized addressing system." An intimidating and nearly unpoliceable tangle of streets would, at a stroke, take on newfound three-dimensional clarity. Nearly every room in every building would be assigned its place in an abstract model that could then be studied by the king, looking down upon his territory as if he were a set of all-powerful eyes floating in space. A police helicopter, of sorts, before the dawn of aviation.

But police use many techniques other than counting streets to find burglars, Burdette continued. He explained that if a helicopter crew responding to a burglar alarm sees something like a big piece of plywood leaning up against the outside wall at the site, then "that tells me right away that there is a possibility of a tunnel job." Someone has carved, knocked, or drilled a hole through the wall—a "tunnel," in police speak, means any deliberately created hole, whether or not it's belowground—and tried to mask the activity by putting up this little piece of camouflage. This might work at street level for your average pedestrian or even a police rookie, he said, "but we, as experienced aircrews, know to look for things like that. That's the sort of thing that an experienced officer in an aircrew can see and then alert officers on the ground, to defeat a lot of really savvy suspects.

"When I came on the job," Burdette added, "my impression of a burglary is that they walk up and kick the door in, or they smash the window and there you go. But most of our burglaries are not like that. Windows aren't used nearly as frequently as you would think. Doors aren't used nearly as frequently as you would think. There are a lot of tunnel jobs. There are a lot of roof jobs. There are a lot of very creative ways of gaining access to restaurants or residences—including driving a car through the wall." Burglars, Burdette had learned while patrolling the city from above, were constantly innovating new ways of using the built environment.

"I've seen people take tools and cut out the back of the Dumpster," he said. "What they then do is pull the Dumpster up to the side of a building and chip away at the wall for several days. They just pull the materials and debris back into the Dumpster with them so that we can't detect it. You can look underneath it and you can look all around it, but you won't see anything because the Dumpster is up against the wall. In that Dumpster they've got a place that's quiet where they can tunnel in peace. But then, sometimes, their goal is not even to get into that building—it's to get into the building that's in the strip mall three doors down from there, but they know that the building they're tunneling into is for lease now." Then, inadvertently likening burglary to a computer game, Burdette said, "That's just the first level. During the next couple of days, they'll tunnel through the inside walls until they get to that last business." All along, the steadily filling Dumpster outside has been acting as their makeshift base of operations.

All these holes and tunnels would be hidden from aerial view, but Burdette explained how being airborne is a real asset: "Burglars look for opportunities. I might see a business where they've got a whole bunch of stuff stacked up behind their building. Well, they're just inviting a roof job. We have senior lead officers in all the divisions, and they work closely with the local business owners. So I'll make a note and say, 'Hey, could you tell that property owner it might not be a bad idea to clean up back there?' Because a person can climb on top of all those pallets they're storing back there, and they can do a roof job. A pallet is a ladder to a burglar. They'll just set it vertically and then stack another one on top of it, and then they're off and running—off and climbing. For anything like that, you look at it from above and you go, 'Okay, if I were a burglar, that's how I would get into that place.'"

On a separate visit to the Air Support Division, I sat down with another tactical flight officer, Mark Burdine, to learn about some of the burglary calls he had responded to over the years. Roof jobs, Burdine explained to me, aren't uncommon, but they tend to happen around one or two in the morning, after the city's gone to sleep and there is little risk of a neighbor's spotting the activity. One case in particular had struck him for its ingenuity and the difficulty of spotting, let alone interrupting, the crime.

A small crew of burglars had gotten into an office building through the roof, accessing the building by its ventilation system; they crawled in and, crucially, closed the vents behind them, leaving no trace on the roof that someone might be inside. Now out of sight, moving deeper into the building like ninjas, they lowered themselves into the main office by removing a panel from the drop ceiling. Then they turned all the motion detectors away from the room itself, rotating them to face the walls. Next they burglarized the place: computers, laptops, cameras, valuables left in desk drawers, whatever else they could get ahold of.

Even after they accidentally tripped an alarm deeper in the building, the police didn't hear anything about it because the security company hired to watch the building's CCTV monitors was based in Texas. By the time they noticed what was happening and had made the right calls to the local business owners and then to the LAPD, nearly half an hour had gone by, giving the burglars ample time to escape.

Examples such as this showed that having an eye in the sky does not make the LAPD invincible, nor can an eagle-eyed tactical flight officer—whether it's Cole Burdette or Mark Burdine—accurately deduce everything happening inside a structure. After all, *Mission: Impossible*–like burglary crews accessing office buildings through air ducts, then rappelling deeper inside by way of a drop ceiling, are hard to detect from nine hundred feet above the streets.

However, new technologies are on the way. An Orlando, Florida, company called L-3 CyTerra has developed a "stepped frequency continuous wave" handheld radar system called the RANGE-R. This device, about the size of a walkie-talkie, allows users to see through walls—or ceilings. It is primarily marketed as a tool of great value for search-and-rescue operations, where firefighters might use it to locate someone inside a burning building or even trapped beneath rubble after an earthquake. However, the RANGE-R is also enthusiastically pitched as a near-miraculous device no SWAT team should be without, offering police a tool for determining "the presence and location of assailants or hostages inside a building prior to entry," the company boasts.

The RANGE-R made national news for all the wrong reasons, however, when, back in February 2013, U.S. marshals used one of the units to determine whether a suspect was inside his home in Wichita, Kansas. The man's subsequent arrest was later disputed in court on the basis that using radar to, in effect, watch him inside his own home was a form of unconstitutional "entry." Its use should thus require a warrant. This argument was based on an earlier Supreme Court case, *Kyllo v. United States*, where the court determined that using thermal-imaging cameras to scan a suspect's home for signs of a marijuana-growing operation was only legal with the appropriate search warrant. The court did not agree, however, that radar should be subjected to the same limitations, and police use of a RANGE-R remains perfectly legal and does not require a warrant.

While RANGE-R radar technology is not—for the time being—used by the LAPD Air Support Division, attaching a high-powered unit to the undercarriage of a police helicopter and using it to peer inside high-rises, suburban homes, industrial warehouses, and even into the sewers beneath city streets would give police a powerful new level of resolution in their 3-D view of the city. Cops don't (yet) have X-ray vision, but something approximating that technology is on its way.

At nearly 10:30 p.m. I was in the police helicopter circling over a house near the banks of the Los Angeles River. In the dark I couldn't see any real detail below and couldn't make out exactly where we were. The moving map on the monitor in the front seat had our position accurately marked, but the pilot and tactical flight officer were arguing over whether they had even flown to the right location. Finally, the pilot decided simply to turn on the spotlight, a blinding, 30-million-candlepower inferno justifiably known as the Nightsun.

There, shining in the LAPD's own artificial daylight, was *The Brady Bunch* house.

"You remember *The Waltons*?" the pilot then said, and we were off again, tracking down not criminals but the bygone sites of prime-time TV. The police radio was still quiet, the city's criminals apparently taking an evening off. Over the next hour or so, we would go on to visit the Bat Cave; we flew over the downtown set from *Back to the Future*, the crashed airplane from *War of the Worlds*, and Charlie Chaplin's old mansion near USC; then we headed back over to that icon of the city, the HOLLYWOOD sign. There, the pilot switched on the Nightsun, and it blazed against the sign's giant white letters; he even circled the helicopter a few times so that I could take a few photos from the backseat. Nearby, they remembered, was Madonna's old mansion—so we flew there, too, even using the Nightsun again as if it were our last chance to do so. They lit up nearly every window of this imposing complex in the Hills as they told me a bit about the home's history, including its connection to gangster Bugsy Siegel and the Luciano crime family. I can't imagine what it would have been like to be inside the house that night, every curtain suddenly blazing as if it were noon as the sky filled with the rhythmic chop of an unexpected helicopter, like an all-out home invasion under way—but, just like that, we left the neighborhood.

I had to remind myself that I was there for an actual reason—doing research for a book, not just gawking at celebrity houses and famous locations—so I began to ask them about the equipment they used: the devices and gadgets on board that literally made the city look different from above, whether it was the forward-looking infrared camera (FLIR), the possible acquisition of RANGE-R technology, or their image-stabilized binoculars.

They showed me how the FLIR worked. This required me to lean considerably far forward, all but pulling myself into the front seat with the tactical flight officer, who inched a little out of the way to help me see. We headed for the darker parts of Los Angeles, flying broadly northwest over the deep canyons of the Hollywood Hills—Laurel Canyon, Coldwater Canyon, Dixie Canyon—deliberately looking for a good place to test the camera's infrared sensitivity. If a human body was down there emitting heat, the camera would find it—but even here we were having bad luck. Nobody was out walking the dog, it seemed, or even sneaking a late-night cigarette, so we continued on over the dark bulk of the mountains until the Getty Museum came into view. The officers realized we'd be better off heading for the ocean, so we made a beeline for Santa Monica—and the effect was unbelievable.

Almost at once, the FLIR monitor mounted in front of the tactical flight officer began to light up with the strangely beautiful thermal flare of human life: white-glowing forms walking along the beach, lying on dark blankets next to one another, even sitting around in a circle somewhere just south of the Santa Monica Pier. We flew on, quite low to the water, as they explained some of the basics of infrared visualization, and I watched as apparently sleeping forms—white-hot—came into sharp focus, curled up beneath lifeguard structures. There was nowhere to hide, I saw; you could be concealed behind the trunk of a tree yet an eerie glow would still surround you, shining like a halo. It was almost moving: a night flight with the LAPD had inadvertently opened my eyes to this extraordinary human glow, as dense knots of blood vessels burned hot in the coastal night like road flares. This all but supernatural vision of animal life is not only being used more and more to track suspects from above—or, technically, to track their thermal side effects—but it also plays an increasingly vital role in capturing suspects before they can get away.

As I looked down out of the helicopter window, the

beach was nothing but blackness, silky and absolute, with not a human being in sight; but when I peered back at the monitor, lights were everywhere. They were like fireflies, these humans huddled around one another and listening to the sea.

Where the Money Is

My time with the Air Support Division had revealed the extent to which pilots and tactical flight officers can identify and, more crucially, interrupt the city's illicit routes and hiding places. Back at ground level, however, I'd become interested in how the city's freeway infrastructure could be used by criminals not just as a possible route of escape from police capture, but as an urban-scale tool for helping them design better crimes.

In an interesting article published by *The New Yorker*, author Tad Friend implies that the high-speed chase is, in many ways, a more authentic use of L.A.'s sprawling road network; by comparison, the daily commute was embarrassingly impotent, an automotively timid use of this extraordinary landscape whose very premise is not safety and convenience but personal liberation. Friend suggests that fleeing from the police—often at lethal speeds—while being broadcast live on local television is, well, it's sort of what the city is *for*. To focus on L.A.'s legendary traffic is to miss a larger and much stranger point: that crime is often a more effective way to use the fabric of the city.

After all, Friend writes, if you build "nine hundred miles of sinuous highway and twenty-one thousand miles of tangled surface streets" in one city alone, then you're going to find at least a few people who want to put those streets to use. This suggests that every city blooms with the kinds of crime most appropriate to its form.

In the 1990s, Los Angeles held the dubious title of "bank robbery capital of the world." At its height, the city's bank-crime rate hit the incredible frequency of one bank robbed every forty-five minutes of every workday. As FBI special agent Brenda Cotton—formerly based in Los Angeles but now stationed in New York City—told me, the agency even developed its own typology of banks in the region. Most notable was the "stop-and-rob": a bank located at the bottom of both an exit ramp and an on-ramp for one of Southern California's many freeways. This meant it could be robbed as quickly and as casually as a commuter might pull off the road for a tank of gas. As Cotton described it, you could jump off the freeway, rob a bank in West L.A., hop right back onto the 405, and be over the mountains—as long as you hadn't timed your crime for the height of rush hour—long before a police helicopter could make it to the scene. This was not possible in New York City, she pointed out, where the city's transportation infrastructure and its pedestrian-friendly streets facilitate a different genre of bank crime in which the perpetrator will flee on foot or even use the subway.

Stop-and-robs are therefore one of those instances where an architectural form—the freestanding bank or credit union—and a piece of urban infrastructure—the ever-expanding Los Angeles freeway network—unexpectedly combined to catalyze something that law enforcement professionals, let alone architects or city planners, had been unable to anticipate. A new kind of crime was now possible—and unsurprisingly, bank crime in Los Angeles began to soar, reaching a spectacular intensity in the 1990s.

In a 2003 memoir called *Where the Money Is: True Tales from the Bank Robbery Capital of the World*, retired special agent William J. Rehder devotes considerable attention to the ways in which the design of Los Angeles facilitates—or even leads to—bank crimes. Like Cotton, Rehder points out that the city's sprawling nest of freeways, offering what he calls "easy mobility" and ultraconvenient connections to literally thousands of banks and credit unions, helped to turn L.A. into a kind of bank robber's paradise. The stop-and-rob was just one symptom of this urban-scale design flaw: the city was peppered with innumerable banks so badly placed from a security standpoint that they could be robbed seemingly at will, functioning almost like ATMs for any criminal who needed quick cash.

Many other factors besides urban design contribute to the sky-high incidence of bank robbery in Los Angeles, of course. Not the least of these factors is that many banks, Rehder explains, have made the somewhat peculiar financial calculation of money stolen per year versus the annual salary of a full-time security guard—and the banks have come out on the side of letting the money get stolen. The cash, in economic terms, is not worth protecting. It's not altogether wrong to suggest that as a conscious business strategy banks outsourced their security needs to already strained local cops and the FBI, who were federally obligated to investigate bank crime. From anecdotes I heard from LAPD detectives and retired FBI special agents, I would say that this was very much the case; the resentment was very real against bank managers and other business owners who sought to save a bit of their own money by not hiring a security guard, knowing full well that some local cop or FBI agent would have to answer their call at 2:00 a.m. and come investigate.

Special Agent Cotton plays only a minor role in Rehder's account of bank crimes in Los Angeles, but through my connection to her I convinced Rehder that we should meet for lunch and discuss his book. Rehder's memoir is a compelling example of what might happen if we were to ask an FBI agent how the design of a city might inspire—perhaps even require—certain crimes. I was eager to make a meeting happen.

On a brief trip to Los Angeles, my wife and I met Rehder for lunch at the Santa Monica Airport, at a restaurant he had chosen. Rehder ordered an Arnold Palmer, called the waitress "darling," and showed us through a small stack of files holding black-and-white photographs, personal notes he'd written to himself in preparation for our meeting, and some newspaper clippings about major cases he'd once worked on. I've come to realize after many meetings with retired FBI agents that they often arrive with files, as if unable to fully leave behind the archives and documentary evidence so central to the

Bureau's investigations. These files are encyclopedic: full of data and references for making narrative sense of the events they describe. Between this and our table at the restaurant's being laminated with aviation charts of the skies around Southern California, our conversation took on a diagrammatic feel, as if we were not only getting an X-ray of the city from a retired FBI agent but also somehow peering into the skies to see the flight paths and holding patterns otherwise known only to pilots and air traffic controllers.

Rehder has stayed busy in his retirement. He now runs a consulting firm called the Security Management Resource Group, which he describes as "a professional firm providing effective and cost-efficient prevention solutions to robbery, violence, and other crimes at financial institutions, stores, and other corporate facilities." Rehder's partner there is Douglas Sims, former head of security at Bank of America. Sims brings decades of private-security work to the position, including a fascinating stint helping to plan urban-scale security protocols for all of Los Angeles during the 1984 Olympic Games.

Rehder's widely known and recognized expertise in all things bank-crime-related led to the surreal accolade of being tapped to serve as an outside consultant on the 1991 film *Point Break*, starring Keanu Reeves and Patrick Swayze and directed by Kathryn Bigelow. He tends to laugh when telling that story. Keanu "didn't really ask anything," Rehder told us, shaking his head. The heists depicted in the film were not unrealistic, he suggested, but the fact that the FBI special agent played by

Reeves assists with a bank burglary struck Rehder as so morally absurd and professionally unbelievable as to ruin any claim to veracity the film might otherwise have had. Rehder's colleagues ribbed him about it for years afterward.

I asked him about the stop-and-robs. If these are an unintended side effect of the design of the city's transportation infrastructure, do other aspects of city planning inadvertently influence the crimes hatched there? Having started his career in Cleveland, and now spending a great deal of time giving talks or consulting with banks and credit unions in other countries, he has had ample time and opportunity to compare the urban contexts of international criminal activity.

He responded with a rhetorical question: "I'd say, how did the city grow? What are the architectural dimensions, if you will, or spatial aspects of the city itself? Los Angeles, for instance, is basically built on a horizontal level. Everybody needs an automobile—including to commit their crimes." Compare this to Chicago, he said, or Boston or New York, where a bandit—the FBI's preferred, albeit amusingly antiquated, term for bank robbers— might aim to get on public transportation, melt into the crowd anonymously, and cross the city as just another citizen or resident. "In New York . . ." He paused, and I expected some oracular insight into the future of Gotham. Instead, he said, "It's not easy to park a car in New York City! Getting stuck in traffic there is a major problem. Your bandit needs to find a different way to make his getaway, which means he'll choose different targets in the first place."

And cities were continuing to change. With ATMs and cybercrime, the target has shifted. Banks are still hit for their physical resources—cash—but, often, entire ATM machines are stolen or, at the very least, cut open from behind to get into the cash stocks. Unexpectedly, Rehder referred to robbery in biblical times—a historical perspective that I found not uncommon with people working in the security industry, less because of an entrenched cultural conservatism in the field, I would suggest, and more out of a resigned cynicism about the perennial role of crime in human society. But Rehder's point, as if indirectly citing the title of his own book, was simply that people go where the money is: whether it's the Jewish merchants Rehder specifically referred to, being robbed on the road two thousand years ago as they transported their stock from place to place, or bank franchises at the bottoms of off-ramps in contemporary Los Angeles. "This is not something new," Rehder emphasized. "This is something very old, and it will continue." As long as there is money, there will be bandits—and there will be people like Bill Rehder on their tail. All that changes is the form the crime takes, molded by the need to overcome the legal and spatial constraints of a particular time and place.

One spectacular case came up again and again as we talked: the still-unsolved crimes of the so-called Hole in the Ground Gang from Los Angeles in the late 1980s. Rehder confessed that he was unable to let the crime go, and that he had originally hoped his book would inspire the perpetrators to come out publicly and identify themselves. Their crimes are now well beyond the statute of limitations. As Rehder put it, these particular bandits could strut into LAPD headquarters in downtown Los Angeles tomorrow morning, brandishing all the maps, photos, diagrams, and tools they once used, and they could not be arrested for their crimes. As Rehder jokes in the book, "All we could do is take them down to the Scotch & Sirloin and buy them a no-hard-feelings beer." Alas, the Hole in the Ground Gang has not been so forthcoming, and Rehder is still itching to solve the mystery of their L.A. bank tunnels. (His offer of a beer still stands.)

In June 1986, employees at a First Interstate Bank in Hollywood, at the corner of Sunset and Spaulding, in a building that now houses a talent agency, began to report strange mechanical sounds coming from the ground near the vault. Neither police nor the bank's security team could find any evidence of wrongdoing or attempted entry, however, and crucially, none of the vault's internal sensors had been tripped. Later, when Rehder conducted interviews with bank employees as part of his investigation, he learned that the police had dismissed the sounds as "just a rat running around inside the walls or something," and no investigation at all was pursued. Another week went by and the noises continued. The power occasionally went out, as did the bank's telephones. Then the internal Muzak system abruptly kicked in late one evening, startling a manager who was there alone working overtime. The employees began to joke that the bank was haunted by a poltergeist, a supernatural force short-circuiting the electrical networks, blocking phone calls, and playing music at odd hours of the day. Incredibly, as the bank's security company still found no breach of the vault itself, the possibility that the bank was haunted seemed more likely than that someone was tunneling up from below.

In reality those sounds were caused not by the ghosts of transactions past, but by a group of three or four men—no one knows how big the team was—who, several theories now suggest, were at least to some degree professionally trained in mining. This was an apparently close-knit, secretive, and disciplined crew, perhaps from the construction industry, perhaps even a disgruntled public works outfit who decided to put their knowledge of the city's underside to more economically lucrative use. After all, while their route into the bank was via a brute-force excavation, they also employed a sophisticated retracing of the region's buried waterways. They had accessed the neighborhood by way of L.A.'s complicated storm-sewer network, itself built along old creek beds that no longer appear on city maps.

The bandits must have had access to Los Angeles County storm-sewer maps, as the connections were by no means obvious; knowing that a manhole several blocks away from a bank might take you within just a few hundred feet of the vault is not something you can simply deduce from walking around on the sidewalk. But even more interestingly, the sewers themselves were not built haphazardly through the canyons of Hollywood; they were constructed to follow the old streams and waterways of the natural landscape, a landscape now buried, invisible, beneath the streets. The ancient watershed of Los Angeles still flows, but it has been entombed in concrete and forgotten. The most well-known—and still the most extraordinary—example of this is the Los Angeles River itself, a controversially paved landscape now more widely seen as nothing more than an arid speedway, hosting dramatic car-race scenes in films such as *Grease*. But the surface of Los Angeles actually hides a capillary-like network of lost creeks, almost all of which have been diverted, combined, and encased in huge tunnels we tend not to think twice about. Yet they're down there, secretly connecting things in the darkness—and they can be used.

A particularly evocative example of this phenomenon was pointed out by landscape architect Jessica Hall, coauthor of a blog called *LA Creek Freak*, in a 2006 interview with *LA Weekly*. Hall asked, "Do you know why there's sometimes fog at the intersection of Beverly and Rossmore?" She was referring to a well-trafficked intersection near the Wilshire Country Club. This is "because there's a perennial creek that runs through the country club there. It goes underground beneath Beverly, and comes up again on the other side." This subterranean presence lets itself be known through a diaphanous mist in the air above. The city gives off signals, provided you know how to read them: something as innocuous as an early-morning fog bank might actually be a clue, revealing sewer tunnels or lost creeks in the neighborhood around you.

Thus, if you know the creeks and their routes, even after they have been encapsulated inside storm sewers, you also know clever and unexpected ways into the buildings above them. For a burglar—or bank bandits such as the Hole in the Ground Gang—these surface indications of underground geography can be used for nefarious purposes, to find ways to navigate the city and plan future heists, tracing old, buried streams until you reach your final target.

In addition to all this, Rehder explained, the Hole in the Ground Gang bandits would have needed intimate knowledge of the ground itself, the actual geology of Los Angeles. As LAPD lieutenant Doug Collisson, one of the men present on the day of the tunnel's discovery, explained to the *Los Angeles Times* back in 1987, the heist "would have had to require some knowledge of soil composition and technical engineering. The way the shaft itself was constructed, it was obviously well-researched and extremely sophisticated." Rehder goes further, remarking that when Detective Dennis Pagenkopp "showed crime-scene photos of the core bit holes" produced by the burglars drilling upward into the vault "to guys who were in the concrete-coring business, they whistled with professional admiration."

In Rehder's file "Tunnel Job" were a handful of glossy color photographs that seemed to have been taken quickly, with less-than-ideal lighting. Sometimes they weren't even in focus. They showed bewildered FBI agents looking at a ransacked vault, the doors of its safe-deposit boxes torn asunder. Standing next to them were members of the

LAPD Burglary Auto Theft Division (BAD), described by Rehder in his book as "an elite unit of fifteen or so detectives who specialized in high-end break-ins and property theft: purloined payrolls, jewelry store burglaries, commercial safe-crackings, fine art thefts, high-profile heists of every description."

The photographs also revealed how impressive the scale of the tunnel was. With its tight, snaking corridor chipped through the sandy ground of subterranean L.A., it bore an uncanny resemblance to the catacombs of Rome or Cappadocia. The tunnel torqued down and around and finally ended at the featureless concrete pipe of the storm sewer. The burglars had driven Suzuki four-wheelers through the claustrophobically tight sewer tunnels beneath West Hollywood, tunnels that were only barely wider than the four-wheelers themselves; the bandits would have been hunched over like horse jockeys, driving nearly blind beneath the city, navigating tight turns and hoping—praying—that they would not bump into any obstructions or hit a dead end.

Those four-wheelers were the workhorses of the entire operation, hauling equipment in and booty out—more than $172,000 in cash and as much as $2.5 million worth of personal belongings ripped from safe-deposit boxes. You can still see the open storm culvert that the crew used as their original point of entrance; it's found just slightly north of the intersection of Nichols Canyon Road and Hollywood Boulevard. Although the FBI believes that this is where they lowered their four-wheelers into the storm sewer system, you can also follow this culvert north up Nichols Canyon until you get to a Department of Public Works drainage basin; with a sloping concrete ramp that leads straight into the culvert, this also affords a convenient entry point to the subterranean heart of Los Angeles.

In their tunneling, the Hole in the Ground Gang had to get rid of the more than three thousand cubic feet of loosely compacted earth. They achieved this through a quick bit of improvisational hydrology, constructing a small dam at the beginning of their work every night; this blocked the head of the storm sewer and caused even the smallest trickle of water in arid Los Angeles to build up— and up and up—throughout the night, while they dumped all the excavated dirt and sand farther down the sewer line. Then, upon breaking the dam—destroying this rogue plumbing in the darkness beneath Sunset Boulevard— the resulting torrent of water washed away all the debris (and, perhaps even more usefully, their footprints). Finally, explaining the flickering electrical supply in the bank and the shorted phone lines that led employees to suspect an electromagnetic poltergeist had taken up residence in the walls, they tapped into the bank's own wiring from below, using it to power their tools and lights.

"There was a lot of technical knowledge," Rehder said wistfully, or perhaps regretfully. "These guys had to be in construction—maybe mining—but they had to know construction. They knew how to construct a tunnel that went one hundred feet underground in L.A., and they didn't shore anything up. Their tunnel was fantastic." He showed me the photos again, pointing at details and remembering the strange day of the discovery.

It still ate at him. They had gotten away with it.

The methodology of the Hole in the Ground Gang bears superficial resemblance to an earlier heist on the other side of the Atlantic. Over the long Bastille Day weekend of July 1976, a team of burglars successfully broke into the vault of the Société Générale bank in Nice, France, stealing nearly $8 million worth of cash and goods from the safe-deposit boxes inside. They had been tunneling for two months. Led by Albert Spaggiari—who later escaped from French custody by jumping out of a courtroom window, landing atop a parked car, and speeding off on a prearranged motorcycle, never to be seen in person again by European authorities (legend has it, he flashed a peace sign as he sped away)—this spectacular underground crime remains a textbook example of criminals bending a city to serve their own devious needs.

Spaggiari and his team began their tunnel in an underground parking garage, chosen because of its proximity to the city's deep drain system. Plans of the drainage network were freely available to inquisitive members of the public; all you had to do was ask. Armed with these, Spaggiari then cased the city for weeks, exploring the actual sewers when he could and making a note of any security cameras or other difficulties along the way. These regular reconnaissance routes would have included verifying that the ground conditions beneath the chosen bank were suitable for tunneling. Given accurate geological knowledge of a city, a person could determine right away which banks are worth trying to hit and which are geologically impregnable. Bank vaults built on heavy Manhattan bedrock are not going to see many tunnel jobs; those built on soft London clay, crumbly Berlin sand, or the fertile soil of South America are immediately vulnerable, provided one is willing to get one's hands dirty. Tunnel jobs—true tunnel jobs, not just drilling holes through drywall but carving your way forward through the earth—are as much about geology as they are about transportation infrastructure, buried creeks, or a lack of CCTV.

Spaggiari soon discovered that the drains beneath Nice were not merely storm sewers, but were an integral part of the now-buried Paillon River. This river, long since covered over by leafy streets in the center of town, was lined with two large underground maintenance roads that mirrored the routes on the surface. As above, so below. These streets beneath the city would let Spaggiari and Co. drive their way to freedom, emerging on the Paillon's natural riverbed in a different part of the city nearly two miles away.

One great detail from the Nice heist involves precisely that buried river. Once Spaggiari's team got down into the drains, they had to find a way to ford the waters to reach the roots of the bank itself. The river was almost like an underground moat, a protective serpent coiled around the bank's foundations. This meant bringing with them a small armada of inflatable plastic rafts and inner tubes. They would use these colorful beach toys as a floating bridge to ferry tools and equipment from one side of the river to the other. Then, like the Hole in the Ground Gang—who tapped into their target's electrical system to power their digging equipment—Spaggiari's crew plugged a chain of heavy-duty extension cords into a power outlet inside the parking garage, pulling electricity down into the tunnels and across the inflatable bridge, and powering a few lights along the way.

The eventual discovery of Spaggiari's bank tunnel in the wake of the successful heist led to a step-by-step revelation of all the spatial short-circuits his team had engineered beneath the surface of the city. Tracking the perpetrators meant following their tunnel down from the bank vault into the city's drains, following their extension cords out across the buried river to the parking garage, then following the underground roads from beneath the Promenade du Paillon all the way to the gang's ultimate point of exit. By the time the police got there, of course, the burglars were nowhere to be found.

Forensic Topology

Our sandwiches cooling, our drinks now on their third or fourth refill, retired special agent Rehder revealed one final detail in the saga of the Hole in the Ground Gang. Not only had they succeeded; not only had they utterly disappeared; but they then came back more than a year later to strike again. This time, it was at the intersection of La Cienega and Pico, where the crew were attempting to burglarize two banks simultaneously. Here, things did not go so smoothly. The group actually did make it into one of the vaults—but without all of the preliminary false alarms and the reported poltergeists of the First Interstate Bank up in Hollywood, when they finally tripped the vault alarm, it was taken seriously. The gang were interrupted right before they could make off with their haul, narrowly escaping back down into their tunnel network, where— once again—they rode their trustworthy four-wheelers to freedom. An abandoned Suzuki Quad with its serial numbers filed down would later be discovered nearly seven miles away, at the mouth of a concrete sewer outflow leading into Ballona Creek beneath Dauphin Street.

They remain at large to this day.

The stakes of this second robbery were huge; Rehder writes, "They could have gotten away with a face-value take of anywhere from $10 to $25 million. It could have been the biggest bank burglary in the history of the world." What is so memorable about this latter attempt—on top of the sheer hubris of tunneling into two banks simultaneously—is the disoriented, almost psychedelic, reaction of Rehder, one of the first FBI agents to arrive on the scene. The presence of two bank tunnels, the second of which was only discovered hours after the first, inspired an uneasy, vertiginous sense that yet more tunnels might— in fact, probably would—be found. Rehder and his colleagues "started getting these nagging mental images of a network of tunnels under every bank in West L.A., of the ground beneath us laced like a prairie dog village with holes and chambers and secret passages, of waking up one morning and finding five or ten or a hundred bank vaults simultaneously breached and stripped, and legions of bankers and boxholders screaming for vengeance and immediate compensation. Every sewer line in West L.A. would have to be searched, every patch job inspected."

The FBI's unsettling discovery of a hidden topological dimension tucked away inside the city is a stunning moment—the realization that, on a different plane, point A might illicitly be connected to point B, and that it is the burglar's role to make this link real. Recall the aerial view of the LAPD helicopter crew, moving through the city freely along the x, y, and z axes and thus seeing connections others have either ignored or simply missed. Rehder's experience with the Hole in the Ground Gang made it clear that burglars, too, can intervene in the built environment along unexpected paths, turning the city itself into a tool for breaking and entering.

The burglar is a three-dimensional actor amid the two-dimensional surfaces and objects of the city. This means operating with a fundamentally different spatial sense of how architecture should work, and how one room could be connected to another. It means seeing how a building can be stented: engineering short-circuits where mere civilians, altogether less aggressive users of the city, would never expect to find them. Burglary is topology pursued by other means: a new science of the city, proceeding by way of shortcuts, splices, and wormholes.

Gazing in unsettled awe at the streets of Los Angeles and realizing that this apparently solid surface hides holes, tunnels, routes, knots, and other unlawful passages leading from one location to another made Special Agent Rehder almost woozy in adversarial appreciation of what lies below. Policing the city, in that moment, became as much about preventing unauthorized spatial connections from emerging—new and illicit diagonals leading from one point to another—as it was about watching its surfaces for crimes yet to occur. As Rehder recalled, the investigation quickly descended into a giant game of Whac-A-Mole, with federal agents and local cops both popping out of manholes throughout the area as they tried to figure out exactly where they were, lost in the underside of the city, the bandits by then long gone.

If George Leonidas Leslie has shown us that burglary is built into the very bones of the modern metropolis, then the Hole in the Ground Gang managed to blow that revelation up to the scale of infrastructure—a shadowy world of buried flood-control basins, storm-sewer outflows, and the very foundations of Los Angeles transformed into the ultimate criminal tool. By burrowing into the ground and riding their 4x4s for miles beneath the streets, they also revealed that it's not just rooms or floors that can be linked together by a clever criminal; whole neighborhoods sit atop vast switchboards of connection that the manic ambitions of a burglar can make real.

Spatial thinking at the scale of the city can reveal a

universe of unexpected, secondary uses—potential crimes (and ways of foiling them). To truly understand the built environment, we might say, even the most law-abiding citizen can stand to learn a thing or two from the urban-scale cat-and-mouse game of cops and robbers, who share this one fundamental strategy: not just to see the city as it is, but to see the city as it could be—then forcing those possibilities to happen. It is burglars and police, not architects or urban planners, who most readily and consistently show us these unseen possibilities, these other routes and spaces hidden in some unrealized dimension of the metropolis.

However, if all cities already contain the crimes that will occur there, then, taken to its logical conclusion, this suggests there might be a kind of Moby-Dick of crime, a White Whale of urban burglary: a town or city so badly designed that the entire place can be robbed in one go. The stakes would be massive. I spoke to an urban information technology adviser, for example, who has worked on several new "smart city" projects under construction around the world, primarily in northeast Asia. When I asked him what burglary might look like in these cities of the future, his answer was shocking. Requesting that he remain anonymous due to the nature of his answer, he explained that the operating system of New Songdo City, Korea—or what he described more specifically as the software that supports the technical fabric of the city, allowing communications between buildings, urban infrastructure, and portable devices—was legally required to be backed up and held in a safe-deposit box (alas, he would not tell me where). If one of the city's founding partner companies went out of business, or if an act of God wiped the city of its digital innards, this backup would be in its bank vault, waiting. You could then reboot the city.

Or rob it.

Consider for a minute the implications of this. By breaking into just one safe-deposit box, you could steal the code to New Songdo City—the operating system of an entire metropolis. In a scenario straight out of science fiction—the heist of the century—the digital engine behind every electronic door lock, every elevator, every streetlight, every fire alarm, every subway tunnel, every bank vault, and every surveillance camera would be under your control. You could rob every building in the city. It's enough to make even the most hardened burglar swoon.

Think of *The Score*, Richard Stark's classic heist novel from 1964. A character known only as Edgars introduces his fellow burglars to a small town in North Dakota called Copper Canyon. He uses a slide projector and old mining maps, as if giving a university lecture, and he seems almost too excited by the outrageousness of his plan to say what it is out loud. However, as more maps of Copper Canyon fill the projection screen, a stunned burst of realization passes through everyone seated around the table.

There's only one road in and out of the place, Edgars explains. There's only one small police station, and it can easily be commandeered. There's the fire department, but it can be avoided. Edgars means the *entire city* is the target. They'll simply drive in at midnight and "pop every safe in town," he says. Parker, the novel's antihero, pretends to consider the job with reluctance and sobriety—but, smiling and clearly swept up in the sheer mania of the idea, he thinks to himself, "Knock over a city. A whole goddamn city. It was so stupid it might even work."

3

YOUR BUILDING IS THE TARGET

At the height of his career, self-proclaimed master cat burglar Bill Mason was an excellent watcher of buildings. He kept an eye on the people, of course, to see who was wearing what—which meant scanning the wrists and necks of strangers for expensive jewelry. But, for Mason, it was the buildings those people lived in that held all the appeal.

After the publication of his memoir, *Confessions of a Master Jewel Thief*, in 2003, Mason appeared on CNN to look back at his long and successful career. When asked by Wolf Blitzer why he did it—what had motivated

Mason to become a jewel thief in the first place—his answer was almost entirely architectural, a modern-day spin on George Leonidas Leslie. "Well, Wolf," Mason began, as if this fact alone would explain it all, "I was in the real estate business, and I knew apartment buildings." While working as a building manager, he "started thinking about crime," Mason explains.

"I liked buildings," he finally states, especially high-rises. Buildings meant that "you could go in and achieve something, bypass a lot of security. And it was a game, it became a challenge, sort of an adrenaline rush that I got addicted to." No matter where the heists took place—Mason broke into hotels, apartments, and high-rise towers from Ohio to South Florida—every heist and the structure it took place within was an elaborate spatial puzzle waiting to be solved. Each caper was like a new level in the game, with its own rewards and obstacles, its secret pitfalls and watchful guardians.

"Once I began thinking about how to pull off a dangerous and difficult heist," Mason writes in his book, "I wasn't much different from a research scientist or an inventor: Hell or high water, I would find a way to solve the puzzle and then I'd do it." The buildings drew him in, as if the jewelry was almost secondary.

On the prowl for new places to hit, Mason would often go out alone at night casing private homes and high-rises, looking for such things as conveniently placed balconies, ledges, or rooftops easily accessed by rope or ladder. He would then zero in on little details that most people might miss, like the exact spot at which a drainpipe might supply a solid handhold or the way an overhang didn't quite protect the terrace below, thus offering a safe place to drop down from the roof.

But why this obsession with buildings? Mason explains that, as a kid, he "became friendly with a lot of maintenance men and building superintendents," learning from an early age the literal ins and outs of different types of structures from the people who knew them best. Not residents, architects, or landlords. "People who take care of apartment buildings," Mason suggests, "are underappreciated masters of many arts. They do the work of electricians, plumbers, carpenters, masons, painters, locksmiths, glaziers and machinists, often all in the same day." They knew how buildings actually worked, but also that buildings consist, for the most part, of sprawling back labyrinths of maintenance rooms and side corridors that residents—even the most dutiful of apartment owners—never visit or realize exist.

For a burglar, these spaces on the outer margins of architectural consciousness are like the dark matter of the built environment. Laundry rooms, fire escapes, employee staircases, emergency exits, rooftop boiler rooms; the list goes on and on. An overlooked hinterland nonetheless central to any building's ability to function, these sorts of facilities permeate hotels and apartment complexes. From a burglar's point of view, these sorts of spaces are temptations: secondary passageways and points of entry over which few people feel they have responsibility. Connect them together just right and these kinds of spaces can be the difference between a sack of free jewelry and a year's salary in one take, or a long night of frustration spent tossing and turning in bed, visions of impregnable buildings interrupting your sleep.

Those early mentors also taught Mason perhaps the most important thing of all: if you give it enough time and thought, you can figure out any building. Even better, you can learn to feel that you belong there. To feel comfortable. Calm. You don't need to panic as you look for whatever impediment or problem might hold you up next—whether it's the location of the safe hidden in an apartment's master bedroom or the way the alarm system works (in Mason's experience, alarm systems were rarely turned on). If you just go about your business, you can reach a kind of architectural Zen, just letting the spaces around you reveal their secret workings. Give it enough time and attention, and any building will expose itself to you from within.

Or from without. Mason was a first-rate spatial voyeur, an autodidact of architectural exteriors. He "liked buildings"—that we already know—but what sorts of things was he looking for? Why would he hit one building and not the one next door?

His book includes scene after scene of his checking out buildings from the parking lots or walking paths nearby, looking for hiding places or handholds, for signs that someone might be out for the night at a party or expensive dinner. Mason's memoir opens with his trying to find a way into multimillionaire Armand Hammer's Florida condominium, from which Mason hoped to steal a trove of valuable jewels. Mason stands outside, optimistic despite the building's doormen; he takes his time, sometimes feigning sleep on a lounge chair on the beach while secretly watching the building, or even, he jokes, just smiling at the bikini-clad women walking by, his actual target looming large behind them. That's when he notices a tiny ledge on the outside of the high-rise, one that seems just wide enough for a grown man to stand on. It wraps all the way around the building, he sees, leading from balcony to balcony, each with a set of sliding glass doors promising easy (and most likely unlocked) entry to the pickings within. It was really that easy: he sat on the beach, plotting the perfect burglary, a daring and ultimately successful heist for which he would never be arrested, while getting a nice tan.

Another example shows how this peculiar form of architectural criticism, conducted with a burglar's eye for detail, really worked. Another year, another heist, and now we see Mason contemplating how he might break into the complex in which retired actor Johnny Weissmuller owned an apartment. Weissmuller was most famous for playing Tarzan, and swinging into his apartment from a ledge outside had a wild irony, like some new Tarzan of the concrete jungle updating the character for an urban age. Mason goes through the motions all over again, scanning the building for hints, playing the game. "It looked to me as though it would be an easy task to climb up one corner of the building and then walk from patio to patio until I got to Weissmuller's," Mason writes, as if this were the most ordinary thing in the world to be considering. Try it yourself, just to get a hang of it, and see how it feels: go for a walk around your neighborhood and select your targets. Look for well-placed windowsills and tree branches, or for lintels and ornaments that might make clever handholds. Or just go to a real estate website, such as Corcoran or even Curbed, and search through exterior photographs of apartments for sale. How could you get into that building without using the front door? What details stand out to you?

All those little architectural minutiae then need to be strung together in a sequence as you plot your burglary, like choreographing a dance or anticipating your forward route as a rock climber. This phase of the planning is all about timing. "It was just a matter of making sure there was nobody home in the correct combination of units," Mason recalls, as if describing an advanced level of *Donkey Kong*. As this suggests, one of the biggest risks of choosing a multitenant building is all those neighbors, always on the verge of popping out into the hallway, coming and going at odd moments, stepping off the elevator or just jogging downstairs with the evening's trash as you emerge, bag in hand. There you are—busted. But "that was easy, too," Mason drily quips, his sense of humor emerging, "all I had to do was hang out on the golf course and watch the interior lights. To top it all off, there was excellent parking available."

It was as simple as that: just park on a golf course and watch the apartment lights, as if the building's exterior is a giant LED screen broadcasting the presence or absence of people within. Then—when the sequence is right—go for it.

Cracking the Code

Midway through researching this book, I received an e-mail from someone calling himself Jack Dakswin. He introduced himself as a burglar—or a reformed one, at least, someone who had given up on crime despite himself and now worked in, of all things, the security industry. He lived in Toronto. He explained that the name he had given me was a pseudonym, to help protect himself from any legal ramifications and because his current employer was not aware of this criminal background. What followed was one of the most interesting conversations I had during my two and a half years of immersion in the world of breaking and entering.

Dakswin's interest in burglary was even more explicitly architectural than Bill Mason's, and it came down to a close reading of building exteriors and a detailed understanding of the regulations that shaped them. Dakswin had learned to use the city's fire code as a kind of inadvertent burglary tool: a targeting system for determining which specific building to hit next.

As Dakswin explained it, he had spent so much time studying the city's fire code that he could now anticipate, to a remarkably accurate degree, what awaited him inside a given building. He had begun to notice patterns. He explained, for example, that the location of an external fire escape or emergency door, including how many of each a building had, were burglary clues hiding in plain sight and were the easiest signs to look for. These would indicate everything from how many apartments you might find per floor, to how big you might expect those apartments to be. Knowing the maximum legal distance an individual apartment could be from the nearest emergency door meant that you could also deduce the building's layout from the placement of those exits. You could then judge, in advance, where the entryways to different apartments might be on one floor, then plan your path through the building accordingly. All this could be done before setting foot inside the building: Dakswin could all but sketch a floor plan simply from looking at a building's fire escape system from the street. "I don't know how many guys go through as much detail as I do," he admitted.

These urban fire codes also govern which internal emergency exit doors in a building are meant to be left unalarmed. For example, in high-rise buildings, such as multiunit condominiums and even offices, the emergency fire-exit stairs will not be alarmed on every floor. "Sometimes it will be the first floor, the fifth floor, the ninth floor—it will go up in a pattern," he pointed out. If Dakswin had just broken into an apartment on the fifth floor of a building and he now needed to get outside, fast, he could just open the unlocked emergency-exit door and flee down the stairwell—without setting off an alarm. On the fourth floor, however—or the sixth floor, or the seventh—he would not have been so lucky. This also means that residents on those floors would do well to learn whether their emergency-exit door is one that remains alarmed at all times; if not, they might want to invest in a little extra home security. "Understanding the fire regulations has been extremely helpful," Dakswin said, "because the last thing you want to do when you're leaving a building, or even going down a floor, is to set off an alarm."

I was reminded of a strange book called *Local Code* by architect Michael Sorkin. *Local Code* was Sorkin's attempt to design a whole city from scratch—with one big twist. The whole thing had been written as if it were the byzantine, nearly impossible to follow codes and regulations for an entire, hypothetical metropolis. The effect is like stumbling upon the source code for *SimCity*. Sorkin's exhaustively made point was that, if you know everything about a given metropolis, from its plumbing standards to its parking requirements, its sewer capacity to the borders of its school districts, then you could more or less accurately imagine the future form of that city from the ground up.

What was so interesting about Dakswin's approach was that he, too, had been poring over the city's fire codes and building regulations, as if reading a sacred text, and that he was doing so not as a prospective architect or city planner, but as a burglar. The keys to the city were in its code—and Dakswin was determined to find them.

He introduced me to the most common tools he would use for gaining entry to different rooms and buildings. He told me stories of hitting hotels during major business conventions, and how easy it was to spoof the magnetic key reader in each door. The deep interiors of buildings such as hotels tended to be relatively unprotected, in his experience; this meant that once you got past the entrances and lobbies and had wandered farther into a building's core, you could expect to find fewer people walking around, whether they were guards on patrol or residents taking out the garbage. Every building had its rhythms. These service corridors were the internal hinterlands—the architectural dark matter—so beloved by Bill Mason.

The Internet has been a godsend to burglars, Dakswin pointed out. He had been going online to research different neighborhoods, zooming in to see specific buildings on Google Street View to scope out everything from window heights—and thus potential routes into someone's home—to the presence of fences and shrubbery that could provide welcome cover. Even more useful, he said, had been the rise of building-industry websites such as Emporis. Emporis describes itself as "a global provider of building information" that "collects data on buildings of high public and economic value." It's practically tailor-made for burglars.

Dakswin told me that he would turn to Emporis only when putting together high-stakes burglaries, what he described as jobs "where you need to know what the walls are made of." You might need to know how thick the walls are, for example, because you have to drill through one, and you want to be sure you bring the right equipment, or you want to be sure that the other walls are thick enough that you're not going to be heard. Emporis will point you to the specific construction companies who built that high-rise or that apartment block, and "they have records of everything," Dakswin said. "They basically have it all laid out on paper. They built these buildings. It's a matter of getting those records from them, either through persuasion or through other means," even if that means "breaking in to where they keep their records and getting your hands on those." From Dakswin's experience, construction companies are not very security conscious. "You'd be shocked if you knew how easy it was," he told me.

Other times, you don't need to go to nearly as much effort to get the spatial information you need. Before new buildings begin construction, Dakswin pointed out, they have to be approved by the city. So building designs are filed at city hall or even in the municipal water department. Then it's just a question of social engineering, of convincing someone else that you need those plans. Dakswin described how essential this has been for him in the past: he actually registered a fake company—he wouldn't say where, but I had to assume it was in Toronto—with the generic name of a legal services firm. He then contacted a local construction company saying that he needed to obtain a set of blueprints due to an impending lawsuit over broken water pipes in an apartment complex they had constructed. With his legally registered company, Dakswin got his hands on the blueprints—then used them to plan his way into the building.

The longer we talked, however, the more it seemed clear that Dakswin had retired from burglary—or so he claimed—less because he was worried about getting caught and more out of an unexpected professional melancholy. He lamented that, to his mind, burglary seemed to have lost its cultural appeal, its romance, its hold on the popular imagination. Now people just steal PINs or send phishing e-mails. Dakswin is at least quantitatively right: burglary is on the decline. According to the NYPD, it has plummeted nearly 85 percent in the last twenty years alone in New York City. This is true to the surreal extent that international financial magazine *The Economist* ran a feature article in July 2013 asking, somewhat mournfully, "Where Have All the Burglars Gone?"

Dakswin seemed to long for the old feeling that intelligent, complex burglaries were still, if not increasing in number, at least keeping pace with other criminal statistics. He repeatedly claimed to feel that he was the last of a dying breed, someone once surrounded by colleagues—however anonymous or invisible they might have been—only to find himself now totally alone. He wasn't happy about it. *Where have all the burglars gone?* For him, this was an existential dilemma, as if he had woken up to find himself the last fluent speaker of an extraordinary architectural language that no one else cared about or could even remember wanting to learn.

Then he told me one final story. He said he now owned a small family house in the country, maybe an hour and a half outside Toronto, where, every few weeks, he would install new types of alarm systems borrowed from work. This was both to familiarize himself with how they worked, so that he could troubleshoot any potential problems and answer technical questions from his clientele, but also, he said, so that he could test his skills in beating them. I laughed. Aren't you retired? I asked, referring to his burglary career. He paused, then said he enjoyed the practice too much.

The Magic of Four Walls

As Mason and Dakswin both reveal, much of the work of a good burglar may already be done before ever setting foot inside the final target. That said, one of the most remarkable aspects of contemporary burglary law is the difficulty of determining when you have, in fact, entered a building. *Inside, outside*: these terms are by no means self-explanatory, and the exact moment of crossing an invisible plane from one to the other can be surprisingly hard to identify.

If breaking and entering requires someone to pass from one space into another, then at what point have I actually "entered" your house or office? Is it after I've walked fully into the middle of the room, or is it when even the barest tip of my shoe crosses the threshold? Conversely, have I really "broken in" if the front door was left ajar and I just casually stepped inside—or, say, if I've reached in through an open kitchen window? What if I grab something out of the passenger seat of a convertible with its top down parked outside on the street? Have I gone "inside" the car? How about if I take a shortcut across your front lawn on a rainy night, and while doing so, I knowingly pass beneath an overhang or walk under an awning—have I actually "entered" a space?

Unless you are Franz Kafka—or perhaps a quantum physicist—inside is inside and outside is something else entirely. Yet one of the peculiarities of burglary law is how it calls into question some of the most obvious and common beliefs we might have about what constitutes architecture—an interior versus an exterior, a private domain versus public space. A house, a shop, an apartment tower—sure, these are buildings. But a fenced-in garden, a houseboat, a backyard shed, even an unattended Jeep Wrangler—do these also constitute *buildings* and can they, too, be burglarized? Burglary has an uncanny spatial power, forcing us to rethink fundamental beliefs we might have about the built environment, from how we define a house to the way we might choose to move from one floor to another within a building.

This is because burglary, as we've seen, *requires architecture*: without an inside and an outside, there is no such thing as burglary. There is larceny—even petty theft, robbery, or vandalism—but burglary is a crime only possible in a world that has legally recognized walls and ceilings. This makes burglary spatially peculiar—and it leads to an interesting, if not entirely unsurprising, legal side effect. If to be accused of burglary requires you to have entered a work of architecture, then are we sure we all agree on what "architecture" is? An act apparently as clear-cut as entering a building quickly disappears down a rabbit hole of legal interpretation. Oddly enough, for example, the outermost limits of a private household are not universally established. The seemingly simple question of how a home is defined, and where a private interior ends, has instead led to a dizzying efflorescence of legal documentation, of arguments and counterarguments often hilariously overspecific in their examples and bewilderingly abstract in their imagery.

Burglary as defined by the FBI sounds relatively straightforward. It is "the unlawful entry of a structure to commit a felony or theft. To classify an offense as a burglary, the use of force to gain entry need not have occurred." So far, so good.

But at least two factors now complicate this definition. First, this is merely the federal definition of burglary. It is not necessarily the way that individual U.S. states will define the crime. Each state has its own, often highly elaborate, classification of burglary where the FBI's misleadingly simple "unlawful entry of a structure" is endlessly overdefined, nearly word by word, from what constitutes "entry" to how we might recognize a "structure" when we think we see one.

The second problem is that the FBI's definition presents us with an unusually succinct and streamlined description of burglary, one that buries the crime's long and complex history. This is by necessity: overly complicated explanations of popular crimes would be a pointless, even dangerous distraction from the business of enforcement.

But according to Anglo-American common law—the cumulative body of decisions and rulings agreed to and expanded upon by judges—burglary was originally only possible in a *household* or *dwelling*; the very word contains an etymological variant on the Latin *burgus*, for "castle" or "fortified home" (from which other words, such as *burgher* and even *borough*, also derive). Common law definitions of burglary also originally required the person to break into a house or dwelling *at night*. Giving historical burglary an oddly vampiric dimension, you could not, legally speaking, be a burglar while the sun was still out.

But let's start with a car. In the February 2011 ruling of *State v. Beauchamp*, the Illinois Supreme Court was presented with an apparently simple spatial problem: they had to define where the inside began of a car whose rear window had been completely smashed. The contents of the damaged car had then been raided by a thief—or had it been a burglar? Had the person "entered" the car? An intact rear window would have made the distinction between inside and outside legally obvious—and the crime, therefore, clearly a burglary. However, with nothing there to serve as a physical threshold, how was the court to decide where the space outside the car should end and the inside of the car should begin? This would decide whether the case was theft or burglary, with substantial legal repercussions for the accused.

Here the notion of "breaking the close" comes in. Breaking the close means crossing the outer limits of a space, whether it be the private interior of a home or the inside of a parked car. As law blogger Nate Nieman, from the Northern Illinois University College of Law, explained, the Illinois Supreme Court's answer to this dilemma was almost magical in its simplicity. The court, Nieman wrote, "answers this question by creating an imaginary plane which stretches across the open space of a 'specific enclosure' like a spider web." The resulting imaginary plane would thus reseal the broken window, creating a legally recognized threshold that could serve as evidence in a court of law. Think of it as an invisible geometric shape perceptible only to lawyers—a conceptual pane of glass that might not have kept the rain out but could, for legal purposes, be used to define the original limits of the car's interior. This is *the close*, and defining it is ultimately just a form of connecting the dots: drawing an imaginary line from the corner of an open window to the edge of a nearby wall to the front gate of a home garden, and so on.

Breaking the close thus constitutes entry into a "protected interior" or "specified enclosure," Nieman writes, whether or not the close is a physical thing. The close can be a complex and entirely hypothetical mathematical shape—but if you narrate it correctly and if you justify your explanation, perhaps even using clever diagrams covered with arrows and dotted lines, then even purely speculative architectural forms can be admitted in court. The close is a kind of architectural fiction, an abstract shape whose legal recognition can determine whether the accused is guilty of burglary.

Despite offering this definitive explanation of the

notion of the close, Nieman seems almost instantly wary of the narrative possibilities opened up by its creation— unconvinced by and deeply skeptical of the elaborate, invisible geometries that hopeful lawyers are now able to cast upon each other's clients, like crystalline spells of hot air, in a ruthless attempt to win the case. Nieman warns that these spiderwebs of private space, described in minute detail, open the door to useless proliferations of unlimited, otherwise invisible shapes and combinations that might threaten the validity of burglary law itself. Like angels dancing on the head of a pin, this entire system of managing architectural edges, limited by nothing but a lawyer's for-profit spatial creativity, "could eventually become unworkable when imaginations run wild in trying to draw the boundaries of these imaginary planes."

It is not hard to imagine some utterly gonzo future court case in which ambitious lawyers square off against each other, describing increasingly unwieldy architectural shapes based on the geometry formed by branches of trees and household shutters, of far-flung property fences and automatic garage doors, all woven together in some unbelievable spatial narrative that nonetheless results in a person walking down the sidewalk being accused of burglary.

For a glimpse of legal imaginations run wild, we needn't look any further than the constantly growing list of structures inside of which burglary can now legally occur. The recognized list of burglary targets has become a surreal cascade of seemingly random constructions, from telephone booths to fishing boats. Explaining all of this with the patient voice of a disappointed parent, attorney Minturn T. Wright III wrote for the *University of Pennsylvania Law Review* in December 1951—nearly seventy years ago—that the list of possible legal targets for burglary was, even then, already getting out of hand.

Wright laments that burglary law has strayed from its original, specific, and spatially limited use. Legal theorists have since lost the plot, Wright suggests, engaging in a generation's worth of free interpretation, "as if they took special delight in inventing hypothetical situations" and the spaces those situations would occur within. "Burglary was becoming less a criminal problem and more a mathematical exercise," he warns. Wright calls this "useless conceptualism."

His text soon explodes in a riot of footnotes, more like a David Foster Wallace short story than a legal brief. Individually referencing nearly every phrase back to a specific legal case, he details the ways in which the definition of breaking and entering has mutated over time. We're back to angels on pins, lawyers quibbling over what Wright calls, as if rolling his eyes, "the nature of an aperture, or the invisible line of the threshold." It is more theology than legal theory, he suggests, more abstract physics than anything that should be admissible in a court of law. In many ways, though, this is an architectural argument in an exquisitely pure sense, reduced to narrative descriptions of volumes and openings, negotiations over area and edge, as if deliberately "leaving loopholes and creating anomalies," Wright adds, for the sheer rhetorical joy of it (and the resulting spiraling legal fees).

Wright recounts a "comprehensive list of buildings and structures" that can now be legally burglarized, citing, in particular, a Nebraska statute. Like the fictional "Chinese encyclopedia" of Jorge Luis Borges, Nebraska's burglary statutes are bafflingly specific—and they do not stop at dwellings. Far from it. Nebraska's statutes fractally expand to include smokehouses, slaughterhouses, schoolhouses, storehouses, chicken houses, malt houses, meetinghouses, barns, mills, potteries, railroad-car factories, railroad cars themselves, "private telephone pay stations," and public telephone booths. Considering both cultural and historical influences on lists such as these, it would not be hard to continue unspooling one in the present day, from wine cellars to cheese caves to Pilates studios to home golf simulators. Even airplanes can now be burglarized.

Wright, remember, was discussing burglary from the perspective of 1951. Since that time, it is not just Nebraska whose burglary laws have become bewilderingly overdetermined. Illinois, for example, defines burglary as a crime in which someone "without authority . . . knowingly enters or without authority remains within a building, housetrailer, watercraft, aircraft, motor vehicle, railroad car, or any part thereof, with intent to commit therein a felony or theft." New York State goes out of its way to define the word *building*. "In addition to its ordinary meaning," the state's lawmakers explain, a building "includes any structure, vehicle or watercraft used for overnight lodging of persons, or used by persons for carrying on business therein, or used as an elementary or secondary school, or an inclosed [*sic*] motor truck, or an inclosed motor truck trailer."

So we've got "inclosed" trucks—potentially used for business or sleeping—as well as housetrailers, watercraft, secondary schools, elementary schools, and more. California law actually adds to this list. In California, burglary can be charged of anyone "who enters any house, room, apartment, tenement, shop, warehouse, store, mill, barn, outhouse or other building, tent, vessel . . . floating home . . . sealed cargo container . . . or mine or any underground portion thereof, with intent to commit grand or petit larceny or any felony." Think about this: if you step into an abandoned mine "or any underground portion thereof" with no plans to steal anything, but instead simply intending to shoot an unlicensed handgun (a felony), you are legally guilty of burglary. Why? Because it took place inside a legally recognized artificial structure (the mine).

Wright himself points out that even a hole in the ground—in this case, a powder magazine for storing explosives—could be considered a building for the purposes of burglary law. "A company stores property in a cave dug out of a hillside," he writes, referencing *People v. Buyle*, a 1937 court case in California. "An employee tries to make off with some of the goods. A burglary has been committed." Indeed, the court's instructions for the case specifically stated that a small bubble of negative space dug into the landscape, even if lacking a complete front wall, "is none the less a house merely by virtue of the fact its walls and roof may be produced by an excavation in the hillside." *None the less a house.* Because of burglary law, architecture is suddenly everywhere. We are surrounded by invisible buildings.

While this might, at first, seem like a minor point to have made at such length, stop to consider its implications. If something as simple as a negative space carved into a hillside, without any defining exterior wall, can legally be recognized as a burglarizable architectural interior, then a whole new cavalcade of spatial questions arises. What is the smallest size such a space must be— would a thimble-size depression in the ground inside of which is a glass marble that I've pressed into the soil be considered a structure that could be subject to burglary? Conversely, what's the largest size such a space can be before it's no longer considered an interior but simply a landscape? For example, if I've removed hundreds of tons of earth from a mountainside in order to flatten the site for future construction, is anyone who steps across the invisible boundary into this formerly solid mass subject to a charge of burglary?

Having heard more than enough of this kind of fantasy architecture even in his own era, Wright concludes, "The inclusion of buildings other than dwellings represents a significant departure from the common law definition of burglary." What's unique about Wright's disdain for endlessly proliferating microdefinitions inspired by and based on other microdefinitions is that he eventually, casually, and seemingly offhandedly suggests at the end of his article that we could simply rewrite the law altogether and eliminate the crime known as burglary. Some men just want to watch the world burn.

His logic rests on the fabulous conclusion that, legally speaking, architecture is a form of "magic," one that has no place in an otherwise rational system. Architecture is the "magic of four walls," he writes, referring to its power to fundamentally transform how certain crimes are judged and how their perpetrators can be sentenced. He describes nine examples in which someone was convicted of burglary. "In none of these cases is there conduct which the lay mind would consider a burglary." They are, he emphasizes, "burglaries only by virtue of the 'structure' involved in each case . . . True, other crimes may still have been committed, but that is exactly the point." Why not simply indict on the strength of these other crimes alone and be done with accusations of burglary? "The magic created by four walls should not be so strong," Wright drily concludes.

Why, then, is burglary so beloved by lawyers and police? As Wright explains, it is often easier to convict someone of burglary than it is of other crimes, including, he specifically notes, rape. What's more, a burglary charge also frequently increases—sometimes quite drastically— the possible sentencing. Think of burglary perhaps as something like an augmentation spell, always ready to be cast upon the crimes at hand: a little special something a prosecutor can tack on to any felony charge as long as it occurred inside a legally recognized architectural space. Conclusively determining a crime's precise architectural circumstances—demonstrating unimpeachably that the accused was inside a built structure at the time of commission—thus takes on great forensic and punitive importance.

Rather than giving in to the spatial magic of architecture, endowing it with unreasonable power over legal sentencing and criminal indictments, Wright suggests that we could, instead, get rid of burglary altogether and replace it with varying degrees of trespassing, larceny, and theft. Crucially, Wright's new classification of these crimes would no longer be determined *spatially*: where a crime occurred, or what its relationship was to architecture, would never again be a factor in sentencing. His ultimate goal was to eliminate the arbitrary nature of burglary, where all lawyers had to do was search for anything at all resembling an architectural structure—a telephone booth, a cubicle for selling train tickets, even a bathroom stall— in order to augment an already-existing criminal charge. As Wright despairingly described this legal tendency, "Place four walls around property, and the magic of the law will give it this added protection."

Although the situations Wright describes took place more than half a century ago, a recent indication of how flexible the spatial circumstances can be for determining whether someone has committed burglary came after an escapade in New York City in the summer of 2014. Early in the morning of July 22, two American flags mounted atop the city's iconic Brooklyn Bridge were mysteriously replaced with white flags. After two German artists claimed responsibility for the act a few weeks later, NYPD deputy commissioner Stephen P. Davis remarked to *The New York Times*, "At a minimum, it's trespass, but there is a possibility you could charge burglary. If you go into a fenced-in area for the purpose of committing a crime, that legally constitutes a burglary."

In this case, the artists climbed into a fenced-in portion of the bridge at the base of each tower. Neither of these spaces has a roof, as they are little more than chain-link cages open to the wind—yet this is considered an architectural interior, in the eyes of the law, transforming mere *trespass* into *burglary* with one enchanted close.

It does not take much imagination to suspect that, someday, an altogether-too-clever team of lawyers, police officers, and architects will combine forces to devise any number of speculative wall-like barriers peppered around the city so that other people can, rightly or not, be charged with burglary after stepping "inside" these imaginary spaces. Burglary, then, would fully and absurdly have become everything Minturn T. Wright III feared back in 1951: a pointless mathematical exercise in which unreal architectural forms are brought forth into the world in a form of legal sorcery.

Wright's sarcastic notion that discussions of burglary risked becoming nothing more than a mathematical exercise came literally true in the November 2012 issue of *Mathematics Teacher* magazine. In a one-page geometry exercise called "The Burglar in the Suitcase," columnists Kristyn Wilson and Chris Achong relate the tale of a Polish man—the eponymous burglar—who had been sneaking onto buses at the Barcelona airport by hiding inside a standard traveler's suitcase. Once the bag was locked in the hold of the bus among the other luggage, he would unzip it from within, rifle through everyone else's goods, and steal whatever seemed of worth. He'd then curl back up inside his suitcase, zip it closed, and wait for an accomplice to pick him up at the next bus stop.

This idiotic plan was interrupted by police, and the man and his accomplice were promptly arrested. Other passengers had apparently noticed a man struggling with his suspiciously heavy suitcase—perhaps even speaking to it—and they called security.

But Wilson and Achong sensed an opportunity here for a creative mathematical exercise and outlined a short geometry tutorial based on the dimensions of the suitcased man. They even provided a line diagram of him, seen in profile, wrapped up inside the case, with measurements down to the tenths of an inch. After you or your students have calculated the internal volume and the available head space of the suitcase, you are then instructed to "research the luggage restrictions for some airlines." This is presumably to make the lesson more difficult, but it inadvertently also indicates which airlines might be easier to rob due to overgenerous baggage allowances.

"Would the burglar's suitcase meet the restrictions or be flagged?" they ask. "Justify your answer."

The Code of the Burglar

Now that the minefield of burglary law has been at least partially explored, and some indication of burglary's strange spatial power has been revealed, let's step away from all the abstraction, put our feet back onto solid ground, and look at the actual architecture of burglary: the kinds of buildings most often targeted by burglars and the factors that might make your home more at risk than your neighbor's.

Despite clear warning signs, why particular buildings are chosen rather than others remains ambiguous and not easily answered. Constantly shifting factors are at play, some of which are rationally premeditated; some burglars, who may not be in the most coherent state of mind, simply make spur-of-the-moment decisions.

Still, if you look closely enough, a few patterns emerge, and a helpful checklist can be developed; this is backed up by research by criminologists such as R. I. Mawby, Paul Cromwell, and James N. Olson, as well as by my interviews with officers from the LAPD and the South Yorkshire Police. The likelihood that your house will be burglarized—and not that of the family across the street—can come down even to the nature of the local streetscape. A complex neighborhood street plan, full of curved roads, dead ends, and culs-de-sac, can deter prospective outsider burglars by reducing their ability to navigate. If the burglars don't know where they are—if they don't know how to get away in a hurry without making wrong turns or doubling back upon themselves—then they're substantially less likely to try to break into a house there.

The caveat, however, is that everything I just described also explains why police patrols can be so thin in those neighborhoods. Burglars will, ironically, have more time to get away and are also far less likely to be caught in the act by a police car coincidentally driving by. During an afternoon spent with the Burglary Special Section of the LAPD—a tight crew of veteran detectives assigned to some of the country's most difficult burglary investigations, from diamond thefts to stolen Picassos—I met an enthusiastic detective third grade named Chris Casey. Over multiple conversations with Detective Casey about burglary in Greater Los Angeles, I filled nearly half of the notebook I had been using at the time—a notebook I'd been expecting to last me through several weeks' worth of reporting—with stories about returned-merchandise schemes targeting Home Depot, San Fernando Valley pawnshop burglary rings, and even a man whom Casey and his colleagues had dubbed the Copper King, committing industrial-scale retail fraud from a warehouse-size machine shop somewhere in Los Angeles.

One of the high points of Casey's career, he told me, had come from a bizarre burglary case back in the 1990s, when a prized baseball signed by Hall of Fame pitcher Sandy Koufax was stolen from a home in the Hollywood Hills. Casey and his partner at the time, Detective Mike Fesperman, convinced Koufax to sign another baseball for the bereaved homeowner; it arrived in a protective plastic case. Casey still laughs when he tells the story. But he was unequivocal that—as the theft of a baseball from a home even in the mazelike, twisting streets of the Hollywood Hills shows—burglars go where the money is. Or, the autographed baseball. They're not going to waste time overthinking something like the local street layout, especially if they just need some quick cash.

Nonetheless, let's continue with the checklist. Is your house on a cul-de-sac? If so, you're less likely to be hit, as a burglar can easily be boxed in: the police only have to block one street. Or is your house on a corner? Bad news: houses on corners are more likely to be broken into, as they offer multiple escape routes and clear lines of sight in all directions, allowing burglars to look out for returning residents or a patrolling cop car. Is your house set back farther from the street than the other houses around it—perhaps even within a ring of large bushes or luxuriant trees? If so, you're more likely to be a target: lush landscaping offers prospective burglars the same privacy as it gives you, wandering around in your robe at night, glass of bourbon in hand. The importance of clear visibility both into and out of your home was strongly emphasized to me when I spoke with Mark Saunders, one of five crime prevention design advisers working full-time with the Surrey Police in England. Saunders's role is to advise local homeowners on how to discourage the attention of passing burglars, even offering architectural input into how suburban homes and downtown business districts should be designed to deter future crime.

Perhaps your house is close to an on-ramp, bus stop, subway station, or train depot. If so, it is more likely to be burglarized: think of all those strangers coming and going through your neighborhood, given such an easy way to get both in and out. If that just sounds like a cynical attack on public transportation—access to public transit often makes land values *fall* in parts of Los Angeles out of fear of itinerant criminals—take heart from the conclusions of a study written by former U.S. secretary of housing and urban development Henry Cisneros, suggesting that pedestrian-friendly environments are less likely to be targeted by criminals. While his research offers a great argument for rethinking neighborhood design, it also somewhat ominously implies living in a community where everything you do is under surveillance. "To deter crime," Cisneros explains, "spaces should convey to would-be intruders a strong sense that if they enter they are very likely to be observed, to be identified as intruders, and to have difficulty escaping."

Further on the checklist, is your house near a school—and thus more likely to receive police patrols or to be carefully watched by paranoid parents? Is a park or a forest nearby—offering a broad swath of darkness into which a burglar can quickly disappear? Does your house have a back door or a garage? Those are common routes of entry for residential burglars. Further, is your back door a sliding glass door? Sliding doors can easily be popped off their tracks without breaking the glass—then just as easily reset upon departure. Perhaps burglars have already broken into your house using this all-but-undetectable method of entry, and you just haven't noticed yet what they stole.

None of these factors is universal, and you have probably begun to see the contradictions already: a pedestrian-friendly neighborhood might offer a degree of protection from burglary—unless a subway stop or a train station is nearby. Grids are bad—unless you live on a cul-de-sac. Lush landscaping gives burglars more privacy once they've broken into your house—unless those trees also seem likely to prevent them from seeing whether the police are on their way. Any golden rule is fallible when it comes to predicting or deterring burglary. To say that walkable, nongridded urban environments are somehow resistant to crime would make absolutely no sense in England. England is hardly a global hot spot for rationally gridded, car-centric towns, yet it boasts the highest rate of burglary in the entire European Union. Italy, another nation not known for its automobile-dependent, gridded megacities, is a close second for residential burglaries (in some years, it is actually worse than England). On paper, they should be nearly burglary-free.

When seen through the eyes of a burglar, many architectural features take on an unexpected dual role. Such things as back doors and side windows often double as potential getaway routes, for example, and experienced burglars will often only target houses with at least two points of exit. Burglars have been known to walk through a house and, before stealing anything at all, unlock another door from within or pop open a window—to ensure a quick escape route.

Even the type of glass in your windows can matter. Do you have storm windows, for example, thus doubling or even tripling the amount of glass a burglar would have to shatter? Multiple panes can make so much noise when broken and pose so much more of a safety risk that good windows can deter even the bravest criminals. Of course, some burglars will carry a roll of tape, throwing up a quick X across the window glass—as if anticipating a hurricane—before shattering it. That way, broken pieces of glass will just hang there, stuck in a web of tape, far less likely to fall and noisily shatter. In one unsettling example, criminologists Cromwell and Olson met a burglar who once worked for a glass-repair company; his specialty had been in expertly replacing whole windowpanes. He, like George Leonidas Leslie, realized that he could use his skill and training for nefarious purposes. He could remove an entire windowpane without causing any visible damage, then reaffix it in its frame on his way back out. You might never even notice that you'd been burglarized.

Now, what about the actual layout of your house? If your house is architecturally unique, or in any way confusing, it can be a less tempting target. But if you live in a suburban development where only two or three original home plans were used, then once a burglar knows these few, he or she knows all the houses—down to where the bedroom closets are and where safes or jewelry cabinets are most likely to be kept. Your neighbor's weakness is your weakness, too. The same is true for large apartment complexes, where each unit's floor plan will be repeated multiple times from floor to floor, giving burglars advance knowledge of where to look and greatly decreasing the amount of time they might need to spend inside the building. Repeat burglaries on the same building are so common as to be expectable, and this is sometimes considered proof that burglars will go back to what they already know, familiar with a given house, its floor plan, its entries and exits.

Think that means you're safe because you live in a unique home or apartment design? All a savvy burglar often needs to do these days is look at the website of your home builder or the property agency in charge of your apartment building to pull up a floor plan; these innocuous online tools ostensibly made for real estate bargain hunters are also amazingly helpful burglars' guides.

Alternatively, perhaps the burglar has already been inside your house and is already familiar with its layout. Perhaps he or she once delivered a package there, did housework for you (or the previous owner), decorated one of your children's bedrooms, fixed the plumbing, painted the living room, or performed any number of other home renovations—perhaps even because he or she is one of your friends or family members. Do you keep track of everyone who comes and goes, and do you really know where all your extra sets of house keys have gone?

One burglar interviewed by sociologists Richard T. Wright and Scott Decker in their book *Burglars on the Job* admitted that he used to work as the family gardener at a particular house; he had a duplicate key cut for access to the house, but he had since used the key over and over to reenter the house and steal things. Incredibly, the house had changed ownership twice since he was last employed there nearly ten years ago, but the door lock had never been replaced; this meant that the ex-gardener no longer had any connection to the current homeowners. His methods were equally devious, making his crimes hard to detect. He would steal only one thing at a time, which helped make it all but impossible to tell if something had been stolen or simply misplaced, if your kids had innocently moved it or if your spouse had put it away somewhere without telling you. You might think it's memory loss or early-onset senility; it's actually a patient burglar robbing you and your family in slow motion.

A burglar's typical list of considerations gets slightly more obvious from here. Do you own a dog? BEWARE OF DOG signs are, in fact, effective deterrents. Is anyone currently home? If not, are your neighbors around and likely to see something? Do you have a burglar alarm? One burglar explained to Wright and Decker how he would react to burglar alarms—and it certainly wasn't with the desired level of fear. If anything, alarms signal to burglars that you own something worth protecting and that your house is thus a good target. As that same burglar reasoned to Wright and Decker: "If they got alarms, then you can look for gold and silver and tea sets. If there's an alarm on the first floor, it probably ain't hooked to the top floor. If it's hooked to the top floor, then it ain't hooked to the attic or it's not hooked to the exhaust system." In that case, following a rigorous process of elimination, he would just go in through the exhaust system. As we already saw with Bill Mason, every building is a puzzle for a burglar to pick apart.

At the same time, these considerations also get more subjective, becoming unique to each burglar and to his or her own fears or financial circumstances. Does the burglar need money *right now*? Does he or she have an addiction that needs to be serviced immediately? Incredibly, as many as 70 percent of residential burglaries are estimated to be committed by drug addicts.

Many burglaries are inspired simply by seeing someone leave a house. Think of the burglar who was just standing waiting for a bus one day when he saw a couple walk out of an apartment across the street, carrying suitcases. On a whim, he let the bus pass, waited till the couple had driven off in a taxi, then promptly broke into their place. He hadn't been looking to commit a crime when he woke up that morning; he didn't see it coming until the very moment he noticed the couple walking out their front door with their luggage, presumably thinking of anything but home security. But now he knew they weren't there—so he struck.

Human variability aside, the idea of discovering some secret law of the built environment that will reveal exactly where and when a burglar will strike next has an undeniable appeal. The police in the U.K. think they are close to cracking the code, and they have instituted a remarkable architectural sting operation as a result.

Capture World

You first spot the apartment from afar, thanks to a light still shining in the kitchen window. Walking closer and pulling the brim of your hat down closer to hide your face, you see the top of what appears to be an open laptop computer sitting on the kitchen table. No one is there, working or surfing the Internet; in the minute or two you've had to study the place, you haven't noticed any movement inside, no other lights turning on or off. In fact, it looks as if only one light is on in the whole apartment.

You step up onto a small brick perimeter wall across the street to get a better look—just a low fence framing the yard of a multistory housing block—and sure enough, the laptop is sitting there alone, without an owner to be seen. Astonishingly, a digital camera has been left out on the table next to it, as if someone had been transferring photos from one device to the other, only to leave, maybe for the whole night, maybe just for a quick errand. Either way, no one's there right now, and that makes this your best opportunity.

Best of all, a living-room window partially hidden behind some bushes is slightly ajar—meaning that whoever lives there has taken zero precautions against burglary and thus practically deserves to be robbed (you tell yourself). It's instant karma—payback for his or her absent-minded naïveté. So it's now or never. With one final scan of the surrounding street and a quick squint up at other windows in case someone might be watching, you confirm you're all alone. It's time to go. You cross the street, pop open the window, and slide in.

It's almost too easy. Immediately, you head for the bedroom, both to make sure no one is there sleeping and also to grab a pillowcase to stuff everything in. While you're in there, you notice it's oddly furnished; it's almost as if no one really spends a lot of time here, as if it's just a place to crash, because nothing but a bed and a nightstand are in the room. It feels strange—but you're in now, so it's all about getting the job done, then getting out.

Quickly, you open the bathroom medicine cabinet, hoping to find some medications—but there's nothing. Then you go into the kitchen to pop open the cupboards one by one. Almost nothing is in them, which again seems strange, and you've also noticed that everything feels vaguely dirty, as if whoever lives here hasn't cleaned in a while. Anything you've touched—a doorknob or cabinet handle—has made your fingers feel oily, your palms a bit slick with something you can't see. If not for the laptop, which you head toward to grab, this would not have been worth it; now it's time to go.

Which is exactly when you hear the front door of the apartment burst open, and that word you've been hoping to avoid your whole criminal career echoes into the room around you: "Police!" Two officers sweep through the door, and it's far too late to get back to the open window and escape.

You're trapped—or *captured*, as the case may be.

"Capture houses" are fake apartments run by the police to attract and, as their name implies, capture burglars. They are furnished to be all but indistinguishable from other apartments, with the important difference that nearly everything inside them has been tagged using a chemical residue only visible under UV light. These chemical sprays and forensic coatings—applied to door handles, window latches, and any portable goods found throughout the properties, including TVs, laptops, and digital cameras—are also known as SmartWater. Tiny Web-connected cameras film each room from various angles. Finally, a small team of officers waits patiently nearby, usually in an apartment next door or across the hall.

The perverse brilliance of a capture house comes from the fact that only the most abjectly paranoid burglars would ever suspect that the home, business, or apartment they've broken into is somehow not real, that it is not quite what it appears to be—that they have broken into a decoy, a mirage, or trap. Capture houses can be so carefully designed that a burglar might never experience the slightest sensation that something's not right or somehow out of place; they might thus never guess that they're inside a house or apartment secretly run by the police.

It helps that these capture houses are not isolated places, glowing like film sets on the outer edge of town; instead, they are normally flats in busy, multiunit buildings and on otherwise unremarkable streets. If you live in the U.K.—or even if you've only traveled there—you may well have seen a capture house yourself, but never suspected anything amiss. Perhaps a police-run apartment is in your very building.

The capture-house program began at the end of 2007 in Leeds, England, under the direction of Chief Constable Sir Norman Bettison of the West Yorkshire Police. Having proved successful in Yorkshire, capture houses are now spreading to nearly every major metropolitan region of the U.K., including such cities as Birmingham, Nottingham, and even London itself.

Just south of Leeds, in the city of Rotherham, Detective Chief Inspector Dave Stopford of the South Yorkshire Police described to me how the program worked, what its strengths and weaknesses have proven to be, and where it might go next. Individual capture houses are most often set up by a technical team of civilians working for the police, he told me. Technicians and local contractors with the necessary expertise install hidden cameras, microphones, fiber-optic or Wi-Fi networks, twenty-four-hour infrared cameras, and even the SmartWater sprays. Each capture house is then fully stocked, complete with electronic equipment, lights on timers, and bare but functional furniture. This makes the apartments something more like an elaborate ploy of interior design and electrical engineering—a wired-up simulation of contemporary British domesticity, all but indistinguishable from the real thing.

Laughing, Stopford explained that his officers once lacked the funds they needed to get the furniture and home goods to stock another new capture house—so one of his officers simply went around the police station, desk to desk, requesting any unused or soon-to-be-discarded personal furniture. Most of the officers contributed at least something—a bedside table, an old couch, a tattered carpet past its prime—thus creating what could be thought of as the ultimate distillation of a police officer's apartment: a space furnished only with things taken from local cops. If only the burglar later captured there had had an eye for law enforcement taste in interior design, he might never have broken in. It was as police-like an apartment as you could get.

Once apprehended, many of the criminals are shown DVDs of their break-in. This is not only—or even primarily—to embarrass them, but also to show off a bit, to demonstrate the ever-watchful, all-powerful eyes of the British police with their clever lenses hidden inside lampshades and ferns. The surreal, Warholian effect is to make it seem as if the burglars have inadvertently broken into a private film studio meant just for them, their fifteen minutes of fame captured on miniature cameras that only the most paranoid among them would even look for or see.

Chief Inspector Stopford explained that in many cases, a capture house will be set up to catch one specific person. The police will have studied the modus operandi of a burglar—someone who only breaks into first-floor flats, for example, where a window has been left slightly ajar—and they then design an apartment to attract that person. The effort is apparently worth it. A single burglar can raise the crime rate of an entire neighborhood; taking that one person off the streets pays huge dividends in reducing the overall local crime statistics. But it's not always a guaranteed success. Some of the fake apartments Stopford's officers have operated have been open for as little as one day before being hit by a burglar, while others have gone nearly a full calendar year without being broken into even once.

All this means that if you are the burglar in question, the local police have designed and furnished an apartment with you in mind. When you are next out and about, casing homes for a possible burglary, and you feel attracted to a certain property, you have to step back and consider the almost science-fiction-like possibility that it was put there specifically to attract you.

The notion of the capture house is easy to adapt elsewhere, even at different scales. Bait cars are basically the same idea: they are "capture cars," left on the street with their windows down or even with their keys still in the ignition to attract passing car thieves. But if you give in to your baser impulses and try to boost the car, you'll find the doors immediately lock, trapping you inside, while an internal camera has already sent high-resolution images of your face to a nearby police crew. The car is GPS-tagged in case you try to get away.

Back in Los Angeles, Detective Chris Casey explained to me that entire fake storefront businesses have been set up around the city by the LAPD to trap would-be thieves, fences, and smugglers. He described how police officers would pose as pawnshop owners or even as black-market metal buyers to deceive burglars and thieves. The program is elaborate and expensive—but it works. Think of it as an architectural version of going undercover: not just officers wearing civilian clothes and using fake names, but an entire building or strip mall disguised and camouflaged as something else altogether.

What remains so interesting about the idea of a capture house is this larger, abstract notion that the houses, apartments, bars, shops, and businesses standing all around us might be *fake*, that they exist as a police-monitored surrogate of the everyday world, a labyrinth of law-enforcement stage sets both deceptive and alluring. Indeed, beyond just trapping local burglars, the capture-house program's overriding and perhaps most successful effect lies in inspiring a distinct and quite peculiar form of interpretive unease among local criminals: the uncanny feeling that the very place you are now standing in is somehow not real but a kind of well-furnished simulation, a deliberate mirage or architectural replica run by the local police, overseen by invisible cameras recording your every move. As Chief Inspector Stopford somewhat over-confidently explained to me, even if you're looking for signs that a given home or apartment is a capture house, you won't find them. You won't know you've actually broken into a simulation until the police themselves come crashing in, looking for you.

The fundamental premise of the capture-house program is that police can successfully predict what sorts of buildings and internal spaces will attract not just any criminal but a specific burglar, the unique individual each particular capture house was built to target. This is because burglars unwittingly betray personal, as well as shared, patterns in their crimes; they often hit the same sorts of apartments and businesses over and over. But the urge to mathematize this, and to devise complex statistical models for when and where a burglar will strike next, can lead to all sorts of analytical absurdities.

A great example of this comes from an article published in the criminology journal *Crime, Law and Social*

Change back in 2011. Researchers from the Physics Engineering Department at Tsinghua University reported some eyebrow-raisingly specific data about the meteorological circumstances during which burglaries were most likely to occur in urban China.

They found, for example, that burglars tended to strike when the temperature was "in the range of −7°C to 27°C," or approximately 19°–81° Fahrenheit. This is not entirely surprising, given that this corresponds quite well to the expected thermal window for most of the country. In a sense, it would be unusual to do *anything* outside of these temperatures. Undaunted by the inherent absurdity, the authors also found that instances of burglary could be correlated to a set of average wind speeds (for example, burglars seem to hit on days when the wind is blowing less than four meters per second in China, or roughly nine miles per hour) and even relative humidity (burglary, we read, is most likely to occur when the humidity is between 15 and 85 percent, another meaninglessly all-encompassing range).

Their conclusion is impressively vague. They write that burglary is "more inclined to occur in a comfortable circumstance," although quite a few burglaries also occurred during "extreme weather." Sadly, although the authors mention barometric pressure as a further influence on burglary statistics, they don't delve into any hard numbers.

But perhaps we shouldn't be so cynical. It's all too easy to mock these attempts at statistical measurement. It might sound ridiculous, for example, to learn that burglary can be correlated to the phases of the moon—as if crime has its own lunar tides—but this, in fact, is borne out quite regularly. The reason is simple: a new moon equals less light to be seen by, and thus an easier time sneaking around someone's property or through an empty part of town.

No less a figure than legendary magician and escape artist Harry Houdini confirms this in his 1906 book, *The Right Way to Do Wrong*. Houdini describes the burglar as a kind of occult psychogeographer, someone uniquely attuned not only to the rhythms of the streets but to the phases of the moon above. Houdini writes that an accomplished burglar would have "consulted the almanac" before heading out for plunder, using astronomical timetables to help coordinate his heist with the orbit of the moon around the earth. Every bit of darkness helps. Then, when the almanac is right and the shadows are deepest, this astrologist-burglar with one eye on the stars and planets would make his fateful move.

Yet even a new moon works both ways. Burglars are humans, after all, and they are not immune to fear when wandering into a house in utter darkness. A great deal of the sociological literature indicates that too little light is as unnerving to a burglar as it would be for a homeowner to hear someone rummaging around in the dark. Think of the hapless burglar—one of my favorite examples yet—who called the police himself when he became convinced that someone else was in the house with him. He thought another burglar was somewhere out there in the darkness, tiptoeing through the unlit rooms, perhaps heading straight for him.

Lunar phase aside, the question of when to strike a particular building is at least as important for burglars as where that building is located or how it is designed. If you don't want to read every issue of *Architectural Digest* looking for hints about which houses to strike, then you might want to look elsewhere for clues about who, what, where, and when to burglarize—such as reading people's Twitter feeds or Facebook updates.

In 2010, as social location services such as Foursquare achieved mainstream appeal, a semiautomated Twitter account called PleaseRobMe popped up. It began retweeting people's social status updates, but only those that seemed to indicate when that person was no longer at home. "Showing you a list of all those empty homes out there" was PleaseRobMe's tagline. Its point was not criminal, PleaseRobMe hastened to add, but sociological, showing how "oversharing," as it's termed, can have real-world security consequences, not the least of which is letting anyone in the world know when you've stepped out to a bar, a museum, a friend's restaurant, or a nightclub—or all of the above, in a multihour bender—and thus are no longer inside your apartment. All a burglar would have to do is check their target's Foursquare account (or Instagram or Twitter or Facebook feeds) to see how much more time they've got to get in and out undisturbed.

Consider burglar Tricia Schneider. According to the sheriff's office of Posey County, Indiana, Schneider "admitted using Facebook posts to pick her targets" in numerous counties throughout southwest Indiana. Sheriff Greg Oeth explained to local media outlet WECT that online oversharing entails risks: "It's posting, 'Look how much fun we're having on the beach today. Here's photos of us at a very unique restaurant.' Those sorts of things [are an] indication that you're away from home and that your property is unprotected."

Or think about the New Jersey man who was also busted for using social media to choose his targets. Known by Hunterdon County police as the "Facebook burglar," Steven Pieczynski would wait until his own Facebook friends had posted holiday plans before raiding their empty houses. Note that these weren't, technically, strangers; they were people who had accepted Pieczynski's friend requests.

An even more astonishing example of social tracking comes from the case of the jewelry-store owner in Kansas City whose shop was robbed of up to $300,000 worth of merchandise. During the ensuing investigation, police found that the owner's car had been tagged with a GPS device—even her son's car had a tag—with the implication that their movements had been tracked for days, if not weeks, as the thieves waited for the perfect moment to strike.

It gets weirder. In the summer of 2014, a young man was arrested in Columbia, Tennessee, for having pretended to be a woman on social media. Luring local men into fictional dates, using pseudonyms such as "Young and ready 234" and "Lilwhitegirl1132," he would send his prospective suitors literally down the garden path, giving them elaborate instructions to find, for example, "the end of Oak Park Drive and meet on a barely noticeable garden path on the dead-end street." They were then instructed to wait there. Meanwhile, the nineteen-year-old female impersonator was actually back at the target's house, stealing cash, jewelry, and other valuables. As Columbia Police lieutenant Joey Gideon instructed *The Daily Herald*, "The basic moral there is not to disclose anything online unless you know who that person is."

This sort of thing needn't only be online or even digital. In his 2001 study of burglary, criminologist R. I. Mawby learned that one burglar would actually pay other burglars to photocopy vacation rosters when they broke into offices late at night so that he could take note of any upcoming vacations. This can be extended to your own home: a common piece of advice for vacationing homeowners is not to write their exact vacation dates on their home calendar, precisely so that future burglars won't learn that you'll be gone for another three days, giving them all the time in the world to rifle through your valuables. Think of the burglar out in Joshua Tree, California, who drank all the beer in the kitchen before taking a nice hot shower, or even the Easton, Pennsylvania, burglar from 2010 who not only drank all the beer in the fridge and took a shower but, awesomely, *gave himself a haircut*. When the homeowner came back, she found him just sitting there, calmly watching TV, freshly shorn. If burglars know how long you'll be gone, they can basically move in.

Obvious oversharing aside, if your goal is to leave no clues for burglars—to make sure that they can never figure out when you are or are not at home—well, frankly, you just might not be able to do much about it.

In a study of how domestic systems such as home heating can be used by burglars to determine whether you and your family are away on vacation, a team of researchers presenting at a 2012 conference on computer security pointed out that you just can't hide that you're not at home. Given the right devices, they explained, "anybody with sufficient technical skills to monitor real-time energy consumption patterns in an entire neighborhood"—and they explain how this is possible—can determine when a particular house sees a precipitous drop in energy use. Either the residents have died or they're off on vacation somewhere, but either way a huge bull's-eye has appeared on their house. Automatic meter-reading technologies have very real security implications, the researchers conclude, and even this overlooks the ease with which someone could physically check your electricity meter to see if your monthly use has dropped off.

With this many possible signs to remember to check for, protecting yourself from research-oriented burglars can, to put it mildly, seem a bit overwhelming. Still, you can take some important and basic technological steps. For example, you can use a timer to turn lights on and off in your absence, and you can also buy a device called FakeTV. FakeTV is more or less exactly what it sounds like: a single-purpose lighting appliance that mimics the shifting colors and motion of a regular television set. The result? It looks as if someone is home watching late-night television, with flashes of action and color flickering through the drapery. Set it on a timer, and your house has what sociologists Wright and Decker call "the illusion of occupancy," even though no one's home but machines.

Again, though, technical devices such as these risk being as obvious a clue as vacation photos on your Facebook page that you're not at home. Consider an article from 2013, published in the *Observer*, where we read about wealthy families in the Hamptons of Long Island all looking for a ritzier place to spend their holidays. Apparently so many people now leave the Hamptons for Europe each season that "whole neighborhoods are on timers." Every night, an otherwise empty neighborhood thus "lights up like the Christmas tree at Rockefeller Center." One exasperated resident points out that the people next door "need to reset their light timer." Why? "They forgot it's no longer daylight savings time." The house anomalously switches on every night a full hour too early, making it even more obvious that, for all the light and electricity, no one's home.

What burglar could resist the appeal of such a scenario—the ultimate suburban heist, moving from home to home like some new Robin Hood of the Hamptons, timing one's entry and exit with the automated table lamps of families vacationing far away? You could break into every house in the neighborhood—unless those homeowners could find a way to keep their neighborhood off the map altogether. A different sort of social media use suggests a way that small cities or entire neighborhoods might, in a relatively literal sense, remove themselves from the view of prospective burglars.

A passing remark in Mike Davis's *City of Quartz* led me to the city of Bradbury, California. This is in itself ironic, as Bradbury—a private, gated suburb north of Los Angeles—has a careful policy of taking itself off the media radar. It does not want to be discussed. As Davis points out in *City of Quartz*, unless you are buying property there, Bradbury would prefer you don't know it exists.

Reporting on the town back in 1988, the *Los Angeles Times* remarked that, following a handful of crimes in the 1970s and as civic culture in nearby Los Angeles went from bad to worse in the eighties, Bradbury's "city officials and residents decided to become more closed-mouthed about their community. Each time an article appeared, they said, it drew attention to the city and the number of burglaries increased." The city managers therefore agreed not to speak to the media, effectively removing their neighborhood from public conversation. Already physically gated to prevent entry by strangers, Bradbury would now be subject to a kind of urban-scale nondisclosure agreement. Out of sight, out of mind—and out of the reach of burglars.

The aptly named Hidden Hills—another secluded semi-city in the economic orbit of Greater Los Angeles—has found a different way to remove itself from public scrutiny. Like Bradbury, the town does not appear on

Google Street View. The invasive cameras of the search-engine giant are not welcome on the private streets of either neighborhood, something not uncommon in the wealthier, private subdivisions and celebrity-dense developments north of L.A. The equestrian-oriented Bell Canyon, for example, also wealthy, private, and keen to stay off the maps of ambitious burglars, has joined them, opting out of representation on Google Street View. This secrecy only adds to their property values (presumably attracting the unwanted interest of future burglary crews).

Despite all the publicly available data, the disappointing truth is that burglaries more often than not are impulsive and unplanned, based on spur-of-the-moment decisions made in response to some immediately noticed detail: the window of that house was left open, that man clearly just left for work, likely leaving an empty house, or that the street is totally deserted and you have a pressing need for cash. The vast majority of burglaries are not particularly exciting (this book exists to shed light on the exceptions, not the rule). Statistically, burglary is far more likely to be committed by an opportunist drug addict smashing a pane of glass to steal a pair of diamond stud earrings and a DVD player than it is to be an organized gang of topology-obsessed underground-mining aficionados burrowing into a building from the structure next door.

There simply is no cut-and-dried rule for when, where, and under what circumstances you can expect a burglary to take place. Even the most general parameters are only moderately useful for predicting when and where a burglar might strike next. Worse, trying to protect yourself against these outliers—against the special cases, the unpredictable break-ins, the addicts, and the impulse burglars—means that you run the risk of fortifying yourself against only the most outlandish scenarios.

Burglars of the Ancient World

The question of how to protect and even fortify your home against a burglar's intrusion is a question as old as the home itself. Jerry Toner, a classicist at Cambridge University, teaches what he calls "history from below": looking at the popular entertainments, bodily sensations, and even the disaster-response plans of ancient Rome. One particularly memorable course focused on the lost smells of early Christianity. I learned that Toner was writing a new book about crime in imperial Rome, from vandalism and riots to murder and burglary, and thus thought it obvious that I should talk to him about breaking and entering in the ancient world. After all, no less a figure than famed Roman orator Marcus Tullius Cicero once asked, "What is more sacred, what is more inviolable, than the house of every citizen?" The injunction against breaking and entering is encoded in the very foundations of civic discourse.

Toner began by reminding me of a book I'd last read in my high school Latin class: *The Golden Ass* by Apuleius. A major secondary story line of that book is the tale of three thieves who steal the titular donkey—they technically steal a homeowner who has accidentally turned himself into a donkey during a conjuring trick gone awry. As Apuleius describes it, this proto–burglary crew would use axes not only to cleave open locked trunks, but to knock down or undermine the walls of private residences. The origin of the word *undermine* is straightforward and quite literal here, as it means digging a tunnel or mine under the walls of a building or city, causing those walls to collapse. They wouldn't bother with merely breaking the close, to return to the language of legal argumentation; they would obliterate the close altogether in a cloud of wood splinters and dust.

While peering out at a neighbor's house, our narrator sees "three great thieves attempting to / break down his walls and gates, and to open the / locks to enter in, by tearing away all the doors from / the posts and by dragging out the bolts, which were / most firmly fixed." They were dismantling the building, taking architecture apart in a literal act of breaking and entering. This would seem to make *The Golden Ass* a candidate for one of literature's earliest tunnel jobs, a second-century heist aligned with present-day police definitions of breaking through walls.

This example was just a prelude to a lengthy discussion by Toner of the criminal environment of Rome, a discussion that he prefaced by pointing out some key limitations to our knowledge of exactly what kinds of burglaries would have occurred there. First of all, Latin had no word for *burglar*; there were only variations on *thief*, implying a lack of attention to the spatial circumstances of a given crime. This is not to say that there weren't home invasions or that private residences were somehow considered impregnable. On the contrary, even the presence of window shutters—useful for more than just offering privacy—was evidence that some degree of home fortification was considered advisable against potential break-ins.

Roman popular culture provided would-be burglars with plenty of ideal opportunities to strike, Toner explained. Consider the astonishing popularity of Rome's chariot races: it is estimated that nearly 75 percent of the city's residents would attend the stadium on race days, leaving an all-but-deserted metropolis behind them, its homes unwatched, its private goods there for the taking. An urban standing army of what we'd now call police was thus called up to fan out into the streets of Rome, moving against the swarming tide of humanity who pushed and shoved their way toward the Circus Maximus. Again, I was struck by a more recent echo: An excited burglar pointed out to criminologists Cromwell and Olson in their 2004 study, "Man! Wait until football season. I clean up then. When they are at the game, I'm at their house." Two thousand years later burglars are still using the same modus operandi.

After Toner described the chariot races, I mentioned Stanley Kubrick's early film *The Killing*, from 1956, in which a heist at the local horse race sets up a disastrous sequence of events for the perpetrators. Surely, I said, such a plot could be altered and rewritten for the ancient world, where villa after villa and mansion after mansion are systematically and expertly looted, emptied of their every valuable. It would be the largest heist in history—a veritable sacking of Rome. If only Kubrick were still around to direct it.

Toner was only half-convinced by the scenario, this *Ocean's Eleven* of the ancient world. The first problem, he began, and there were many, was with what the burglars of the time could actually steal—what luxury goods would have existed at the time, not to mention which were valuable enough to target—and how the criminals could carry it all through the city without being spotted. This would, in turn, have had an effect on which buildings they chose to rob, and even which streets or neighborhoods—such as those closest to the Tiber River, so that they could plot an aquatic getaway and just float to distant safety. Burglars even back then would have made decisions based not only on a building's perceived vulnerabilities or how easy it might have been to scale the outside walls (or to knock them down), but also based on what those thieves thought they might realistically find inside worth stealing. I was reminded again of Bill Mason and the various details he would look for before choosing to hit a certain high-rise, struck by the continuity of ideas that seem to have underlain burglary for millennia.

The great temples, Toner explained, would have attracted a lot of criminal attention. Temples served a role not unlike the banks of our day; those institutions were not just used as a place to conduct religious activities but as communal holding spots where valuable items, civic gifts, and even personal property could all be stored. They were like building-size safe-deposit boxes for the wealthiest members of society—and, thus, perfect targets for an enterprising troupe of burglars.

In fact, he added, the looting of temples—albeit at a military scale and perpetrated by heavily armed and well-trained soldiers, not small criminal gangs—was quite often the climactic and deliberately humiliating end to intercity warfare. A metropolis such as Rome or Jerusalem would be sacked of its belongings, its most prized possessions paraded away on the shoulders of triumphant enemies. Sacking a city was nothing more than militarized burglary—breaking and entering applied to an entire metropolis. Look at Troy, for example, its walls breached, its soldiers deceived by a hollow horse. In retrospect, it's not entirely inaccurate to suggest that the Trojan War was decided by an ingenious act of burglary now enshrined in popular mythology through the metaphor of the Trojan horse—the original and most consequential burglar's tool in Western history.

Perhaps the most interesting takeaway from my conversation with Toner was the implication that the fear of being burglarized while everyone was away from home at the chariot races helped to catalyze the growth of a metropolitan police force. Without all those quiet streets and empty homes to protect, armed guards on specifically timed, routine patrols would not have become such an urgent necessity then in urban history. It's as if the city itself, and the behaviors and institutions through which it was regulated, coalesced around the activities of criminals, like irritating grains of sand around which an oyster gradually grows its pearls. Burglary, placed in the expanded context of thousands of years of urban development, helped to catalyze a kind of evolutionary cat-and-mouse game through which cops and robbers inadvertently collaborated, reacting to one another and shaping the legal, fictional, and literal dimensions of the built environment.

4

TOOLS OF
THE TRADE

Picking the Bridge

On a Saturday afternoon at the end of summer, a loose group of recreational lock-pickers met halfway across the Brooklyn Bridge to help "save" hundreds of love locks. One hundred and fifty years after construction began on the Brooklyn Bridge—150 years after George Leonidas Leslie arrived in the city—the bridge was now the target of a mass lock-picking attack, a kind of burglary flash mob in clear view. Their plan was to remove hundreds of old padlocks that had been attached to the bridge's rails before the city's cleaning crews could dispose of them; then to store those locks in red, Valentine's Day–colored nylon bags and to reattach them later to a future public sculpture, a specially made "tree" on which all ensuing love locks would be latched. The group called this "love picking."

Love locks are padlocks, often with names, initials, or messages of love written on them, that have been clipped onto pieces of urban infrastructure as a public sign of romantic commitment. Some have been expensively laser-etched; others have simply been written on with a Sharpie. "Carrina, will you marry me?" "Zach+Julie, Always+Forever." The result can be quite beautiful—lush, multicolored, roselike clusters—but they're also doomed. In nearly all cases, love locks will be removed by city workers.

Over the last decade, locksport—the organized recreational picking of locks by amateur enthusiasts—has grown tremendously in countercultural appeal. Participants, by definition, are not professional locksmiths. This puts what they do in a legal gray area that they are quick to discuss and defend; in addition to possessing nimble fingers and impressive attention spans, locksport enthusiasts try to remain fluent in local burglary law. Indeed, while emphasizing that they "are not lawyers and this page is not offering legal advice," TOOOL (The Open Organization Of Lockpickers) maintains a webpage linking to broad summaries of individual state laws.

Almost all of these come down to the question of *intent*—of what you were planning to do with those lockpicks. This is often deduced using a loose and far from rigorous constellation of factors. In addition to your lock-picking set, for example, do you also have a crowbar, sledgehammer, flashlight, or balaclava in the trunk of your car? If so, that combination of objects might imply clear intent to commit a crime—even if you were just heading over to a friend's house to help fix his deck on a dark winter's day—and you could be facing arrest. Perhaps you have lockpicks in your backpack and nothing else—except for a well-worn map of a certain neighborhood, complete with handwritten annotations detailing the times of day someone won't be home. If so, you could be legally suspected of intent to commit burglary—even if the lock-picks had been sitting unused in your bag for six months, and the map was to remind you of what days you had to go feed your aunt's cat. Or perhaps it's the time of day that makes you seem a bit suspicious—for example, being seen walking behind a closed Walmart at 2:00 a.m. with a set of lockpicks in your back pocket. No matter that you were only taking a shortcut home through the local shopping mall after a long birthday party at a friend's house where you were given a set of lockpicks.

The vagaries of determining criminal intent—or the willingness of a police officer to listen to and believe your story—can be extremely hard to predict. No matter what your own state laws or city statutes might be, any reader would do well to consider the consequences of being caught roaming the streets with a set of lockpicks (or, at the least, to have a good lawyer on call). These are lessons many members of TOOOL have learned the hard way.

Several weeks before the event on the Brooklyn

Bridge, a Facebook page was created. Messages of support were sent and forwarded. Then, as the day drew near, a change of tone set in: the group's e-mails went from high-spirited anticipation of an outdoor lock-picking party hosted in the late-summer sun to a slightly stunned, what-have-we-done? careful consideration of legal specificity. The group's lawyer was cc'd. Interested attendees were urged to "be polite"—even to stay at home if they had any open warrants. They were advised to arrive sober, to be well behaved, and to pick locks, not fights: no arguments with cops or curious bystanders would be tolerated.

The group was not easy to find. Despite the suggested 4:00 p.m. kickoff, it was nearly 4:30 before it became clear that anyone had shown up. Unsurprisingly, perhaps, for an introverted tribe of technical specialists, the lock-pickers had dispersed along the bridge, their backs turned away from tourists and other walkers. They stood, hands at waist level, fidgeting unobtrusively with tiny objects on the outer rails. It was like watching a strawberry harvest as hands delicately popped the locks and moved on, foot by foot, toward Brooklyn.

I introduced myself to the group's ostensible conductor for the day, a well-known lock-picker and author of several books on hacking and security who calls himself Deviant Ollam, or Dev. He had driven up from Philadelphia that morning with his partner, who goes by the nickname Lady Merlin. Dev is on the board of directors of TOOOL. He was dressed in a black polo shirt, a TOOOL logo prominently displayed on his chest, with dozens of laser-printed "love picking" leaflets slipped neatly into the pockets of his cargo shorts. Wrapped on one wrist was a magnetic bracelet to which he could affix his picks, swapping one tool out for another in an instant, a performative mix of off-grid survivalist gear wed with the quirks of urban maker culture.

"Love picking," as I was shortly to learn, is by no means universally sanctioned among the lock-picking crowd. A vigorous and far from polite discussion had been developing on the social news website Reddit for the past month. The event on the Brooklyn Bridge had initially been proposed as a kind of antigraffiti gesture by an otherwise anonymous Redditor called Bobcat; Bobcat is a get-off-my-lawn, gun-rights type who had been roused to anger by what he considers a blatant misuse of city infrastructure. Love locks accelerate rust, he railed. They're ugly. Bobcat is not a romantic. Only later was he able to secure the support and interest of Deviant Ollam and TOOOL—but even then, it wasn't easy. After all, for an anarchic group of fringe hobbyists keenly aware that most people see what they do as illegal, stealing these tokens of public love would only make things worse. Everyone already thinks we're criminals, they complained; now everyone will think we're assholes.

Some New Yorkers did stop to watch, and a few even interrupted to ask why a small group of people had suddenly appeared, picking locks on a Saturday afternoon. A couple walked by, getting their photograph taken for a wedding album; families strolled slowly down the middle of the bike lane, snapping photos of each other on iPads. Who were these mysterious people, dressed mostly in baseball hats and black T-shirts, hunched over alone by the pedestrian rails, picking love locks?

Schuyler Towne, one of the earliest popularizers of locksport in the United States, got in touch with me soon after he saw my photos of the day popping up on Instagram and Twitter. He seemed exasperated. Locksport has two primary rules, he emphasized to me, and everyone is meant to follow them. Think of these as pledges of locksport chivalry. One is, never pick a lock that isn't yours. The only exception is when you have the clear and specific permission of that lock's owner. The other rule is, never pick a lock that's actually in use. Even if it's your own lock, you might damage it—and you don't want to incapacitate your front door or some other lock you rely on for everyday safety. Seemingly embarrassed by his belief in the poetry of it all, Towne insisted that all those Brooklyn Bridge love locks *are* being used—admittedly not in the traditional sense. But couples are using them to symbolize something, Towne emphasized, and it shouldn't be up to a group of out-of-state locksport hobbyists to decide otherwise.

Worse, he added, TOOOL had informed its members of New York State law only; but according to New York City Administrative Code 20-301, it is "unlawful for any person other than a licensed locksmith to open any lock for which a key or combination may have been lost." Thus, Towne explained, each participant had unknowingly been "marching out onto that bridge to commit a crime, and for no particularly good reason." This is worth repeating: in New York City, possessing lock-picking tools is not, in and of itself, evidence of criminal intent—unlike, say, Mississippi, Nevada, Ohio, and Virginia, where, as of this writing, it is illegal to possess lockpicks. However, in New York City, if you are not a licensed locksmith, using your tools to pick someone else's lock—even if you're just helping a friend get back into his or her apartment for the night—is against the law.

By the end of the day, the group had removed nearly eighteen pounds of padlocks, lightening the infrastructural load of the bridge by approximately the weight of an infant and, as Bobcat enthusiastically emphasized on Reddit, reducing the future threat of rust and patination. However, within a week, shiny new padlocks were already appearing on the bridge like little buds of steel fruit, undaunted either by this rogue locksport crew or by the bolt cutters of the NYC Department of Transportation.

❦

What brought me out onto the Brooklyn Bridge that day wasn't an interest in love locks; I went because I wanted to learn more about the tools people use to subvert barriers, slip through openings, and gain access to architecture without waiting for a key to the front door. I wanted to know more about the specialty equipment that enables people to pass through the built environment like fog through a forest—like ghosts, like neutrinos. Indeed, the very existence of a legal category of object known as the *burglary tool*—a strangely compelling phrase with an air of mystery to it—implies that a whole parallel class of hardware exists, unavailable for sale in the aisles of Home Depot. What were these tools and who made them? Whom would you have to talk to, to get hold of some? Naturally, I thought, if I wanted to learn about burglary, I should follow the tools—and that meant talking to lock-pickers, a whole crew of whom would be gathered together in one place that Saturday afternoon in New York City.

In the popular imagination, no self-respecting burglar could operate without a set of lock-picking tools, to the extent that these tiny metal picks that look like something a dentist might use to clean your teeth have become all but synonymous with the crime. Indeed, the heavily worn lockpicks used by President Richard Nixon's burglary crew to break into the Watergate Hotel in 1972 are on display even today as nationally important artifacts in the Gerald R. Ford Presidential Museum. The Watergate lockpicks not only came to represent an era, with all of its conspiracy, paranoia, and betrayal; they also seemed to prove, once and for all, that burglary requires lockpicks.

Following my afternoon on the Brooklyn Bridge, I set up a meeting with Schuyler Towne at the John M. Mossman Lock Collection at the General Society of Mechanics and Tradesmen in Manhattan. John Mossman had grown up the son of a safe and lock manufacturer and would later become a vault designer during the heyday of George Leonidas Leslie's gang. Mossman's extensive personal collection of locks was slowly assembled over his professional career, forming a kind of greatest hits of global locking mechanisms.

Under high ceilings inside a nineteenth-century building that originally housed a boys' school, dusty glass cases today host hundreds of delicate instruments. At times, the fluorescent lights of the room catch their polished brass and steel at just the right angle, and they glint like pieces of jewelry. The locks span thousands of years of human history, from ancient Egyptian door locks made of wood to the world's first time locks, by way of magnetic locks, Chinese padlocks, and some of the first modern cylinder locks, encompassing samples up to the early 1900s—yet few people seem to know the museum even exists. In the few times I have since been back to browse the collection, I have not seen another visitor.

Victoria Dengel, executive director of the General Society, met us in her office to give Towne and me a brief tour of the space. She told us that when the building was first constructed, it had an outdoor courtyard, which was eventually roofed over, absorbed into the building's interior to serve as a dramatic location for the society's library. This had a peculiar effect: the administrative offices, located in an older part of the original building, now look out at the other rooms through glass exterior windows and what appear to be old exit doors. The offices are a building within the building. Smiling out of apparent embarrassment, Dengel said that one day she had locked herself out of her office—but, thankfully, because those glass windows could easily be unlocked and slid open, she was able to break back into her own office, sneaking in like a burglar through the window frame and unlocking the office door from within. Amid all these locks, illegal entry seemed perversely de rigueur.

Dengel soon left us alone to examine the displays,

and Towne took on the mantle of temporary museum guide with visible relish. He led me nearly lock by lock through the entire collection, describing the inner workings of each and narrating, step by step, how they were meant to operate. We were not allowed to handle the actual mechanisms, which meant that Towne would look at each device the way a lepidopterist might look at pinned butterflies: he would lean in, concentrate, and, in an assured voice, start describing how something might work, but then—"Oh!" he'd exclaim like a character from a Sherlock Holmes story, and he'd start all over again, with different emphases, speaking faster, amazed and sometimes literally laughing from surprise and delight as he finally figured out how a particular locking sequence would most likely have worked. Towne would then talk me through the exact steps by which that lock could be opened—and explain, in equal detail, how it could probably be picked.

We moved from lock to lock, giving some only fleeting attention, before—"Oh!" Another realization with Towne's accompanying cry, and we'd both crouch down in front of another case. He was remarkably quick at determining which elements were integral to a lock's action and which were just decorative metalwork—swirls of frivolous brass added for aesthetics—and he'd launch from there into a series of assumptions about what each lever, tooth, or wheel might do. Sequences would build; it was like listening to someone recount an elaborate chess game, narrating moves and countermoves with one eye always on what would happen a few more steps down the line. He would describe things to me in precisely detailed

sequences, hoping I would come to see these intricate geometries the way he could, every metal-on-metal contact
and even the tiniest of grooved surfaces invisible within
the lock itself. For Towne, each lock could clearly be blown
up to the scale of a megastructure, a palace the size of a
city block, its inner gates and cylinders like cavernous hallways and rooms his mind could then wander through. He
seemed to hold a detailed, three-dimensional model of
each lock in his head, and he could manipulate it back
and forth, round and round, like a hologram rotating in
space.

A catalog of the Mossman locks was published in
1928, written by Alfred A. Hopkins. Like Towne, Hopkins
was a true enthusiast for the subject; indeed, his book
was called *The Lure of the Lock*, as if he were aware that
locks possessed a strange attraction (and that those charms
were perhaps something that ought to be resisted). He
describes the locks as "handsome," "remarkable," and "extraordinary." Also like Towne, Hopkins was not afraid to
admit when he did not necessarily know how a given lock
was meant to work, pointing out when his descriptions
began to veer into speculation and conjecture. The interior of a lock "seems" to operate a certain way, he'll write,
or he'll explain that he tried to ascertain how another lock
worked but that those attempts were "without success."

Hopkins also goes out of his way to discuss the bur-
geoning arms race that had developed, even before his
own era, pitting lock designers and vault architects against
canny burglars intent on breaking through their most ambitious defenses. As early as the 1920s, and presumably far

earlier, a design war unfolded, waged between defense and offense. It was "a war that knows no armistice," an article in the book's back matter moans, fought endlessly between "the planners of safes and vaults, and the safe, vault and bank robbers." Various battles and skirmishes in this ongoing clash were described in the "Mossman Papers": newspaper clippings, leaflets, and technical papers meticulously filed away by John M. Mossman himself and only partially digitized at the time of Towne's and my meeting. Mossman seemed obsessed with bank crime, I noticed, having saved articles of even the most fleeting relevance to major break-ins, including some that involved George Leonidas Leslie, such as the great Manhattan Savings Institution heist of 1878.

Towne knew the papers well. Toward the end of our visit, Victoria Dengel reappeared to ask how everything was going, and he enthusiastically asked if we could see some of those old books and manuscripts. Dengel was more than happy to oblige—but quickly discovered that the key for those cabinets had been misplaced. Visibly concerned, she joked that she might have to ask Towne to pick the lock—something he said he was very willing to do. Towne began to explain exactly how he'd pick it, down to the specific tools he would need, even asking Dengel if she had the necessary tensioning tool (she did not). I was a bit taken aback by this display of enthusiasm, as the lock was currently in use—an explicit no-no in terms of the moral code of locksport—and, perhaps more important, because Towne would have been breaking New York City ordinances. Thankfully, though, after a short discussion over walkie-talkie and before any moral lines were irreparably crossed, the missing key was located by the building's maintenance crew.

We spent a little more than an hour looking through some of Mossman's voluminous private archives. Towne's eye for editorial detail came out as he sifted through the bound books and loose documents, looking for things he either wanted to show me or to see for himself. He had, after all, once edited a small zine called *NDE*, or *Non-Destructive Entry*, and he was also kicking off a new project, the X-Lock Project. In this entirely archival undertaking, Towne is attempting to recover—in some cases, even reconceive—patents for locks lost in a catastrophic fire at the U.S. Patent Office in 1836. Those lost patents are an obsession for Towne—in public lectures, he refers to it as his "personal mission" to piece back together as many of the forgotten locks of American history as he can, hoping to restore them in the record of the U.S. Patent Office. This is as much detective work as it is speculative mechanical design, as it requires Towne not only to discover impossibly obscure bits of paperwork that might help flesh out what locks existed, when they were invented, by whom, and how they operated, but also to conjecturally reproduce their inner mechanics in the absence of hard historical data.

It felt, not for the first time, like Towne was looking for something far larger than just a complete record of lock patents lost to fire, that he had embarked on something much more metaphoric than a forensic understanding of how certain locks might work. These devices had taken on an almost mystical status, it seemed, becoming more like relics or charms, complex objects that seemed to prove for him that humans are capable of great feats of creativity and invention when they finally apply themselves. Someone once joked on Twitter that Towne was "a machine for turning locks into anthropology." Locks meant something to him in a literal sense, in that they were mechanical messages passed down across human generations—provided you knew how to read them. No wonder recovering the lost patents of locks was so important to him; they were like hieroglyphs. He was standing in the shadows of history, trying, not always successfully, to interpret this language for others.

I let myself get lost in his descriptions of "x-locks" and patent diagrams, of forgotten documents and papers yet to be digitized, as if listening to a rabbi describe the exact dimensions of the Temple of Solomon—a mythical work of architecture that probably never existed yet is still, even today, a spur for intensely esoteric arguments over its every spatial detail. All the while, Towne and I flipped through the crumbling sheets and cracked bindings of a part of Mossman's archive normally kept away from public view.

Even Mossman, designer of newfangled vaults, had been fixated on heists and burglaries, I said, pointing to several stories and news clippings saved in his papers. To what extent are burglars the ultimate lock-pickers? I asked. Is locksport, I wondered aloud, something of a gateway drug for people intent on thwarting dead ends or crossing boundaries? I couldn't quite bring myself to phrase it this way, but what I wanted to know was, is locksport basically a training ground for burglars?

Towne, not one to hide his displeasure, knew exactly what I meant—and he seemed deeply, even morosely, unimpressed by the question. Clearly, he—indeed, almost all locksport enthusiasts—had been asked this multiple times, like heavy-metal fans having to defend themselves against yet another accusation of Satan worship in the suburbs.

In retrospect, I see how naive a question it was—how naïve all of my assumptions were about locksport—but Towne, to his credit, patiently explained to me how an interest in picking locks was by no means the same thing as an interest in stealing other people's property. The two are entirely unrelated, he emphasized. It would be more accurate to think of locksport enthusiasts as like an organized puzzle-solving group: people united by a shared ambition to understand and solve specific technical challenges that happened to take the form of locks. It was about understanding how a mechanical object worked; it was not about how to enrich oneself by robbing others. This was morally clear to him, and he reminded me of what he had said earlier, that locksport has a code: again, you never pick a lock that isn't yours, without explicit permission to do so. Using lock-picking skills to become a better burglar would be a clear and obvious betrayal of the sport—I couldn't help but point out, however, that there would be little to stop you. You're not supposed to learn karate to become better at mugging people, but there's always a risk that the wrong kind of person will sign up for martial arts.

In any case, Towne continued, and this was painfully obvious by the time he said it, a burglar simply isn't going to sit there listening to every pin and tumbler inside your front-door lock, artfully finessing his way into your house. Even professional locksmiths, Towne pointed out, usually avoid picking any lock to open it; it would take too long. They'll just drill through your lock (collecting a much higher fee, now that they need to replace it)—and that's assuming the door they're trying to get through has an analog lock in the first place. I was reminded of an anecdote from cat burglar Bill Mason, who once convinced an international lock-manufacturing company to send him a digital master key that would work for an entire hotel in South Florida. Faced with digital smart locks and even biometrics, lock-picking is a weirdly anachronistic activity.

Towne wanted me to understand that locks are more like objects to be contemplated: hypnotic knots of gears and teeth that exert a visible spell on people intent on understanding them. It was like appreciating the inner workings of an ornate but, in this era of Apple, obsolete Swiss watch, or geeking out over the internal gears and counterweights of a grandfather clock. Another, harsher way to put this would be that locksport is basically useless: it is less an example of cutting-edge contemporary security research and more a kind of amateur antiques society, more romantic and even nostalgic than it is tactical.

You'll see, was Towne's overall message—but not

until you start doing it yourself. Pick a few locks, he suggested, and burglary will be the last thing on your mind.

Secret Keys Hidden in the Objects Around Us

TOOOL was founded in the Netherlands by security researcher and lock expert Barry Wels. TOOOL describes itself as "a growing group of enthusiasts interested in locks, keys and ways of opening locks without keys," and now has a handful of chapters around the world. It runs free monthly workshops at various locations throughout the United States, from Austin to Los Angeles, the Bay Area to Philadelphia. Chicago also has a chapter.

On a windy evening punctuated by mist and light rain, my wife and I drove out to a quiet residential neighborhood on Chicago's northwest periphery, passing endless low-slung warehouses and new brick lofts. That month's TOOOL gathering was being hosted in a space called Pumping Station: One, or PS:One. PS:One is a six-thousand-square-foot, garage-like space with a ramshackle meeting room in front. It is furnished with old couches and some worktables. A small warehouse full of equipment stands in back, with the air of a permanent Maker Faire. Scanners, 3-D printers, welding stations, multiple laptop computers, custom-made plywood bunks and shelves, and other random pieces of gear await their next user; these assorted bits and bobs included a half-assembled DIY vending machine, a remade soldering iron that burned images into wood, and some behemoth piece of machinery—more like a stranded whale—in the far background that I was unable to learn anything about. By the time we all left, a little before 10:00 p.m., the back room was still buzzing. Empty beverage cans proudly touting their drink's caffeine content seemed as good an indication as any that the folks chipping away at their latest projects were used to tinkering well into the early morning.

Our instructors that night were Patrick Thomas, his wife, Krystal, and John—known as Jack—Benigno. The other attendees included two teenage boys who had driven in from the suburbs—apparently more than an hour each way—a few couples in their late twenties, and a handful of enthusiasts who had come armed with their own, self-made picks. At one point, all the action in the room stopped so we could admire a set of handmade, bamboo-handled picks brought in by one of the attendees; we passed the set around to whistles of admiration.

Our evening began with a slide show giving us the most basic overview of what makes a lock function: how it works, what the cylinder is, how to find each individual locking pin, and the purpose of the different lock-picking tools at our disposal. There was no music and the lights were bright. Arrayed before us on heavily worn worktables were padlocks and cylinder locks, the latter labeled with numbers corresponding to their level of difficulty. The most basic had two internal pins only, and these were astonishingly easy to pick; these then went up to six-pin locks, beyond which a range of spooled locks and padlocks awaited us.

The types of picks are seemingly endless. The most commonly found ones are used for opening pin-tumbler locks. There are rake picks and snake picks, hook picks and ball picks. There are full diamonds and half diamonds—also known as triangle picks—but also diamond rakes, hooked diamonds, and offset Deforest diamonds. There are snake rakes and ball rakes. Bogotá triple rakes, Bogotá quad rakes, Bogotá single picks, Bogotá Sabanas, and Bogotá Monserrates. There are long reach hooks and slant hooks. Beyond these larger families of picks and pick types, the tools rapidly diversify, leading to ever-stranger and more specialized one-offs and mutations. There are snowman rakes, half snowman rakes, wave rakes, postal picks, long ripple picks, bogie picks, long reach rakes—the list goes on and on. And that's before you get into the world of automotive-entry picks, warded lockpicks, double-sided picks, et cetera, et cetera, ad infinitum. There are as many picks as there are keys—in fact, there are probably more.

An individual pick is usually named after its profile. You might consider this to be the pick's skyline, so to speak: small metal bends and shapes in the metal, when viewed from the side, resemble tiny buildings or hillocks sticking up over the horizon. With the aid of a tensioning tool—a separate piece of metal, used to apply tiny amounts of torque to the lock's inner cylinder or tumbler—you insert a pick into your target lock. Those little shapes that give each pick its profile—all those ripples and diamonds and waves and half circles and hooks—are then used to locate individual locking pins, each of which is a different height, which you push up out of the way using the pick.

When all of a lock's internal pins have been pushed above what's called the shear line, the lock can finally be turned. It has been picked.

I'm proud to say I was not that bad, picking my way quite rapidly through the first five levels of a six-lock set, but I was permanently stymied by level six. Along the way, our instructors, disarmingly polite and not at all stand-offish despite their advanced lock-picking skills, explained some of the folklore that accompanied the individual tools. The Bogotá rake, the one that I would ultimately use the most throughout the evening, was so named because its waves and bends apparently resemble the mountains surrounding Bogotá, Colombia, where the tool was invented. This made the nickname a no-brainer—but it also means that this widely used lock-picking tool is a portable topographic model of the Andes, a landscape in miniature.

As a host, Jack Benigno was something of a slow-burner. At first quiet, he became more animated and even quite talkative as the night developed. About half-way through the event, Benigno took over the front of the room and began telling us how to make the most effective lock-picking tools. The best sources of metal for these tools were ordinary objects, he explained, things we'd probably never have imagined could be transformed into something that would let us break through doorways: the underwires of bras, for example, or the inner blades of discarded windshield wipers, and, best of all, the rough brushes of street-cleaning trucks. Individual bristles are occasionally knocked loose during operation and left lying on the street. All of our instructors that night admitted, like addicts confessing to extreme behavior, that they had followed Chicago street-cleaning crews around, often for hours at a time, waiting for a bristle to break free. Benigno suggested that, for those of us without the patience to follow a truck all day, a good place to find metal is simply in the Dumpsters of auto-repair shops. Just lift up the lid, grab handfuls of old wiper blades, and be done with it.

As I was beginning to realize, the master tools of real-life breaking and entering are typically just everyday objects, reimagined and transformed for criminal purposes. Consider the shockingly successful Antwerp diamond heist back in February 2003, when more than $50 million worth of diamonds were stolen from a high-security vault in the center of that city's well-protected jewelry district. To a great extent, the extraordinary ease with which that crime was carried out came down to simple objects bought from the local hardware store. A broomstick, a brick of polystyrene, some black electrical tape, a can of hair spray: these were enough to subvert and neutralize more than a million dollars' worth of high-tech security sensors, as if a rewards shopper at Home Depot had somehow managed to rob Fort Knox.

Think, for a second, about how frustrating this would be: you install some futuristic motion detector in your underground supervault and a bunch of anonymous strangers get around it by sticking a piece of Styrofoam on the end of a broomstick; stand that up in front of a motion detector while the lights are still off and it won't see anything move for weeks. It's embarrassing. You could try to catch the bad guys using your state-of-the-art thermal camera—something space-age and intimidating—but they've got a can of hair spray. They uncap it and coat your fine-tuned electronics with a sticky film of aerosolized beauty products and render it useless. So you turn to your light sensor, something so sensitive it can pick up even the glow of an uncovered wristwatch—but your ingenious adversaries have arrived with a roll of electrical tape. They rip off a few inches, wrap it around your sensor, and all that gear is now totally obsolete. The vault is theirs to ransack. They have spent less than fifty bucks at a hardware store, yet they've caught your million-dollar setup with its pants down.

Or take Phil Christopher, a self-described "superthief" who explained in a 2006 biography how he and his partners thwarted the exterior alarm bell of a bank in Laguna Niguel, California. Did he have some ingenious spy gear, like something out of a James Bond film, capable of neutralizing electromagnetic circuitry? Nope. Bringing to mind the classic French heist film *Rififi*—in which burglars use fireproof insulating foam to silence the alarm of the store they've carefully broken into—Christopher and crew simply filled the alarm box with a squirt of fast-expanding liquid polystyrene, eliminating at least one threat of early detection.

Burglary tools are effectively everywhere, hidden in

plain sight. Street-cleaning bristles, broomsticks, electrical tape, liquid polystyrene: in the right hands, everyday items have an unexpected secondary function, able to become something like skeleton keys with which we can gain entrance to any building or thwart the world's most sophisticated security systems. The dark promise here is that if only you can assemble the right tools in the right combination, you'll find yourself holding keys to everything around you.

This can be quite literal. A set of master keys to the infrastructure of New York City popped up on eBay back in September 2012, leaving media commentators and city officials alike concerned for the safety of the metropolis. These keys promised universal access to urban infrastructure, from subways to skyscrapers—true "keys to the city" that should never be let out into the wild.

After an undercover reporter for the *New York Post* purchased the set, the paper published a photograph of them captioned "What you could do: Take over the subways." The *Post* suggested that it was "what a terrorist might call a dream come true," feigning outrage next to their own high-resolution photograph of the key set. Indeed, that very photo could easily have been used to duplicate the keys, and it was removed from their website shortly thereafter.

The newspaper had purchased a cluster of five keys "that would allow control of virtually any elevator in the city," they explained. The keys "could knock out power to municipal buildings and skyscrapers, darken city streets, open subway gates and some firehouse doors and provide full access to 1 World Trade Center and other construction sites."

The reporter claimed to have done his due diligence, verifying that "most of the keys did, in fact, work." Among them was "the all-purpose '1620,' a master firefighter key that with one turn could trap thousands of people in a skyscraper by sending all the elevators to the lobby and out of service, according to two FDNY sources. And it works for buildings across the city. That key also allows one to open locked subway entrances, gain entry to many firehouses and get into boxes at construction jobs that house additional keys to all areas of the site." Also found on the key ring were city electrical keys that would give access to streetlights, "along with the basement circuit-breaker boxes of just about any large building."

While these were not hacked together from everyday objects—being, instead, actual keys used by fire departments and city electricians—they fulfill the promise of the key to end all keys, something that makes every door transparent and every building open for entry. Even Jack Dakswin had specifically fantasized about getting his hands on a set like this. In Canada, he explained, they are known as Crown keys. These are issued to Canada Post workers, used to enter (and deliver mail inside) multiunit apartment buildings. Give a burglar a set of Crown keys, and you've given that burglar keys to half the city. Dakswin added that obtaining Crown keys is often the suspected goal whenever a Canada Post worker has been mugged.

Superkeys are out there, in other words, whether they're something we piece together ourselves from other tools and objects, or they're official city equipment that has somehow ended up on eBay.

Benigno, sensing that he'd gotten our attention, began more freely telling stories about how he had taught some of his colleagues at work to pick locks—and that he was now beginning to regret passing on that knowledge. He said that he had come into the office one morning, for example, only to see that one of his colleagues had picked open a cabinet—"but that's where we keep all the shotguns!" he roared, laughing. Another day, he came in only to find that someone else had picked open yet another cabinet—"but that's where we keep all the AR-15s!" We all laughed, but I was more confused about what on earth this guy must do for a living, to have so many guns lying around the office.

It turned out he was a cop: a young detective with the Chicago Police Department with an enthusiasm for picking locks (and teaching other people how to do so). On the back of his neck, in solid black letters, with no attempt to disguise or hide it, was the word PAR•A•NOID tattooed just above the collar line. If anything would conclusively prove that locksport is unlikely to be a training ground for tomorrow's supercriminals, it was that the guy teaching me to pick locks was a police officer.

I got in touch with Benigno a few days after the event to learn more about his current job and how he got there.

His story was surprising. Improbably, both Benigno and I have a master's degree in art history from the University of Chicago, where we graduated within only three years of each other. We even studied with a few of the same professors. But, like me, Benigno did not want to spend much time talking about art history, so we quickly got back to the topic of lock-picking.

I dispensed with the most obvious questions first. What does it mean, for example, that he was leading workshops in lock-picking but was simultaneously a Chicago cop? Was there any sort of conflict of interest there? Benigno laughed. Not at all, he explained. Emphasizing several times that he was speaking to me now purely as a civilian, giving me his own point of view, not that of the Chicago Police Department, he reminded me that possessing lock-picking tools is not a crime in Illinois, although possessing bump keys is. A bump key is basically a regular, blank door key that you insert into a lock, then, as you turn it slightly with one hand, you give it a solid bump with a hammer or even with the heel of a shoe; if done correctly, this bounces all the pins up out of the cylinder, and the lock will open. It is disconcertingly easy to do; multiple YouTube videos of bump keys at work will make you question why you put any faith in your home's locked doors.

Then Benigno asked if I had noticed at the event that when I'd asked if I could use one of his lockpicks, he did not directly hand it to me. Instead, he had set it down on the table and talked to me for a few seconds before I picked it up, as if trying to make me forget that I had even asked to use it. I had noticed this—but I had interpreted it as nothing more than a slight hesitation in letting me, a total stranger, use one of his personal tools. Perhaps I would damage it or even slip it into my pocket. But, no, he said; it is illegal to transfer lock-picking tools to another person in Illinois. This means that he would technically have been breaking the law if he had handed the pick directly to me. If we were to hop into a car and drive over the nearby state border into Indiana, then we could legally hand lock-picking tools back and forth to each other as long as we wanted. We could then just drive back over the border into Illinois—and no one would be the wiser.

The longer we spoke, the more Benigno's academic background began to emerge. For example, several times he mentioned Michel Foucault, a French philosopher whose notion of "discipline and punish" explored the state's ability to coerce certain behaviors from its citizens. Foucault's analysis of law, imprisonment, and state surveillance is well-known among academics and political activists, but it is unusual, if not rather extraordinary, to hear a rank-and-file Chicago police officer quoting critical theory while discussing his work. All of which led me back to the question of burglary: Was it possible that Benigno had been helping out at these lock-picking events as a decoy tactic, acting as a double agent for the Chicago PD? He could simply note who was in attendance, and even what sorts of questions they might ask, and the police department's central dossier would continue to grow. So stressed-out was he by this dual role, he had been reduced to permanent paranoia—and thus the tattoo . . .

He laughed again, appreciative of the narrative investment—but, no, he said. He just likes lock-picking. He likes the people; he likes the events, such as Locktoberfest, an annual gathering of locksport enthusiasts who hang out over beer, brats, and padlocks. He likes solving technical puzzles, the way other people like solving crosswords or Sudoku.

But he understood where I was going with my questions, and the final moments of my earlier conversation with Schuyler Towne began to replay in my head. Lockpicking is not a gateway drug for burglary. About this Benigno was unequivocal. From his experience as a street cop, burglars simply aren't out there picking locks—or, if they are, it's noticeable precisely because it's such a rarity. Real burglars are breaking windows or kicking doors in; they're cutting holes through walls and roofs. They'll slip in through a half-open garage door before they'll pick a lock in full view of a watchful neighbor. Not even locksmiths are picking locks anymore, Benigno said, repeating something Towne had specifically mentioned. It's not worth their time.

The only people Benigno knew who picked locks at all were the hackers, tinkerers, and security aficionados who came to monthly meetings such as TOOOL's—and the other cops whom he had taught to do it. If I wanted to learn about the tools people really use to get into buildings, he said, sensing my disappointment, I would have to look elsewhere.

Zen and the Art of Door Annihilation

The tools of burglary are more varied than one might expect. In his book *The Right Way to Do Wrong*, Harry Houdini described the "sofa game." This was simultaneously "a confidence game and a first-class burglary job," employing a hollow piece of furniture. In this game of domestic Trojan horse, you show up at the home of a wealthy family, claiming to have a piece of furniture that they've inherited from a distant relative. It's quite urgent, you would say, as you have to make several other deliveries before the day is over, and the deliverymen are all getting tired—can you let them drop it off? It won't take a minute. If your story works, you deliver the sofa and depart—before you return an hour later, feigning humiliation. My God, you say, we had the wrong address—it's the right street, and you even have the same last name, but we're in the wrong part of town entirely. We have to get our sofa back. We're so sorry for the inconvenience.

Inside the sofa all along had been a woman—slender, lightweight, and hidden where the springs should be—curled up in "a hollow compartment of considerable size." The woman would have emerged from her hiding place to pocket as much silver, jewelry, loose cash, and fine art as she could get her hands on. She would then climb back into the sofa—just in time for her apologetic co-conspirators to return, hats in hand, begging for their sofa back. Dozens of pounds heavier, it would be hauled down onto their moving cart, and the gang would disappear.

Boom: sofa job. Incredibly, this heist-by-furniture apparently worked.

Trumping sofa jobs in ambition, however, was the "lodging lay." As Houdini describes it, in a lodging lay the leader of a burglary crew would convince a prospective landlord that a scam artist was a wealthy, worthwhile tenant. Having secured access to a new home or apartment and having forgone payment of a deposit thanks to pure charisma, the tenant would then gut the residence. Marble fireplace lintels, exotic wood cabinetry, and even, in one famous case, an entire carved staircase would all be carted away. If the landlord came by in the meantime, demanding to know what was going on—well, it was just a quick renovation. After all, this mysterious tenant would explain, I'm going to be here for the next ten or twenty years, and only the best will do. Surely you don't mind if I renovate the place?

A week later, the entire interior of the house has been stolen.

Gaining access to buildings by means other than keys has been refined since Houdini's day. Indeed, breaking and entering is the explicit specialty of so-called rapid-entry teams, small tactical units sent out by such organizations as the FBI and ATF to forcibly enter a structure in which a suspect might be hiding. Ironically, I would soon get a glimpse of the real supertools used to access architecture—not among burglars at all but deep inside the world of law enforcement.

One name came up again and again during my conversations among the lock-pickers: Marc Weber Tobias.

While some people accused Tobias of arrogance—of holding on to potentially devastating knowledge about vulnerabilities in commercially available locks, even while knowing that thousands of people continued to put their trust in them—all admired his legendary lock-breaking skills and his encyclopedic knowledge of the field. *Wired* has described him as the "ultimate lock picker," a man who "can pick, crack, or bump any lock," and he has earned this reputation through a number of thrilling, high-profile exploits. These include his most famous feat: the alarming discovery of vulnerabilities in Medeco high-security locks, which are relied upon by the U.S. government to secure military and nuclear sites.

Tobias is also the author of *Locks, Safes, and Security: An International Police Reference*, an exhaustive—at times, exhausting—catalog of doors, locks, and the tools used to break them. This huge, fourteen-hundred-page, two-volume set is priced well out of reach for your everyday reader. In a narrative arc that mirrors my own journey through the world of burglary tools, the book also begins with locks and how to pick them, before scaling up to discuss a much wider range of more aggressive breaching tools.

Part of the book's length comes from its sheer breadth of reference: Tobias locates locks and lock technology within a long history of human security. This means he stretches back roughly three thousand years to discuss the treasuries of Pharaoh Ramses III as some of the earliest examples of vault architecture and safe-room design. In only a few pages, he moves from a discussion of vaults able to survive nuclear-bomb strikes to a look at the temples and strong rooms of ancient Egypt, to hydraulic tools used by the FBI for breaking into mob-owned warehouses. Roman padlocks, Mesopotamian keys, a possible spring-loaded bolt lock preserved in the volcanic ash of Pompeii, locks resistant to X-ray imaging, Doppler-based ultrasonic sensors, closed-circuit wiring embedded in a room's wallpaper for detecting any breaches in the walls, seismic alarms—the book's language may be dry, but its contents are fascinating.

Tobias points out, for example, that older combination locks had a significant vibrational vulnerability—they could be vibrated into opening. "This was such a pervasive problem," he writes, that during long ocean crossings, these "safes used to open themselves on some ships." The "constant engine tremors" would simply be "transmitted to wheel packs through the metal of the vessel," and the safes would just swing open, as if picked by the swaying of the waves.

Later, Tobias introduces readers to the Europlanet line of safes, which use a proprietary pourable plastic known as Ellox developed by safe-maker Chubb. It is extremely lightweight and astonishingly strong, incorporating small fragments of another proprietary material that Chubb claims is harder than a diamond. The plastic also resists fires of up to 1,000°C—or 1,832°F—for at least an hour before failing. Better yet, it can be molded into larger, complex shapes, "poured to form strongrooms, safes, hasps, and other special items." The architectural implications of this—a kind of bullet-resistant pancake batter moldable into any form—have barely been tapped.

Tobias's advice for architects and building engineers is straightforward but useful: the room next to the actual target is just as important, for security, as the room you are trying to protect. Even the width of certain hallways leading to those rooms should be restricted so as to prevent criminals from using known burglary tools. For example, if a particularly effective breaching tool requires six feet of free space in which to operate, then make your hallway less than six feet wide. Whole classes of attack can be ruled out by architectural design alone.

Tobias describes what he calls a "unique approach" to vault placement: hiding an entire vault in plain sight. In this case, that "involved the placement of a strongroom onto the façade of a high-rise building. The wall that formed the entrance to the strongroom was part of the façade; the rest of the enclosure was constructed to hang in the air." The vault hung off the side of the building, like a room floating in space. Because of this, "only one wall could be tackled from within the building; all other surfaces were situated in the air and could be seen from every side." By exposing the vault for all to see, in theory it became all but impregnable.

Tobias's lists and discussions of the tools used for breaking into the built environment are the most relevant here. What is particularly striking about these devices is that, for the most part, they are off-limits to civilians such as you and me. In almost all cases, when I reached out to companies that manufacture these tools, hoping to learn more about their function and clientele, I came up against an emphatic no: without a connection to law enforcement, I was told, I did not have the right to know anything about the equipment. Their sale is also tightly regulated. Merchants as well-known as Gerber, a manufacturer of camping knives and multitools, also have a "tactical" division where many items are marked "Credentials Required." This is true across the board; forced-entry and breaching tools are officially controlled items, meant to be available only to first responders, law enforcement, and the military (although a quick trip to eBay reveals that many of these tools will occasionally, like the keys to the city, turn up on the open market).

In a nutshell, if you want to get into a building fast, you don't mess around with lockpicks—and if you need to breach something truly well fortified, don't bother looking for a tensioning tool or a Bogotá rake. You have to take things up a notch and use equipment seemingly more appropriate for laparoscopic surgery, including flexible borescopes for peering deep into a lock's inner gear. Or you get your hands on some drilling templates for specific safe designs—the year, make, and model. These function almost like an acupuncture diagram: just overlay them onto the doors of target safes to reveal the exact order and depth to drill for each place. Such templates are easily available from safe and vault companies and locksmith-supply warehouses. Or get yourself an electric arc welder, which is basically a portable plasma-cutting device— available at any high-end industrial tool shop—with the added bonus that you are technically using the controlled introduction of a fourth state of matter to slice your way through vaults and walls. Or you could also use a so-called burning bar to do the same thing the old-fashioned way; DIY instructions for building these tools are available all over YouTube and even *Make:* magazine.

The burning bar—also known as a thermal or thermic lance—is an interesting piece of equipment. It was originally developed after World War I to help cut through battlefield ruins, dismantle tanks, and demolish concrete bunkers. A burning bar is basically a long bundle of steel rods encased inside a larger steel tube through which oxygen is then blown at high pressure; the steel at one end of the tube is ignited using an oxyacetylene torch, causing the internal rods to begin to melt. Push this sparkling bundle of slowly melting steel rods forward into virtually any obstacle, including solid granite, and it will burn a hole straight through; you can use a burning bar to cut through train tracks, solid-steel industrial machinery, and the walls of safes and bank vaults.

Perhaps you've seen Michael Mann's 1981 film, *Thief,* starring James Caan. *Thief* includes an extraordinary scene showing this tool in use. Toward the end of the film, Caan and his cohorts have broken into the faux-rococo apartment of their adversary, complete with marble floors, ornate furniture, and period chandeliers. After piling all of the furniture in the center of the room, they don head-to-toe, dark, hooded outfits, like high priests of a Satanic cult about to perform a Black Mass, and they ignite a thermal lance. Burning their way forward through the vault door, they produce a frothing soup of liquid metal that bubbles and drips away. The heist has the feel of science fiction—the set looks like something from the end of Stanley Kubrick's *2001*—as these black-robed astronauts of crime melt their way ever deeper into a locked room they plan to rob.

Tobias singles out a firm called Broco several times for its various product lines. Broco's website—part of the Broco-Rankin corporate umbrella—is something of a fever dream for anyone who might want to dismantle the built environment; all architects should spend at least a few minutes there simply to see the tools capable of taking apart their most prized creations. Broco runs a specific division for military and tactical products marketed to Special Forces teams, armored units, search-and-rescue crews, combat engineers, and police tactical squads. As with Gerber, these products are off-limits to anyone without security credentials. "Today we offer a full line of forced entry products that follow the natural progression of breaching, ranging from mechanical, to saw, to torch, to dynamic hydraulics," Broco proudly proclaims. *The natural progression of breaching.* Somewhere, a wishful burglar is flipping through a Broco catalog and making a holiday gift list.

Among many other things, what's remarkable about much of this equipment is the extent to which it resembles the everyday arsenal of a well-stocked fire department. This includes hydraulic doorjamb spreaders (in a different context, popularly known as the Jaws of Life), so-called Halligans and other pry bars (available on

Amazon.com), and even circular saws and angle-grinders (stop by Lowe's next weekend to pick up your own pair) that any fire crew would use to ventilate a structure or rescue people trapped inside a crashed vehicle. The somewhat obvious implication is that firefighters have at their disposal house-breaking technology that could easily be repurposed for burglary—or that, should you want to commit the ultimate act of breaking and entering, you might want to rob a firehouse first and liberate their best equipment, including elevator keys and tactical cutting-torch kits.

How these sorts of tools are developed, tested, and used was explained to me by Special Agent Kenneth Crotty of the ATF during a workshop held on a rainy winter day in New York City. As part of a packed agenda, from canine demonstrations to anti-explosive workshops, Crotty described a series of pop-up training exercises run by the ATF where field agents practice and develop door-breaching techniques. This is known within the field as Tactical Explosive Entry School, or TEES. One of the most common classes could be thought of as Zen and the art of door annihilation; usually a temporary facility is built entirely out of doors, featuring multiple examples of the typical door types, materials, and styles most likely to be encountered during a home raid. Resembling an avant-garde architectural installation, these structures are often nothing but doors and doorframes standing in the middle of open parking lots.

Rapid-entry teams are then supplied with an array of tools that they use to break through those doors as quickly and efficiently as possible; this not only tests each agent's particular skills, it also inspires innovations and improvements in the tools themselves by way of user feedback. Breaching rams, hydraulic jaws, sledgehammers, even explosive packs that use nothing but detonation cord and water-filled IV bags—everything and anything of potential use is thrown at these surreal labyrinths of doors built in the middle of nowhere to see what does and does not work. Crotty played a few films of various exercises, including an example of repurposed air bags—the same devices that deploy during a car crash—being applied to an inward-opening door; the door is blown out of its frame by the opening of the bag, without any explosives in sight.

Photos of these exercises are proudly displayed on the Facebook pages of groups such as the Tennessee-based Tactical Energetic Entry Systems, as well as a larger umbrella organization called the International Breachers Group. These masters of rapid-entry gather at annual trade conventions like the International Breachers Symposium. Their websites are filled with equipment that would make any organized burglary crew drool. "Built by Breachers for Breachers," one firm boasts. Another company offers a fifteen-hundred-dollar backpack-mounted "entry kit," promising, "With this kit, Nothing Shall Stand in Your Way." Police-product websites offer mini-rams and "break-n-rakes," torch kits and "Wallbangers," "edge benders" and even a Thor-like object known as the Thundersledge.

These tools make the very idea of architectural defense seem absurd. You can put half a dozen dead bolts on your front door and a hydraulic doorjamb spreader will make a mockery of all six of them in an instant. You can hammer boards across the doorframe like something from a zombie horror film, but an air bag will blow the whole thing to smithereens. You can even seal an entire doorway with concrete, but a single burning bar—they even come in handy backpack-size units perfect for ATF or FBI rapid-entry teams—will melt through the concrete in minutes.

As should be expected, the overwhelming superiority of these tools has been met by a series of illegal innovations in the field of DIY home fortification. Crotty described a few unsettling examples, such as the house of a drug dealer where the front door opened not into the building's interior but onto a closed vestibule. Loaded shotguns tied to a trip wire made from fishing line were pointed at ankle height, set to blow the feet off any potential assailants, whether they were federal agents or rival dealers. In other houses, ATF teams had found machine-gun ports in walls and ceilings; in yet others, railroad ties had been set into reinforced concrete to prevent battering rams from breaking through.

Booby traps are illegal—you can wire up as many burglar alarms as you like, but you can't wire up a shotgun to fire if someone kicks open your front door. Nevertheless, traps are not uncommon. Worse, as the tools for breaking into architectural structures become more and more effective, the shields, traps, and defenses only grow more extreme. It's all just part of the infinite arms race, the "war that knows no armistice" that Alfred A. Hopkins warned his readers about more than a hundred years ago, waged between "the planners of safes and vaults, and the safe, vault and bank robbers."

What I didn't yet know was that the next step in architectural defense—something that could resist not just battering rams but C-4 explosives—had already been designed, and that I would find it in a warehouse in rural New Jersey. But if these, not the delicate instruments of locksport, are the true tools of breaking and entering— the torches, saws, rams, and air bags with which anyone can bash or burst into almost any building in the world— then I would clearly need to flip the story once again.

I had already moved from recreational lock-pickers to ATF rapid-entry teams, but I would now have to turn to the people specifically designing architecture to resist the most aggressive attacks. Because if someone is developing new hydraulic doorjamb spreaders, then someone else is building a defensive structure specifically with those tools in mind.

Panic Room

A little more than an hour's drive south of Manhattan, amid a rolling landscape of state parks and golf courses in the woods of coastal New Jersey, Vietnam vet and former New Jersey State cop Karl Alizade owns a small warehouse. Pulling into the parking lot of Alizade's firm, you can't miss the broken safe placed out beside the driveway, its door wide-open, sitting there exposed to the weather like a peculiar kind of lawn sculpture. It's as effective a reminder as any that, to a burglar, safes are often just decorative, offering little more than an illusion of security.

Aside from the safe, it is not easy to guess what happens inside this warehouse set back among the pine trees. But here Alizade runs what architects would call a design-build studio; his is a busy workshop dedicated to conceiving and assembling some of the world's most impenetrable architectural designs. Yet Alizade doesn't think of himself as a designer, let alone an architect. He actually seemed somewhat taken aback when I explained that I was interested in his work from an architectural point of view. Rather, Alizade works in the niche world of the design of safe rooms—more popularly known as *panic rooms*.

Alizade greeted me at the front door in jeans and a half-zip black fleece sweater. He is built more like a linebacker than a businessman. He is stout, broad-shouldered, and has large hands; he gestured with them often as he spoke, twisting and turning them as if solving an invisible Rubik's Cube in order to explain how his products were made. Despite his chosen field of security design and his physical resemblance to someone more likely to be leading tours through the Alaskan outback, he is jovial, prone to quick jokes and laughter.

After graduating with an engineering degree from Auburn University, and following a stint in Vietnam, Alizade joined the New Jersey State police force. During his time as a cop, he was struck by the raw, destructive power burglary had on victims' lives, making it second only to rape, in his view, in terms of its long-term emotional impact. This is supported by much of the sociological literature: that intense feelings of betrayal and paranoia can be expected to follow any burglary, after which even the smallest detail from earlier interactions with neighbors can lead to a debilitating suspicion that perhaps they were behind the burglary. Maybe your neighbor made a now deeply suspicious comment when you mentioned you'd be going out of town for a week, or, in retrospect, a curious observation that you always seemed to be at the grocery store the same time every day—which was exactly when your home was broken into. This can lead to an often paralyzing fear of leaving the house or trusting any of your old friends.

Burglary is a horribly invasive crime, Alizade emphasized, offending the very idea of personal space and dignity. The feelings of embarrassment and violation it can cause are so powerful, he added, that he decided to commit himself to finding a way to help end the crime altogether, dedicating the latter half of his professional career to the design of defensive architecture, devising new and ever-better ways to thwart burglars. Working as a police officer had taught him firsthand that locks don't work. They slow criminals down, sure—but they don't really *stop* anyone. Maybe your lock means that a burglar will need a few more minutes to get inside—but they'll still get inside. If you really want to keep people out of a space altogether— if you want to end the humiliation of burglary—then you need something far stronger than a dead bolt. You need an absolute physical barrier.

After leaving the police force, Alizade began working in the field of safe- and vault-room design. This took him overseas for an intense period of research and apprenticeship, first to London in the late 1970s. There he worked in the safe factories of both Chubb and John Tann, and he studied vaults in the London Docklands—at the time, a brutally rough and industrial part of London—where importers and exporters stored their goods. These were exotic and strong vaults, Alizade explained, sounding almost wistful, and they taught him far more than he could have learned if he had stayed home in the United States, where all the safe factories were still working only with plate steel. Even better, Alizade was beginning to meet—and have dockside drinks with—some of the very people who were targeting those safes and vaults. Everyone there knew he was a former cop, he said, "but I told them I didn't care what happened in England; I cared about keeping stuff safe in America. They thought that was funny." He spent many long nights outdrinking English and European burglars alike, learning their tricks of the trade.

After a few more years in the U.K., Alizade left London to work in safe factories in the Netherlands, South Africa, and even Australia, getting a global perspective on the technicalities of vault design, from advanced metallurgy to the thermal properties of concrete. But things were beginning to change: many of the big foundries and factories he had been so enthusiastic about studying were now starting to shut down, their land sold out from beneath them and handed over to developers. The silver lining? As those factories began to close, a new space in the global market was opening up. Alizade saw an opportunity.

Before returning to the United States, and because of his unusually extensive international expertise, Alizade became a trusted fraud investigator for the international insurance giant Lloyd's of London; this means that, even today, he will regularly be sent out around the world to inspect burglary insurance claims firsthand, analyzing popped locks, broken safes, and even tunnel jobs to verify that they have not been faked. Several times Alizade and I were only barely able to squeeze in a brief phone call before another of his trips to a new site in the UAE or Brazil, two growth markets he spoke about with genuine interest. Customers in Rio, because of the 2014 World Cup and the 2016 Olympics, had begun investing heavily in private fortifications for everything from suburban homes to police infrastructure, and the UAE was attracting in ever-increasing numbers wealth, tourists, and the criminals who prey on them.

These twin interests—physical security and extensive global travel—were fittingly summarized by his office décor. We were sitting in a cozy, wood-veneer room, its windowsills and shelves lined with the spent cases of large-caliber bullets, and a world map on the back wall was dotted with colored pins marking the countries where Alizade had so far traveled or done business. There were a lot of pins.

Since making his way back to the suburbs of New Jersey and founding CitySafe, Alizade has been on a tear of design innovation in architectural security. He has developed new, high-strength concrete recipes, mixing bauxite and metal wire into his concrete to form an intensely abrasive, harder-than-rock conglomerate that can resist .50-caliber sniper rounds and wreck almost any drill head applied to it. He has accumulated an extensive physical collection of destroyed safes, including entire sections of walls removed from crime scenes around New York, in order to study how the burglars broke in.

Early in his career, for example, Alizade had noticed that gold burglaries in Jackson Heights, Queens, were on the rise; the increasingly Indian population of the neighborhood places an unusually high cultural value on gold and had been keeping more and more of the precious metal locked up behind flimsy storefronts, relying on fallible architecture and imperfect safes. Many of those compromised safes and sections of walls completely sliced through by criminals were now here in Alizade's warehouse, forming a kind of criminal cross section of Jackson Heights relocated to the forested hinterlands of New Jersey.

Seeing these architectural sections and broken safes in one place is a bit like walking into a private museum. Alizade's collection rather strikingly resembled an avant-garde architectural display reminiscent of the work of American artist Gordon Matta-Clark. Today, Matta-Clark is known primarily for having cut whole sections out of existing buildings—even chainsawing an entire suburban house in two—then displaying the results in a New York gallery. This was not the first time the field of burglary and burglary prevention would bring to mind the work of

Matta-Clark: the physical results of slicing through buildings, whether it's performed as part of a bank heist or as part of an art installation, are often indistinguishable.

Most important, Alizade designs and fabricates a line of trademarked safe rooms he calls MODUL-X. He had realized during his cop days, he explained, that few people had in those years thought to strengthen anything but the front door of a house or nothing more than a bank's teller window. People seemed to take it for granted that buildings would be used properly—not sidestepped, punctured, or otherwise worked around. You might have the strongest front door in the world, but if I can hammer my way through your wall in two minutes, what good does a dead bolt do? People were looking at architecture all wrong, he saw, acting as if criminals respect a building or treat it like a precious object.

Once he realized how easy it was for burglars simply to burst down through ceilings, or to slice their way through the drywall of a check-cashing facility to steal thousands of dollars, it also became clear how naïve the existing approach to architectural security had been. Something had to be done, and that meant rethinking where, through the eyes of burglars, the entrance to a building really was. Because it wasn't the front door. It was a hole of their own making: a new entrance sliced through the unprotected surfaces that held our vulnerable world of doors in place. Burglars refuse to take that world on its own terms. They can go around it, through it, under it, making every crime a kind of tunnel job, worming their way through architecture while the rest of us just stand there, hypnotized.

They've developed their own tools for this, as well, Alizade saw, not bothering with skeleton keys or lockpicks but misusing or redesigning architecture itself. Burglars are the M. C. Eschers of the built environment, approaching every wall and ceiling as a door-to-be, a connection waiting to happen, then making their vision real with the help of burning bars and Sawzalls.

The next obvious step would be to fortify those walls and ceilings—but why stop there? Why just reinforce— that is, be held hostage by—the mistakes of the original architect? Why not insert *an entirely new room*—a strong- box, a bullet-resistant command center complete with bottled water and emergency phone lines at the ready? Assemble this new space inside an existing home or busi- ness, and voilà—say goodbye to the brute-force thuggery of takeover robberies and late-night home invasions, and say hello to a place of refuge away from the risk of harm. It would be a literal safe room.

Before I visited Alizade, I spent a long time looking through a handful of patents he has filed for the modular defensive structures his firm now constructs. Those patents are for high-security safes slotted together piece by piece, or panel by panel, assembled almost like three-dimensional puzzles or magic boxes. What's so brilliant about Alizade's subsequent work is that he has effectively blown these safes up to the scale of small buildings, simply by adding more—and more, and more—panels until something the size of a jewelry safe has the dimensions of a functional liv- ing room. Because of the modular nature of their construc- tion, these rooms have no realistic upper limit on their size.

Finally, install all this inside someone's house—near the master bedroom, for example, behind a fake wall, or maybe next door to the home office—and you have a panic room. Even better, if you move to a new house, you can unbolt the whole thing from inside, pack up the panels, and take it with you.

Two main strategies are at work in Alizade's MODUL-X line. The modular assembly of the walls themselves—what one of his patents refers to as "a plurality of interconnected panels"—means that they can be bolted together without gaps along tight seams. Additionally, each panel joins up with the others along unusual right-angled edges. Think of a square of chocolate popped into a grid, where each square has a double right angle, like a small staircase, cut along its edges. Those doubled angles mean that you cannot slip any burglary tools through the cracks between the panels—not to mention any orthoscopic cameras for spying inside. Finally, the walls are not only designed to resist simple burglary tools; they can also only be assembled or dissembled, bolted or unbolted, from the inside. Even if intruders have days and days of uninterrupted time, they cannot take the room apart without first gaining entrance.

The spatial premise of David Fincher's 2002 film, *Panic Room*, plays on this promise of true invulnerability. *Panic Room* depicts a burglary gone wrong, as three men break into a brownstone on Manhattan's Upper East Side—only to find that a mother and her daughter have locked themselves into the home's eponymous panic room.

The problem? "What we want," the burglars write on a piece of paper, shown to the mother and daughter by way of a surveillance camera, "is in that room."

The conundrum here is obvious: What kind of heist is possible when the room you're targeting is impossible to enter? Ironically, this reveals what is perhaps any panic room's fundamental flaw: the people who turn to it for protection have effectively entombed themselves there, locked into a space of inescapable claustrophobia. Refusing to believe in the panic room's impenetrability, however, two of the film's burglars begin discussing various ways to get in—despite the fact that, as we learn in an early plot twist, the leader of their crew was responsible for the room's design and installation. "I spent the last twelve years of my life building these rooms specifically to keep out people like us," the man mutters at one point, shaking his head. "It's all so ironic and amusing," another burglar trills—*but how do we get in?* The designer laughs at him. "We can't. You can't get into a panic room. That's the whole point. We have to get *her* to come *out.*"

Achieving this kind of stopping power brings us to Alizade's other signature approach: brute strength. The concrete he uses is remarkable. CitySafe has settled on a slow-curing, proprietary mixture. It resists sledgehammers and drills and is also impenetrable by .50-caliber, high-velocity sniper rounds, rocket-propelled grenades, and, incredibly, C-4 shape charges. This means that even professional demolition teams and small insurgent armies would have trouble getting inside a MODUL-X safe room.

Further, because the concrete mix includes a matrix of metal fibers, the panels will dissipate—that is, neutralize—the directional heat of a thermic lance.

It doesn't seem entirely out of the question to suggest that these rooms, built to resist even the explosives used to demolish high-rise buildings, old casinos, and obsolete sports stadiums, could well be the last architectural structures standing after the collapse of civilization. Among the ruins of human culture, alongside the Pyramids, Stonehenge, and the Great Wall of China, Karl Alizade's safe rooms, surrounded by wastelands of collapsed towers and twisted rebar, would still be intact, their doors still locked from within, impenetrable to future archaeologists and grave robbers, with skeletons of the wealthy sealed in silence, enthroned among their gold and jewels. It's as if Alizade was so concerned about eliminating the threat of burglary from the world that he inadvertently designed an architecture that would outlast humanity altogether.

Of course, his safe rooms are not *truly* impenetrable, and Alizade was clear about this (without sharing any tips for how to defeat their defenses). He emphasized, instead, that impenetrability is the wrong way to think about personal safety: you're not trying to build a pharaonic tomb that will survive to the end of the world. You're trying to buy time. "Any safe can be penetrated," he pointed out, and that applies equally well to any safe room. If the owner of a safe dies and no one else has the key, or if someone locked inside a safe room is for any reason incapacitated and can no longer open the door, you need at least some way to get in. "But that's not the Holy Grail of safe design," he said. "It's *time*—time and the fact that you're making them bring lots of different tools to the scene. That's the Holy Grail. Difficulty. The longer you keep them on that site, the more nervous they get." And the more nervous your attackers get, the more likely they are to lose their nerve, make rookie mistakes, or just run out of time and be caught.

We left the main office and walked back into the attached workshop to see one of Alizade's contraptions standing in the center of the warehouse. The unrelentingly gray, bunker-like box consisted of several dozen two-foot-square panels bolted together like a cubist armadillo. It was pieces attached to pieces attached to pieces. If ever a structure seemed to have been designed using *Minecraft*, this was it. Alizade was clearly happy with his product, as well as delighted by the visible scars left on its side from unsuccessful attacks by prospective clients. He even urged me to pick up a sledgehammer—several were lying about—and try it out myself, to drive home how pointless such an attack would be. It was like kicking a mountain.

These rooms don't only resist all of the major tools used by rapid-entry teams, from sledgehammers and Halligans to burning bars. One of the most interesting things Alizade explained to me was how he tests his products (videos of these tests can be found on his website). Emphasizing the strange asymmetry of global weapons availability, Alizade ships his panels off to be field-tested on a Russian military air base against weaponry, including AK-47s and rocket launchers, designed in the former Soviet Union. This is because, he says, these are the weapons the bad guys have: Cold War munitions have flooded the global marketplace through official and unofficial arms deals, finding their way into the hands of criminal gangs, child armies, and terrorist insurgents.

As Alizade reasons, in addition to standard house-breaking tools and U.S.-made munitions, his products must stand up against these weapons in particular. The MODUL-X system is certified for use by the Department of State and the Bureau of Diplomatic Security, he reminded me, and it has been used to protect not only wealthy businesspeople temporarily posted overseas but U.S. ambassadorial staff stationed in foreign, often highly volatile, countries. If loosely defined groups of terrorists, thieves, gangsters, seasoned criminals, drug-fueled warlords, religious extremists, political separatists, and other stateless movers and shakers of the global black economy are going to use off-market, hand-me-down Soviet military gear against a target, then that target needs to be built to withstand that constellation of weaponry.

This is one of the clearest examples of the *Spy vs. Spy* mentality animating many of the innovations in both protecting and violating private space. To physically build into the architectural productions of his firm resistance to the specific damage profiles of old Soviet machine guns and sniper rifles is to make explicit the arms race between one side and the other, between those who design for security and those who design to defeat it. Architecture, in this context, is just another word for this tug-of-war.

I asked Alizade about his clientele, and he was necessarily cagey. Giving away any recognizable details about who had had a safe room installed would defeat half the purpose of owning one, and it could indicate to a determined observer that something inside must be worth stealing. Alizade did say that several CEOs of pharmaceutical companies had had his rooms installed inside their homes (one of the peculiarities of New Jersey is that its well-forested roads often lead from pharmaceutical giant to pharmaceutical giant).

But, once again, the business landscape is starting to change. Alizade explained that he was restructuring CitySafe, looking for investors, and preparing for a potential move west to Nevada, where the security market was expanding. He also admitted that he had been growing a bit bored with domestic security over the past few years. He wanted to continue working with the State Department and the Department of Defense, and to expand the business accordingly. The home fortifications and safe rooms offered by his competitors made him laugh, they were so easy to defeat. He seemed restless.

As Alizade walked me through his model panic room, pointing out every detail, I was reminded of something Jerry Toner, the Cambridge classicist, had told me. During our wide-ranging conversation about crimes and burglaries in the ancient world, Toner had pointed out that the House of Menander in the destroyed city of Pompeii had apparently featured a kind of safe room: a private underground vault that nonetheless offered no protection from the eruption of nearby Mt. Vesuvius. The home's owner, Quintus Poppeus, had constructed an elaborate villa for himself, the size of an entire city block, complete with a fortresslike safe room belowground. This subterranean chamber appears to have been designed for carefully controlled access, its walls thickened and seemingly impenetrable against any bandits trying to undermine or tunnel through them.

This architectural feature, Toner suggested, indicated that the walls of the private home and the legal cobweb surrounding it, even in the ancient world, would not have been enough to keep intruders at bay—indeed, that human civilizations of all known eras have produced their own Karl Alizades, we might say, people whose interest in the built environment lies in strengthening it and redesigning it to help keep the rest of us safe against intrusion, theft, and humiliation.

5

INSIDE JOB

Groundhog Day

Before they knew his name, they called him Roofman. He would cut holes in the roofs of chain stores and fast-food restaurants—usually a McDonald's—then drop down through the ceiling to rob the startled employees. Sometimes he'd come in through the back wall, slipping in through a hole of his own making, only to pop out in the kitchen or storeroom; but it was mostly the roof and so the name quickly stuck.

The employees he held up were usually teenagers paid minimum wage working the morning shift or wearily closing up shop for the night, getting the day's take ready to be counted. They didn't have much to gain from trying to stop Roofman from doing his job; the risks of being a hero seemed to outweigh the potential gains. In any case, Roofman was known for his gentle demeanor, without fail described as polite—in one oft-repeated example, even insisting that his victims put on their winter coats so that they could stay warm after he locked them all in a walk-in freezer.

An official spokesperson for McDonald's offered perhaps the simplest explanation of the ongoing crime spree: Roofman was just "very brand loyal."

But there was more to it than that. Hidden inside the repetitive floor plans and the daily schedules of these franchised businesses, Roofman had discovered a kind of criminal Groundhog Day: a burglary that could be performed over and over in different towns, cities, and states, probably even different countries if he had gone international, and his skills—his timing, his movements—would only get better with each outing.

For Roofman, it was as if each McDonald's with its streamlined timetable and centrally controlled managerial regime was an identical crystal world: a corporate mandala of polished countertops, cash registers, supply closets, money boxes, and safes into which he could drop from above as if teleported there. Everything would be in similar locations, down to the actions taking place within each restaurant. At more or less the same time of day—whether it was a branch in California or in rural North Carolina—employees would be following a mandated sequence of events, a prescribed routine, and it must have felt as if he had found some sort of crack in space-time, a quantum moment stuttering in a film loop without cease, ripe for robbing. It was the perfect crime—and he could do it over and over.

🐾

Noted designer and architectural theorist Bernard Tschumi would call the predictable repetition of events inside an architectural space a *sequence*: a linear series of actions and behaviors that are at least partially determined by the design of the space itself. Tschumi's idea rests on an architectural truism: that, for example, you probably wouldn't convene a weekly congregation inside an underground parking garage. Why? Because it's designed for parking cars, not for prayer. Or you wouldn't graze a herd of cows inside a church. Traditionally, a building gives clues as to how it is meant to be used—thus all those empty, perfectly car-size parking spots.

Buildings call for certain behaviors—even if their spatial demands are often so subtle that, at first glance, we don't realize we've been obeying them.

Tschumi's larger point is that if the design of a space or a building tends to influence what occurs within it, then the role of the avant-garde designer is to push past this, to find new ways of challenging or disrupting architecture's behavioral expectations. Why not graze cows inside a church—or at least design barns to look like churchyards?

Tschumi began to explore this notion through what he called screenplays: each "screenplay" was a black-and-white diagram breaking down a range of events that might occur inside an architectural space. Tschumi drew them in a way that resembled dance notation or the spatial analysis of a film scene. How do the people move, he wanted to know—how do they respond to one another or to the props scattered around them in space? Where do the actors stand during key moments of narrative drama? Tschumi believed that this was all part of the scenography of architectural design, and the ultimate visual results of his explorations ended up looking a lot like football-strategy diagrams—a comparison he himself has made—featuring abstract geometric shapes that tracked the movement of people past one another and through the rooms around them.

Fair enough. But what does this have to do with burglary? For Tschumi, what we think of as a "crime" typically occurs when a user of architecture does something radically out of sequence, breaking with the pattern that a building might imply—for example, sneaking past security at an airport to board a plane without following the traditional sequence of approach, entering the vault of a bank without first being granted the manager's permission, or, to cite a recent real-life example, jumping the fence outside the White House to enter the president's home by the back door. These are crimes of sequence. They are crimes of space.

Tschumi, writing in the late 1970s, at a time when American cities were falling apart, the Bronx was on fire, and New York City as a whole seemed on track to become the Mogadishu of its day—a city not to settle in but to escape—became obsessed with crime. Crime, for Tschumi, was just another way to use the city. Looked at in a specifically architectural context, crime reveals how people try to use or misuse the built environment. Criminals are more like rogue usability experts, analyzing architecture for shortcuts, hiding spots, and other spatial tricks. As Tschumi once wrote, "To really appreciate architecture, you may even need to commit a murder"—a statement he accompanied with a photo of someone being pushed out the window of a tall building. The building itself would be an accomplice to the crime.

In a way, Tschumi was simply pursuing the interests of an architect to their logical conclusion: he wanted to know how people use cities and inhabit space, whether it's walking up New York's Fifth Avenue or plotting a murder in Central Park. Indeed, such a murder is the scenario he turned to next with a project called *The Manhattan Transcripts*. Now something of a cult classic among architecture students, *The Manhattan Transcripts* diagrams a fictional murder in Central Park, implying that the crime could be used to reveal previously unknown or repressed forensic insights about how people really want to use the city, whether or not what they choose to do there is legal. For Tschumi, the murder mystery was as architectural a genre as any other.

For all Tschumi's obsession with crime and space, however, he chose to write about murder rather than burglary—despite the fact that the latter is the ideal spatial crime, literally defined by its relationship to architectural space. A bank heist or an apartment burglary—not a fictional murder in Central Park—would have been a much better fit for Tschumi's narrative goals. Imagine for a moment planning a heist on the thirty-fourth floor of a New York City high-rise, or plotting a burglary in a popular art museum. These require sequential thinking, elaborate timetables, and precise plans of action that purposefully and strategically differ from the events that are officially—that is, legally—allowed to occur there. Heists and burglaries are the ultimate Tschumian crimes.

Tschumi—Swiss-born and still working internationally—currently lives in New York City. On a blazingly hot summer day, he talked to me about these old explorations of his, looking at the strange inflection point where avant-garde spatial theory imperceptibly blurs into a criminal plan of attack. This is where a burglar's guide to a building becomes an alternative form of architectural criticism, I suggested; burglars simply look for different shortcomings, vulnerabilities, and weak points in the design.

Tschumi didn't disagree—but he wanted to back up a bit, concerned that the phrasing of my question risked making burglars into heroes or role models. "For a long time," he said instead, "my chief interest had to do with cities in general, and the extent to which an entire city could be transformed by an act of creative misuse. I was fascinated by the role of insurgency, for example, from the nineteenth century, or in the 1960s with the student movements, or even in Northern Ireland, with what was happening in Londonderry and in Belfast. I was interested in how people with a particular intent could take over certain parts of the city with an action that could transform the way the city was used." Motivated individuals or groups, he observed, could use "the complexity of the city against itself," uncovering the possible behaviors that a building or space unintentionally allows, then adapting them to stage a protest, overthrow a government, demand political representation, or, yes, simply to commit a crime.

Tschumi became quite animated as we discussed this, taking me back to his original idea of the transcript or architectural notation. Traditional architectural representation, he emphasized—such as sections sliced vertically through a building to show what's happening in every room, or floor plans used to explain how each room connects to all the others—lacks the ability to communicate events in time. It's much more difficult to make an architectural drawing of a riot, a revolution, or a bank heist—but not impossible.

For Tschumi, this inability to represent events in space remains a fundamental weakness in architectural thinking today. The goal of his earlier work had specifically been to find a way for architects to reliably visualize the events that might take place inside their spaces; but it never became an accepted technique, just an art project, a series of avant-garde posters and drawings.

In these sorts of crimes, Tschumi pointed out, the architecture is *always* involved. In every heist film, he said, "The vaults and corridors and elevator shafts are just as important as the characters in the story; one cannot exist without the other. The space itself becomes a protagonist of the plot. There is no space without something that happens in it; and nothing happens without a space like this around it." The same thing is often true for grand public plazas in the hearts of cities: these can be used as nothing but picturesque backdrops for tourists to take photos of each other or as insurrectionary platforms for starting a revolution. It's all about how you use the city— or misuse it, turning the fabric of the city against itself.

In fact, one of the most spectacular art heists of the last decade is thought to have succeeded precisely because of a flaw in a museum's architectural design, which inadvertently allowed the general public to study the internal patterns of the security guards and visitors. The Kunsthal in Rotterdam, designed by Rem Koolhaas's firm OMA, was robbed in the middle of the night back in October 2012; seven paintings were stolen, including works by Matisse, Gauguin, Monet, and Picasso. Ton Cremers, founder of the Museum Security Network, an online forum, put some of the blame for this on the building itself: the museum's expansive floor-to-ceiling windows offered a clear and unobstructed view of many of the paintings hanging inside. More important, they also allowed a constant, real-time surveillance of the internal workings of the museum for anyone passing by—the patterns of visitors and the comings and goings of the guards were effectively on public display. Thus thieves could have sat outside in a nearby park, watching until they found the right moment to strike. The museum had its own internal rhythm of events that the burglars interrupted with a perfectly timed counterevent: the heist. This is the rhythmic space-time of burglary.

I thought of Roofman. In his case, this sort of Tschu-mian analysis would translate into using a business's internal timetable against itself: when managers and security guards walk their rounds, for example, or when employees change shifts. For that matter, I suggested aloud, just think of all the hundreds of film scenes in which bank robbers are shown clicking a stopwatch the instant they burst through a bank's front doors, knowing that they only have a certain number of minutes—even mere seconds—to get the job done before a security response. They uncover and then misuse the existing schedule of the bank's security to help them commit their crime.

🦗

For Roofman, it must have looked as if the rest of the world were locked in a trance, doing the exact same things at the exact same times of day—in the same kinds of buildings, no less—and not just in one state, but everywhere. It's no real surprise, then, that he would become greedy, ambitious, overconfident, stepping up to larger and larger businesses—but still targeting franchises and big-box stores. They would all have their own spatial formulas and repeating events, he knew; they would all be run according to predictable loops inside identical layouts all over the country.

With overconfidence came carelessness, and Roofman was eventually arrested and imprisoned in North Carolina's Brown Creek Correctional Institution. Now the police finally knew his name and backstory: Roofman was Jeffery Manchester, a former U.S. Army reservist with a peculiar eye for spatial patterns. But as quickly as they locked him up, he broke out, escaping from Brown Creek— the first person ever to do so—by hiding underneath a delivery truck. He was carried to safety by the easily memorized and predictable schedule of a package-delivery van.

Manchester made a beeline for nearby Mecklenburg County, North Carolina, where he'd been told by his fellow inmates that sentences for commercial burglary— should he ever want to commit one again—were not as severe as in surrounding areas. There, his architectural proclivities took an especially bizarre turn. His (second) arresting officer, Sergeant Katherine Scheimreif of the Charlotte-Mecklenburg Police Department, spoke to me about his January 2005 recapture.

When Scheimreif and the Charlotte Police found him again, Manchester had been living for several months inside an apartment of his own making, disguised behind a bicycle display in the walls of Toys "R" Us. This was only one of two such apartments: Manchester later abandoned his first hiding place to burrow through the outer wall of the toy store into an abandoned Circuit City next door. There, he constructed a surprisingly well-kept new home tucked beneath a stairwell, a twenty-four-hour burglary HQ hidden inside the walls of an American chain store, taking his brand loyalty to a strange new level of spatial intensity where ever-more-elaborate plots could be hatched.

Scheimreif referred to Manchester's unlikely abode as "his little spider hole," and my first reaction was to assume that this was a condescending analogy, a cop's put-down, as if comparing Manchester to vermin or to a bug. To an extent, it was—but Scheimreif was being amusingly literal. Manchester had been sleeping on Spider-Man-themed bedsheets, with Spider-Man film posters tacked up on his makeshift walls, surrounded by DVDs stolen from the children's toy store next door. This pirate of space-time, ritualistically breaking his way into identical commercial moments across the country, convinced of his own genius, had constructed for himself the escapist bedroom of an eleven-year-old.

But Manchester didn't stop there. He also installed his own, parallel surveillance network inside the Toys "R" Us, using stolen baby monitors to spy on the movements of guards and employees, looking out for rhythms, patterns, and times of weakness as he planned his next blockbuster caper. "He would just watch the baby monitor and know exactly when everyone was coming and going," Sergeant Scheimreif explained. It was a more sophisticated version of his old days as Roofman. "Everything in these businesses is so procedurally organized," she pointed out. "They put the money away at the same time; they cook the fries at the same time. These corporations organize things like this for a reason, but they're not thinking about these other kinds of people."

Think back to Bernard Tschumi's point that all buildings imply a certain kind of use or behavior; this is not just true for art museums and churches. A McDonald's or a Toys "R" Us is designed to facilitate a specific retail sequence in which customers enter, choose their goods, stand in line, and pay. But Sergeant Scheimreif's "other kinds of people" have discovered something like a parallel world hidden inside all of this: these sequences also and entirely accidentally contain a kind of countersequence, a crime nestled in the building's lulls and blind spots. It's the flip side of all those regularized floor plans, daily schedules, and employee rhythms. It's the same dots connected to make a different picture.

With his own surveillance network in place, Manchester made perhaps his best discovery of all: he could actually rearrange and interfere with the building's rhythms until they began to form the pattern he was waiting for. Indeed, Manchester "had become so attuned to his Toys 'R' Us," Sergeant Scheimreif added, "that he actually began changing its security system and changing the schedules of the employees." He was engineering a perfect moment so that he could strike.

In the commission of what would turn out to be his final major crime, however, an off-duty sheriff's deputy unexpectedly arrived, throwing off Manchester's meticulously arranged plans. His Mr. Nice Guy character finally broke, and Roofman resorted to violence, punching the female deputy, stealing her gun, and fleeing the premises. All of a sudden, a slew of random details began falling into place for the police. An earlier false alarm at the toy store had been blamed on a rodent, but suspicions had nonetheless been raised. The Charlotte-Mecklenburg police had already searched the abandoned Circuit City next door—even tugging on an odd piece of drywall that was an entrance to Manchester's burrow. His bizarre hiding spot was now soon discovered.

While going back through his case, including a review

of his behavior at the Brown Creek Correctional Institution before he made his escape, Sergeant Scheimreif found that Manchester had apparently spent a lot of time in his cell drawing up plans for his future dream home. Not a mansion on a tropical island or a fantasy castle somewhere in the Alps, his dream house included a maze of trapdoors and what Sergeant Scheimreif called "escape holes."

Secret passages, "escape holes," apartments hidden in the walls, and makeshift entrances sliced down through ceilings: this was the architectural world Roofman lived within and moved through, a universe of spatial possibilities tucked away deep inside our own. Sergeant Scheimreif laughed and deadpanned, "He definitely had a different way of looking at things."

It should be obvious by now that burglars have their own peculiar ways of using the built environment, not only in how they choose particular targets but in how they navigate buildings from within. However, the predictability of a building's interior and the events that take place inside it can also come in handy for the police.

Retired NYPD detective sergeant Michael Codella's book, *Alphaville*, is a red-blooded police memoir set in the public housing projects of New York's Alphabet City (named after its avenues: A, B, C, and D) during the heroin days of the 1980s. While it won't win many awards for political correctness, it includes several interesting architectural observations. The spatial details recounted in Codella's book make it feel at times less like the autobiography of a retired detective and more like an example of some new, experimental literary genre: architectural criticism by cop, or how easily riled NYPD detectives see and inhabit the built environment.

Codella explains how a special police task force was created in New York back in 1934—originally known as the New York City Housing Authority Police Department, and today as the NYPD Housing Bureau—specifically in conjunction with the inauguration of public housing projects in the city. These were buildings so bewildering—as if the cloning tool in Photoshop had taken on a sinister mind of its own—that, without their own specifically dedicated police force, they would have been all but impossible to patrol. That a new type of building required a new type of police force, with its own techniques of surveillance and its own tactical understanding of the built environment, underscores that an architectural design can present previously unheard-of possibilities for criminal behavior.

The irony here, Codella explains, is that the types of megaprojects most often funded and built by the state inadvertently created pockets of immunity to further state intervention and police control. Public housing became an arena in which the city simply "tried out some new architectural experiment on the mostly immigrant poor," Codella suggests, confining those residents inside meandering architectural labyrinths where the state could no longer reach them.

Codella describes a monstrous residential complex known only as the Site Four and Five Houses: "Site Four and Five was a multistory poured concrete rabbit warren so sprawling and generic that even seasoned cops would get completely lost in its hallways or not be able to give the correct address for where they were when calling Central for backup."

If we recall LAPD tactical flight officer Cole Burdette's interest in clarifying the city's system of house numbers and addresses, Codella is just describing the indoor equivalent: making state-funded megastructures numerically legible to the police forces tasked with patrolling them. Even navigating their behemoth interiors required tactical innovation. Residential tower blocks require what are known as vertical patrols, for example, during which officers will walk the stairways up and down, often navigating only by flashlight, as dead bulbs can go for days or weeks at a time without being replaced. Codella describes how he and his fellow officers would pass acoustic signals to one another by tapping their nightsticks on the walls and railings of stairwells, echoing out to their colleagues somewhere else in the titanic shafts.

However, all this architectural monotony had at least one silver lining for the police. Codella points out that the "impersonal design" of the housing projects meant that repetitive floor plans were stacked one atop the other seemingly without end, so officers could quickly become familiar with the kinds of apartments they might be called to. These honeycombs of near-identical homes meant that officers could have a relatively good idea of the most likely hiding places, whether they were looking for the subject, the subject's weapons, or drugs. The police could therefore refine their tactical responses through sheer repetition, meaning that, ideally, they would not be taken by surprise if someone leaped out from behind a closet door—because the cops would have known that closet was there and it had probably happened to them before.

The repetitiveness and similarity of these individual apartments meant that NYPD Housing Police were something like the Jeffery Manchesters of law enforcement, always storming into the same space in different locations on different days, trapped in a loop not of crime but of its interruption. Unlike Roofman, however, who intervened at a precise moment in an established pattern to commit his Groundhog Day–like burglaries, pulling off the same crime again and again across the country, the police were having the opposite experience: seemingly always breaking up indistinguishable incidents, over and over, kicking their way ever deeper into a kaleidoscope of identical apartments for another drug bust that looked just like yesterday—and last week and the month before—as if crime itself were a broken record, a repetition addiction, a compulsion that only leads to more of itself, ticking away behind closed doors all over the city.

Rhythms of Vulnerability

The question of how deep architectural interiors can be monitored and controlled extends far beyond the realm of the residential. Museums, hotels, and casinos, not to mention pieces of urban infrastructure, such as subways, train stations, and even streets themselves, have almost imperceptibly been transformed into unwitting film studios, recorded not by Hollywood equipment but the high-tech gear of the security industry. Surveillance cameras blur the line not just between public and private, but between architectural structures and optical installations, turning entire casino interiors, for example, into carefully designed stage sets specifically meant to steer you in front of the lens.

Jason England is a gregarious expert in sleight-of-hand magic: dexterous techniques for distracting your target and beating the house. He is also unusually insightful about the strategic, rule-based vulnerabilities inherent in certain games—from dice to poker—and how each requires a different kind of security, whether that means electromagnetic sensors, radio-frequency devices, or simply CCTV.

Speaking to me from his home in Las Vegas, world capital of fantasy heists, England opined that the original architects of that city's iconic casinos "gave almost no thought to security while designing these older buildings. Instead, security managers now have to find a way to retroactively build choke points into the layout and funnel everybody past high-resolution cameras." The result "might not be great buildings, in an architectural sense—but they are great at taking pictures of you."

Those cameras are everywhere. ATM cameras are wired directly to the casino's central security network; check-cashing cameras catch every detail of your appearance (even down to your signature); cameras are on the way to the bathrooms; cameras are at the tops of escalators.

Indeed, escalators reveal one of the casino world's preferred tactics. Subtly guiding people onto an escalator almost immediately upon entering a casino might seem to be an example of bad architectural design, but it works as an ingenious security protocol. Nearly every visitor to the building dutifully lines up to have his or her picture taken, not just once but multiple times, from nearly every conceivable angle, as people are carried from the entrance to the gaming floor.

Recall Bernard Tschumi's point that architecture is constantly making subtle, even imperceptible, demands of its users, pushing them to behave or inhabit the building in certain ways, and now think of all those casino escalators filling up like cattle cars. "Every escalator ride gives them thirty more seconds to take pictures of you," England said. The building itself is a camera.

Darrell Clifton is head of security at the Circus Circus hotel and casino in Reno; *Security* magazine has named him one of the "most influential people in security." Circus Circus is in an old building, designed with anything but security in mind, but Clifton patiently walked me through the many ways he and his security teams can mitigate this. He likes to think of the building in terms of layers, with certain key spaces (cash rooms, retail stores) at the center of concentric rings of security.

At the outermost edge of these layers, Clifton thinks of landscape architecture as a useful security barrier, even choosing certain species and planting regimes not for aesthetics but for their ability to interfere with criminal activity. A thorny plant called trifoliate orange—nicknamed

the Rambo bush—is sold as a low-cost living barrier. It
is marketed under the name Living Fence. Trifoliate orange is so dense and fast-growing that it can stop speeding vehicles; it is used by the U.S. military to help secure
the perimeters of missile silos and armories; and its razor-
sharp thorns make it a great fit for domestic security needs.
Clifton pointed out that protecting every single external
wall and window with its own dedicated security camera
is too expensive, which means that something as simple
as a thorny plant—even a cluster of rosebushes—can be
enough to deter anyone but the most determined criminal from coming near.

That said, it is in the interiors of these structures
where security protocols become most spatially interesting. Clifton described the innermost layers of casino security in terms of views and sight lines. Camera placement
and interior decoration go hand in hand, as furniture,
gaming stations, and retail cash registers are all coordinated for maximum visual efficiency. When you walk
across a casino floor or step into a side shop to buy a bottle
of Coke, you are actually navigating a carefully calibrated
scene assembled not for the eyes of architecture critics
but for the optical benefit of security teams, who are
watching it all unfold from their command center hidden
somewhere else on-site.

Jes Stewart, head of security at the nearby Nevada
Museum of Art and a longtime colleague of Clifton's, also
emphasized this point. Stewart led me through the museum one afternoon as he described the various invisible
forms of security that have been installed there, hidden

in the walls, floors, and ceilings. He explained that even the building's air-conditioning system can pose a security risk, not by offering devious cat burglars a secret route through the walls but by fluttering loose paperwork left behind on someone's desk at the end of the day. Memos, receipts, and other papers, if not secured at day's end, can be blown onto the floor by the HVAC system, setting off motion detectors and making the security team think an intruder is on the loose. Believe it or not—he laughed with frustration—it happens.

We spent some time in the museum's administrative control room, where Stewart let me operate an outdoor PTZ camera—or pan-tilt-zoom—which was so powerful I could zoom in to read the license plates of cars parked nearly four blocks away. Interestingly, this is also how the intermediary urban zones between downtown buildings can be patrolled and linked together without installing publicly funded CCTV; the building, as Jason England pointed out, is a camera, but it's also filming the streets all around it. A sufficiently powerful internal surveillance network is also a useful tool for spying on the city.

Stewart explained that museums, like casinos, also use choke points and funnels to help limit the routes people will use to circulate through a building. Even if you manage to lift that Mark Rothko painting off the wall, he joked, you're still going to have to carry it down corridors or through rooms where the cameras are all ready to film you. Often, he said, these cones of vision are specifically mandated by the insurance companies that underwrite exhibitions or shows. This means not only that the layout

of rooms, hallways, and artworks is at least partially or-
chestrated for the visual benefit of a hidden security crew,
but also that the framing and composition of a specific
scene as viewed on CCTV is, in effect, paid for by an insurance company.

In all of these examples—the casino escalator revealed
as a massive photographic device or the museum interior
seen as a series of deliberately framed tracking shots choreo-
graphed from afar by the insurance industry—architectural
security relies on reinforcing and controlling visitor circulation. It means knowing exactly how someone can move
from one room to the next—and then being there waiting
for that person to arrive at their next destination.

The response of the spatial criminal would, then, be
to operate through stealth: to avoid those cameras, to
refuse the building's suggested paths of circulation, and,
in a sense, to beat the house through spatial sleight of
hand and architectural misdirection. Unless you are deliberately trying to call attention to yourself for the purpose
of distracting the security guards, infiltrating a building's
interior without being detected is central to the successful commission of a burglary. This theme is explored to
great effect in the worlds of art, cinema, and gaming.

Take, for example, a project by Canadian artist Janice
Kerbel that focuses exclusively on surreptitious movement through architectural space. Called *Home Fittings*,
Kerbel's project consists of nothing more than annotated
floor plans that show how a person could navigate the
inside of a creaky, old Victorian building without making
a sound—stepping only on solidly fixed hardwood boards,

for example. Kerbel also notes where a person could stand without casting any shadows. The results deserve comparison to Bernard Tschumi's *Manhattan Transcripts*: they are architectural plans marked up to show potentially illicit human events in space.

Indeed, like Tschumi, Kerbel has an eye for criminality and infiltration. She is most well-known for a project called *15 Lombard St.*, a widely imitated artist's book that explored what it might take to pull off a bank heist in central London. It was motivated, Kerbel explained to me, by her being, when she made it, a recent arts graduate from Canada living in London and utterly penniless. And, as master bank robber Willie Sutton apocryphally once pointed out, banks are where the money is. Kerbel thus spent several months furtively casing a bank at 15 Lombard Street, noting the layout of the bank itself as well as every detail of its daily schedule. Her observations included when cash deliveries were made and what time of day usually saw the most customers.

Kerbel assembled floor plans, photographs, and timetables. She wrote detailed instructions. Her planned burglary was downgraded to a robbery, however, when she realized she had no believable way to access the bank's vault. Instead, she devised a fictional but meticulously detailed scenario in which she would intercept the money by holding up a delivery truck outside the bank. Pulling it off—and getting away with the cash—required an exhaustive study of central London's traffic patterns, of every side street and alleyway, as the design of the city became an unwitting accomplice in her crime.

What remains so interesting about Kerbel's project—with its compulsive multimedia hoarding of plans and photographs, its vast archive of ephemera generated by obsessive attention to a specific building and its urban context—is that it suggests a world in which illicitly annotated floor plans or carefully traced maps of streets surrounding banks in central London could be traded back and forth like architectural samizdat. These underground publications would then provide their readers with alternative or unexpected guides to everyday buildings. After all, why read a Pevsner Architectural Guide to London or an *AIA Guide to New York City* when you could read a burglar's guide to the buildings all around you? Somewhere between an architectural handbook and *Ocean's Eleven*, these would show you not only how to get inside certain buildings but what to do once you find yourself standing in a space you were never meant to access in the first place. Kerbel's work suggests that thinking about architecture as a burglar would, and understanding different ways of moving through space, bring their own peculiar rewards—even if they are not monetary. Seen this way, even the most mundane or overlooked buildings and cityscapes around us can inspire the same level of wonder and admiration we might normally reserve for international landmarks, such as the Eiffel Tower or the Houses of Parliament.

For Randy Smith, a Texas-based game designer and a level architect on the legendary *Thief* games, designing a game environment in order to foreground deeply enjoyable opportunities for criminal stealth, deception, and subterfuge is a complex but rewarding challenge. The *Thief* series, the first of which came out in 1997, is widely credited as introducing the three-dimensional, first-person stealth game. Moving through an architectural interior without being detected was, in many ways, the entire point of the story. The player's goal was not to kill as many people as possible, but to slip past them unseen and unheard. Sound—or, rather, not creating any—became a central design feature of the *Thief* universe.

During our in-depth conversation about burglary and game design, Smith laughed as he explained, "You would think it was our job to design buildings that are hard to break into, but what we actually want to do is design buildings that will channel the movement of the player along different sequences. We introduce deliberate weak points or blind spots where a player can hide, and we make the guards or the architecture itself do weird things to open up more player opportunities." This means the guards are programmed to do things that, from a security manager's point of view, would be completely absurd, such as turning their backs on an important doorway just long enough that a savvy player can tiptoe past. Smith calls these built-in patterns "rhythms of vulnerability." At first, this might seem relevant only to the world of computer games or burglary fiction, but game play in the *Thief* series is not at all unlike the way security worked at Toys "R" Us, for example, with Jeffery Manchester hidden in the walls, staring at his baby monitor, watching the internal traffic of the store ebb and flow, preparing for his moment of attack.

Smith pointed out how incredibly easy it is for a game designer to create an impossible level or an impenetrable environment—a castle gate that no one can get past, a high-rise no one will ever be able to sneak into. The real challenge is to find just the right level of difficulty so that slipping past the guards and maneuvering through the rooms and corridors becomes enjoyable. This is what he meant when he suggested that game designers need to "introduce deliberate weak points or blind spots" into their environments, such as removing the guards from a room at key moments or creating otherwise unrealistic amounts of shadow at the edge of a courtyard so that a player can walk past without being seen. Real-world scenarios also contain weak points and rhythms of vulnerability—but it often takes the eyes of a burglar, or a cop, to appreciate them.

As fellow game designer Andy Schatz looks at it, however, stealth is not the only or most interesting criteria by which a heist game should be judged. While watching people play his burglary game *Monaco*, Schatz saw that breaking the rules of the game's architecture was the essence of a successful heist—not sneaking past the guards, but cutting through the walls themselves. He explained this to me in terms of efficiency: "You could say that following a winding path across your lawn is more efficient if what you're trying to do is keep your shoes clean. The winding path—not the direct path—has different efficiencies and rewards built into it."

In terms of *Monaco*, he realized, "Spending ten minutes of game time digging a tunnel through a wall in order to get just one coin is not the most time-efficient solution—but, for someone who's risk averse, if you want to limit your exposure to security guards or limit your risks in attacking the building, then it might actually be the most efficient way to solve the problem." You just carve your own route from A to B; if there isn't a door, you make one. Schatz even encouraged this approach to the game—that is, treating the architecture as something to cut through, blast apart, or dig beneath—during an "Ask Me Anything" session on Reddit. He emphasized, "There are secret passages hidden all over EVERY level that any character can access. Try pushing on suspiciously thin areas of wall . . . Hint: Find any large area of wall and start digging."

While we were talking about the different architectural strategies that Schatz imagined being used to solve the game's various heists, he said something that sounded like equal parts Roofman and Bernard Tschumi. "Heist games are largely about repetitive but enjoyable actions," Schatz said, "and exploring all the different variations that come from them." This puts a huge emphasis precisely on timing: "The timing on everything comes down to a split second: doing things right and getting away in the nick of time. 'Is he gonna get caught? The guards are coming into the room—can he get to the window in time?' That tension typically drives the heist game or the heist movie."

What this means is that repetition performed across consecutive, often nearly identical heists can become dangerously hypnotic. "You learn how to do something— then you do it over and over again until you get it right," Schatz said. He could just as well have been describing a serial burglar of McDonald's franchises as a dedicated player of heist games. That's exactly why hiding little vulnerabilities and unexpected openings in the architecture itself becomes so important for a game designer. As Randy Smith said earlier, describing his "rhythms of vulnerability," the outline of a perfect crime is usually camouflaged in the environment—you just have to find it.

🏃

Schatz's exhortation to players to move *against* the architecture, not with it, to uncover a scene's possible crimes, is useful not only in the world of games. Ignoring the paths laid out by architects and even remaking a space from within are some of the most fundamental ways in which burglars misuse the built environment.

Recall our friend jewelry thief Bill Mason. The last time we checked in on him, Mason was scaling the fronts of high-rise apartment buildings on the Florida coast and learning about the inner lives of architecture from maintenance personnel and building superintendents. Now, however, Mason will show us a way past the watchful eyes of security guards, as if using the architectural lessons of *Monaco* two decades before the fact.

During one of his heists, Mason experienced a tactical epiphany: he realized not only that he could but that he needed to change his target building from within. Mason chose a target building based on its perceived weaknesses or security flaws—but that didn't mean there weren't ways to make his job even easier once inside. In one of the most interesting moments in Mason's memoir, he sees that architecture can be made to do what he wants it to do; it's like watching a character in *Star Wars* learn to use the Force.

In a lengthy scene at a hotel in Cleveland that Mason would ultimately hit more than once in his career, he explains that his intended prize was locked inside a room whose door was too closely guarded for him to slip through. Then he realizes the obvious: he has been thinking the way the hotel wanted him to think—the way the architects had hoped he would behave—looking for doors and hallways when he could simply carve a new route where he wanted it. The ensuing realization delights him. "Elated at the idea that I could cut my own door right where I needed one," he writes, Mason simply breaks into the hotel suite adjacent to the main office. There, he flings open the closet, pushes aside the hangers, and cuts his way from one room into the other using a drywall knife. In no time at all, he has cut his "own door" through to the manager's office, where he takes whatever he wants—departing right back through the very "door" he himself made. It is architectural surgery, pure and simple.

Later, Mason actually mocks the idea that a person would remain reliant on doors, making fun of anyone who thinks burglars, in particular, would respect the limitations of architecture. "*Surely if someone were to rob the place,*" he writes in all italics, barbed with sarcasm, "*they'd come in as respectable people would, through the door provided for the purpose*. Maybe that explains why people will have four heavy-duty locks on a solid oak door that's right next to a glass window." People seem to think they should lock-pick or kick their way through solid doors rather than just take a ten-dollar drywall knife and carve whole new hallways into the world. Those people are mere slaves to architecture, spatial captives in a world someone else has designed for them.

Something about this is almost unsettlingly brilliant, as if it is *nonburglars* who have been misusing the built environment this whole time; as if it is nonburglars who have been unwilling to question the world's most basic spatial assumptions, too scared to think past the tyranny of architecture's long-held behavioral expectations.

To use architect Rem Koolhaas's phrase, we have been voluntary prisoners of architecture all along, willingly coerced and browbeaten by its code of spatial conduct, accepting walls as walls and going only where the corridors lead us. Because doors are often the sturdiest and most fortified parts of the wall in front of you, they are a distraction and a trap. By comparison, the wall itself is often more like tissue paper, just drywall and some two-by-fours, without a lock or a chain in sight. Like clouds, apartment walls are mostly air; seen through a burglar's eyes, they aren't even there. Cut a hole through one and you're in the next room in seconds.

The irony here is that even someone such as the psychotic, ax-swinging character Jack Torrance from *The Shining* still believes in doors: he hacks his way through the Overlook Hotel by way of preexisting routes laid out for him by others. Even Jack Torrance was too timid, hemmed in by architectural convention and unwilling to question the walls that surrounded him. He should have thought more like Bill Mason. A surreal and altogether more terrifying version of *The Shining* would have been the result, with Jack Torrance hidden somewhere in the hotel, sharpening his ax, unseen—until he comes bashing through the walls again, moving through the building as a burglar would, popping up whenever and wherever everyone else feels most safe.

Nakatomi Space

In an essay called "Lethal Theory" by Eyal Weizman—an Israeli architect and prominent critic of that nation's territorial policy—we find an inadvertent but spatially extraordinary perspective on the misuse of the built environment. While Weizman is discussing military maneuvers used during the Israel Defense Forces' high-intensity 2002 invasion of Nablus rather than a bank heist, the spatial techniques used during that operation are so useful for our discussion of burglary that we'll make a brief diversion.

Weizman describes the movement of the Israel Defense Forces, or IDF, through the city of Nablus as a tactical avoidance of everything we think we know about architecture—that walls are barriers, that doors are openings we're meant to pass through. The Israeli battlefield commanders decided instead to use "none of the streets, roads, alleys or courtyards that constitute the syntax of

the city, and none of the external doors, internal stairwells and windows that constitute the order of buildings,
but rather moved horizontally through party walls, and
vertically through holes blasted in ceilings and floors." It
was a "three-dimensional movement through walls, ceilings and floors," he writes. It was an infestation—a cho-
reography that Weizman calls *walking through walls.*

He compares this to earlier urban conflicts in which
architecture played a central role, including the urban barricades of the Paris Commune in 1871 and the house-to-
house fighting during France's colonial urban warfare in
Algiers. In the latter case, combatants relied on "alternative
routes, secret passageways and trapdoors," Weizman writes.
This technique, known as mouse-holing, seems as much
an act of haunting as it is an act of war.

In the Israeli case, many of these tactics were developed specifically because doorways had been booby-
trapped with pressure-sensitive, improvised explosive
devices—analogous, in our case, to motion sensors or burglar alarms, or to Bill Mason's eyeing that well-guarded
hotel doorway and knowing he could never pass through
it. Moreover, to avoid being seen from above by spotters
hidden on rooftops or in the windows of nearby houses—
comparable, in terms of burglary, to security cameras or
police helicopters—the soldiers needed to achieve a new
kind of invisibility, a kind of militarized stealth. This
meant moving forward using "fractal maneuvers," as a
representative of the Israeli military describes them in
an interview with Weizman, tunneling from one building to
the next or disappearing into the architectural environment

like an insect—or being absorbed into it, we might say, like water into a sponge.

The soldiers were able to navigate through this new maze of openings by leaving spray-painted traces on the walls behind them—arrows and other directional markers that served as military way-finding glyphs offering a clear path through the dust, wrecked furniture, screaming families, and twisted rebar.

As Weizman points out again and again, this approach may be tactically ingenious, but it is also fraught with moral peril and with highly dangerous ethical implications. Indeed, he refers to all this as "lethal theory." By thinking of a target purely as an architectural obstacle—an empty building or depopulated neighborhood you simply have to blast through—the lives of the people residing there become entirely secondary. For Weizman, this turned the city into something more like "a military fantasy world of boundless fluidity, in which the city's space becomes as navigable as an ocean." This oceanic condition is something he compares to navigating a computer game.

These internal routes were carefully chosen based on detailed maps and aerial photographs. In burglary terms, we might say that the IDF had been casing the entire city of Nablus. Since that 2002 invasion, Weizman writes, the army has even developed detailed 3-D models of Gaza and the West Bank, down to the locations of internal doors and windows. Each structure has also been given an identifying number so that the otherwise impossibly complex task of signaling one's location to other troops can be resolved simply by relaying a coded number, a kind of military lat/long for the ocean of architecture into which the soldiers have dived. Recall LAPD tactical flight officer Cole Burdette—or even retired NYPD detective Michael Codella—with his own numerical suggestions for navigating urban megastructures.

One immediately obvious possibility for resisting this—to avoid the tyranny of soldiers armed with 3-D maps or to deter outside invaders and architecturally informed burglars alike—would be to alter the internal layout of a structure so that it no longer corresponds to its official floor plans or existing 3-D models. An anecdotal example of this strategy comes from the work of my wife's great-aunt, Joan Harding, an archaeologist and historian who founded an organization dedicated to documenting historic houses in the English county of Surrey. Harding's job included drawing sets of interior plans for each home and estate—however, publicly accessible reproductions of those plans would deliberately omit certain key details for reasons of security. The drawings would leave out entire staircases, for example, or even every family bedroom, so that intruders could not use these documents to plot a burglary. The upshot of this is that many of England's old country houses have, in effect, secret rooms and stairways—purely because those features do not appear on the buildings' official floor plans.

While this is a different approach from the Israel Defense Forces example cited above—altering floor plans to hide the architecture rather than altering the architecture to diverge from the plans—the overall effect is the same: to disrupt someone's knowledge of what to expect inside a structure.

For all this talk of art theft and military operations, one of Hollywood's greatest heist films actually best depicts Weizman's idea of "walking through walls," taking it to delirious, action-blockbuster extremes. *Die Hard* is easily one of the best architectural films of the past three decades; it is, in many ways, a film about the misuse of architecture.

In the film—directed by John McTiernan and based on a novel called *Nothing Lasts Forever* by Roderick Thorp—a New York City cop named John McClane, while visiting his estranged wife in Los Angeles on his Christmas vacation, moves through a high-rise building, called Nakatomi Plaza, in what seems to be every conceivable way but by passing through its doors and hallways. He traverses the tower via elevator shafts and air ducts, crashes through windows from the outside in, and shoots open the locks of rooftop doorways. If there is not a corridor, he makes one; if there is not an opening, there soon will be. McClane blows up whole sections of the building; he stops elevators between floors; he rides on top of them instead of in them; and he otherwise moves through the internal spaces of Nakatomi Plaza in acts of virtuoso navigation that were neither imagined nor physically planned for by the architects.

This is one of the hallmarks of a good heist film: to borrow a term from Eyal Weizman, good heist films depict space as deeply infested with routes and openings, and with bandits hiding in the walls. People squeeze themselves between floors or into unlit gaps above ceilings; they find handholds inside elevator shafts or burst through walls to move from room to room. They swing from awnings and balconies; they drop down through ceiling tiles, disappear into vents, and radio back and forth to one another from cramped half spaces while the cops chasing them usually stick to the doors and hallways. It's as if heist films always depict two competing methods for the use of architectural space, which then battle it out on-screen for tactical supremacy: the linear versus the nonlinear, the direct versus the indirect, the geometric versus the fractal.

In *Die Hard*, this indirect approach to the built environment pervades the film. Even the SWAT team who unsuccessfully assault the structure do so from its flanks, marching diagonally through a rose garden on the building's perimeter. Meanwhile, the terrorists who seized control of Nakatomi Plaza in the first place do so after arriving by truck through the service entrance of an underground parking garage.

In one of the film's most iconic scenes, McClane evades capture by climbing through an air duct—this after falling down an HVAC shaft when the machine gun he has been using as an anchorage point fails—giving the building's ventilation system a second life as an escape route and adding to the popular mythology of the ventilation system as an overlooked, parallel system of circulation within a building. As we saw with Bill Mason, these vents are part of the architectural dark matter—the invisible backstage—that makes up so much of the built environment.

Indeed, McClane's actions reveal a new type of architectural space altogether—a topological condition that we might call *Nakatomi space*, wherein buildings reveal near-infinite interiors, capable of being traversed through all manner of nonarchitectural means, with their own exhilarating form of boundless fluidity.

As a revelatory look at the labyrinthine, previously unexposed back corridors of the built environment—where the thirty-first floor is connected to the lobby or the twenty-sixth floor leads directly to the roof—the first *Die Hard* movie remains exemplary. Disguised as an action film, it is actually architectural moviemaking at its best and most spatially invested, turning walls, floors, and ceilings—rooms, corridors, and stairwells—into the unacknowledged costars of the picture, demonstrating that heist films are the most architectural genre of all.

6

A CRIME IS NOTHING IF YOU CAN'T GET AWAY

In Franz Kafka's parable "A Message from the Emperor," you—the addressee of this shortest of short stories—are told that an imperial messenger is on his way to reach you.

It seems simple enough: the messenger only has to exit the emperor's chambers, push his way through crowds of guards, find the right doors to the inner courtyard, walk across that, force his way through yet more crowds of attendants, work his way through a new series of doors and courtyards, down vast stairways and halls, hurrying through and around ever more and larger throngs of citizens and servants now spilling out into the town streets, shoving his way past secondary gates and garden palaces, through outer villages and packed squares, trying desperately to get to you—somehow—this now-labyrinthine task that seemed so easy growing more and more impossible by the instant.

It goes on like this forever, Kafka writes, a reverse Zeno's paradox in which there is no real way to get anywhere, any promise of a clear path undone by yet more obstacles at every turn. The messenger is, for all intents and purposes, indefinitely detoured, stuck in traffic, unable to get away.

Outsmarting the City

It's impossible to talk about getaways without talking about traffic: automobile traffic, pedestrian traffic, even boat traffic and congested skies. Traffic is always in the way, seemingly right when you've got the least time for it. However, rather than resign ourselves to the inevitability of obstacles, as Kafka implies, why not look at traffic as a burglar would? If a successful burglary is often one in which the interior of a building has illicitly been rearranged—with new doors sliced through drywall or vertical tunnels opened up, unexpectedly connecting floor to floor—or where the rhythms of a security patrol are used to time the precise moment of a heist, then the same technique can be applied on an urban scale.

Sometimes if you want to get away, you have to redesign the city around you, intervene in the fabric of the metropolis, and reengineer the city's traffic patterns to open new paths of movement for your getaway.

"We could do anything with green lights all the way," a character played by Mos Def remarks in the 2003 remake of *The Italian Job*. All the group would have to do is hack into L.A.'s electronic traffic-control network and make their chosen route through the city the only route there is: a long corridor of green lights leading them, and them alone, from one end of the city to the other. The ensuing computer-assisted getaway relies on a specific sequence of spatial events—such as cleared intersections and open back streets—that will help propel the crew to liberation. It's a vehicular wormhole, a perforation cut straight through the moving mess of Los Angeles traffic, another kind of tunnel job with its own precision timing.

These *Italian Job* fantasies of urban-scale hacking—taking control of a city's transportation network from within—are not just the stuff of Hollywood blockbusters. Consider the case of a fourteen-year-old boy who used what security expert Bruce Schneier described as a "modified TV remote control" to take over an entire tram system in Łódz, Poland. According to the city's police, the boy turned his home remote control into an electromagnetic supertool that gave him command of every tram switch and junction in Łódz. The boy even "wrote in the pages of a school exercise book where the best junctions were to move trams around and what signals to change," police explained. While he did not use this homemade magic wand for anything resembling a bank heist, it would have come in quite handy during a crime spree. As clearly as any example from Hollywood, this otherwise childish prank suggests that the most successful getaways of tomorrow will be achieved by hacking the city.

The technology is already here. At a 2014 security conference in Miami, Florida, self-described "professional hacker" Cesar Cerrudo revealed that he had discovered a security loophole in widely used urban traffic-management technology, allowing him to fool vehicle-detection systems into thinking the light needed to change. Through extensive field-testing, Cerrudo found that his technique worked best within 150 feet of an actual intersection, but that more powerful antennas could also be used. Someone could then spam an intersection with imaginary traffic data from a hiding place on a nearby roof—or, as Cerrudo himself demonstrated, "from a drone flying at over 650 feet" above the target. This security flaw designed into the city itself could clearly be used to engineer the perfect getaway. Indeed, burglary crews and organized-crime rings flying drones over a city to reprogram its intersections from above is something we are sure to see, not only in the real world but coming soon to a silver screen near you. The only question is which will come first. "I would be worried about attacks from the sky in the U.S.," Cerrudo warned.

Spoofing a city's traffic systems or a driver's in-car GPS sensors is an equally effective way to engineer new routes across the city. This means not just overwhelming nearby GPS receivers with white noise, but, in effect, lying to them, convincing a dashboard navigation unit or smartphone mapping app to tell drivers that they are still heading in the right direction even as they veer wildly off course. In his book *Future Crimes*, author and former futurist-in-residence at the FBI Marc Goodman describes how GPS spoofing could be used to lead a delivery truck, street by street and block by block, to the wrong warehouse, where dozens if not hundreds of valuable boxes could be unloaded directly into the hands of criminals dressed like innocuous office workers. The driver is unlikely to realize the mistake—that the truck's GPS unit had been taken over by criminals and that he or she just dropped everything off at the wrong address—until the delivery company is flooded with complaints about missing packages.

Spoofing can also be used indirectly, to open new, unobstructed routes where a road had been gridlocked only ten minutes earlier. For example, if you know your intended getaway route, you can digitally fake a traffic jam along that same street or freeway; the intended goal would be to make traffic apps report a road impassably clogged with vehicles, thus pushing other drivers—even police—away from your chosen street, shepherding them toward any number of nearby roads. A new line of escape is essentially unzipped down the middle of the city.

This exact scenario was successfully demonstrated by two students at the Technion-Israel Institute of Technology back in March 2014. To create the digital illusion of real-world traffic chaos, the students registered thousands of fake accounts on Waze, "the world's largest community-based traffic and navigation app." The students then used those fake accounts to report a well-coordinated series of traffic complaints, all the way down to the simulated movement of fake GPS signals, maintaining the illusion that the accounts were indeed coming from gridlock-trapped drivers. The result? Waze fell for this phantom traffic jam and began to reroute other drivers around the area, effectively guaranteeing that the students' target road became eerily free of traffic, at least for the duration of their imaginary gridlock.

Despite these hacks and spoofs, the power to control a city's traffic usually lies firmly in the hands of the police, with their arsenal of blockades, traffic stops, and road closures. Police powers are increasingly woven deep into the fabric of the built environment and will only grow more pervasive as "smart city" technology becomes widespread. Cantankerous Belorussian technology critic Evgeny Morozov has written that the surveillance powers of the state are so dramatically amplified by the ubiquitous sensors, cameras, and remote-control technology associated with the smart city that urban space risks becoming little more than an inhabitable police barricade. "As both cars and roads get 'smart,'" Morozov wrote in a 2014 op-ed for *The Observer*, "they promise nearly perfect, real-time law enforcement. Instead of waiting for drivers to break the law, authorities can simply prevent the crime."

While these sorts of technologies offer urban authorities powerful new tools to control the modern metropolis, the idea of designing out crime is by no means unique to our era. In nineteenth-century Paris, for example, acting under instructions from Emperor Napoléon III, urban administrator Georges-Eugène Haussmann instituted an extraordinarily ambitious series of urban improvements.

He ordered the demolition of entire neighborhoods, the erasure of whole streets from the center of Paris, and the widespread replacement of them both with the broad, leafy, and beautiful boulevards Paris is known for today. This was not motivated by aesthetics, however, but was explicitly a police project, a deliberate—and quite successful—effort to redesign the city so that the streets would be too wide to barricade, the back alleys no longer winding or confusing enough for insurgents and revolutionaries to disappear or get away. The urban landscape of Paris became a police tool, its urban core reorganized so aggressively that popular uprisings would henceforth be spatially impossible.

This is not the only police project for which Paris is widely known. As historian A. Roger Ekirch explains in his 2005 book, *At Day's Close*, the idea of lighting the streets of Paris back in the 1600s originally came from the police. Streetlights were one of many new patrol tools implemented by Louis XIV's lieutenant general of police, Gabriel Nicolas de la Reynie. De la Reynie's plan ordered that lanterns be hung over the streets every sixty feet—with the unintended side effect that Paris soon gained its popular moniker, the City of Light. The world's most romantic city takes its nickname from a police operation.

Morozov warns that we are living through a kind of digital upgrade of Haussmann's universal street-control project: the inauguration of a smart city that will be able to anticipate—and, more important, interrupt or preempt—certain behaviors, whether that means speeding, committing a burglary, or violating curfew. So-called *predictive policing* has been much discussed over the past few years, whereby authorities use detailed statistics and algorithms—a city's criminal patterns and rhythms—to "predict" when and where a crime is most likely to occur. Morozov is describing a kind of *predictive urban design*, a geospatial policing project where specific activities become impossible to perform: police can turn off your car engine from miles away or redirect driverless vehicles to clog the road precisely when you're trying to escape.

It would be the exact opposite of *The Italian Job*: red lights all the way, an impenetrable phalanx of traffic that only the police can control or navigate.

🏃

As Morozov points out, however, we're not quite there yet. For now, the art of the getaway is still an analog undertaking, one whose most basic outlines date back to a former Prussian military officer named Herman Lamm. In the 1920s, following his emigration to the United States, Lamm developed something like a mathematical science of bank robbery—an ingenious series of clearly defined steps with reproducible results. Much of our present-day mythology of the high-octane bank bandit comes down from the example set by Lamm and his "Lamm technique." This called for the meticulous use of a stopwatch based on the absolute conviction that, after a specific period of time, no matter how much (or how little) money his gang had taken, they were to leave the bank and get away, following a carefully devised set of instructions so as to outsmart the city's traffic as well as any police who might be pursuing them.

Before each heist, Lamm would have spent hours mapping out the best possible routes of escape, specifically recruiting drivers with racing experience and storing an extra fuel tank in the trunk, in case they needed to fill up on the road. As crime writer Duane Swierczynski describes Lamm's method, a map of the getaway route would be attached to the inside of the car, within view of the driver, including detailed marginal notes, all the way down "to speedometer readings for each block and alternate turns to take in case of emergency." There would be getaway routes inside getaway routes, each with its own speed and timing. Lamm's foresight extended even to planning for different weather conditions, noting alternative roads to take (and how fast) if a sudden rainstorm blew in or if the road was blocked by snow.

For Lamm, this well-honed technique seemed unbeatable—but its efficacy could only go so far. In December 1930, after robbing a Citizens State Bank in Clinton, Indiana, Lamm and his group were confronted by a shotgun-wielding vigilante barber before they could get away. Startled by the man's gun, Lamm's getaway driver pulled a sudden U-turn and blew a tire hitting the curb—and things went catastrophically downhill from there. Forced to improvise by an obstacle that even Lamm's obsessive mind had failed to anticipate, the gang stole another car—but a governor installed on the engine meant it couldn't go faster than 35 mph. So they ditched that and stole a truck—but it didn't have enough radiator water to drive. They then stole another car—but it barely had any fuel in the tank, taking them just a few miles out of town before running out of gas. Lamm's previously well-organized gang found itself trapped by the side of the road, surrounded by police. Their getaway was in shambles. Within only a few minutes, Lamm—depending on whose account you read—would either shoot himself dead or be gunned down by police, his eponymous technique having relentlessly failed every step of the way.

Nonetheless, Walter Mittelstaedt points out in his book about Lamm—whom he calls the "father of modern bank robbery"—this kind of militaristic precision and foresight was passed down to a new generation of master burglars, including, most notably, the gang run by legendary bank bandit John Dillinger. Lamm's influence on the Dillinger gang was particularly evident in their planning of getaways. Dillinger, for example, began to "plant gasoline cans along the getaway route—improving, perhaps, on Lamm's way of carrying a can of gas in the back of the getaway car." Dillinger also adopted Lamm's preference for using "only the best late-model cars," so that the gang could get away as fast as possible.

If the techniques of burglary such as those developed by Lamm and later refined by Dillinger aren't scientific, they are at least comparable to a folk art: inherited, improved upon, and always available for others to adapt and use. This is apparently true even for CEOs: bizarrely, the Lamm technique was recommended to business leaders in a 2009 book about corporate management strategies,

The Talent Code. Lamm, that book claims, "was an innovator who taught with discipline and exactitude. He inspired through information." Lamm was "a master coach."

For modern-day descendants of Lamm and Dillinger—those rogue outsmarters of the city, masters of traffic, pioneers of the high-speed getaway—the benefits of new technology extend far beyond a fast car or an extra gas tank, into the dazzling realm of digital camouflage. How can the police track your getaway car if they don't even know it's there? The goal post has shifted from simply being able to drive so fast you can't be caught, to being able to flip a switch and disappear.

GPS jammers are tiny devices you can plug into a car's cigarette lighter to flood the immediate area—usually about thirty square feet—with a white noise of radio signals pitched at the exact frequency of the satellite-based Global Positioning System. This makes a car, truck, or even container ship impossible to track using GPS—forcing police to rely on direct, visual observation—with the flick of a simple switch. Entire seaborne container ships have had their navigation systems disabled by GPS jammers, and trucks filled with consumer goods have been stolen using this digital assistance. Luxury cars are other popular targets. Such a vehicle simply "disappears from radar," professor and police expert witness David Last explained to *The Guardian* newspaper in 2010. However, jammers currently reside in a rather laissez-faire legal area. They are illegal to possess or use in the United States and the U.K., for example, but at least for the time being, it is perfectly legal to purchase them in either country. They are easily available online, as even the most rudimentary search will reveal.

Worse than this is the threat of military-grade GPS jammers that can drown out the GPS networks of entire cities. The resulting effects would be widespread and catastrophic, affecting financial transactions—which are time-stamped using GPS—the ability of airplanes to land at regional airports, the accuracy and even functionality of construction equipment, and, of course, the ability of police to track local GPS signals, whether they're coming from vehicles or from transmitters planted on stolen merchandise. In the case of London, the whole of the Thames estuary could be commandeered, warned Bob Cockshott, former head of location and timing for Innovate UK. Given a sufficiently powerful GPS jammer, gangs could "disrupt navigation in the Thames estuary if they were taking a delivery and didn't want rivals to be able to trace them"—or if they simply wanted to outwit police. Anyone near London planning a getaway by sea would do well to obtain an industrial-strength GPS jammer. As Marc Goodman concludes in *Future Crimes*, "A confused GPS unit equals a successful heist."

Even with such tools at their disposal, however, a canny burglar could still smooth his getaway using analog, old-school spoofing. One of the most interesting attempted getaways of the last few years occurred the morning of September 30, 2008, when roughly a dozen men, responding to a Craigslist ad, met near a Bank of America in the Seattle suburb of Monroe. They were each expecting to find a long day of landscaping work ahead of them, and they'd been instructed to dress in a specific way, in a reflective work vest, blue shirt, respirator mask, and protective eyewear.

Among them was Anthony Curcio, anticlimactically described by the U.S. Attorney's Office as a "former high school athlete." He was dressed the same way and had placed the ad so as to fill the area with all but identical versions of himself. Curcio strayed from this group of unwitting decoys to pepper-spray the driver of an armored truck whose delivery schedule he had carefully researched. Seizing nearly $400,000 in cash, Curcio then sprinted to a nearby creek where, days before, he had installed a steel cable leading downstream. Jumping into an inner tube that he had also strategically cached there—and becoming perhaps the first criminal in history to mastermind an inner-tube getaway—Curcio pulled himself down the cable to escape. It was, we could say, a true landscape job.

Technically, this was not a burglary—Curcio never broke the close of an architectural structure, including the armored truck. That said, if only the bank had put a roof over its loading dock, and if the armored truck had been parked beneath it at the time, prosecutors could have used the legal "magic of four walls," as Minturn T. Wright III described it, to charge Curcio with burglary. But his Craigslist heist presents social camouflage as a different kind of spoofing: by intentionally blending in with the people around him, Curcio made it almost impossible to identify him as the actual thief.

When the story first broke, Curcio's actions were widely compared to the 1999 remake of *The Thomas*

Crown Affair, directed by John McTiernan, of *Die Hard* fame. The film's ultimate heist occurs inside the Metropolitan Museum of Art in New York, where Thomas Crown, played by Pierce Brosnan, disguises himself among dozens of criminal recruits who had all been instructed to dress the same way. Wearing suits and bowler hats, they meander through the museum's labyrinthine galleries, the police now incapable of keeping tabs on Crown himself, this most original of burglars deliberately lost among his copies and duplicates.

Perhaps the most elaborate spoof of all, however, is to get away by staying put. This was the strategy described to me by reformed bank robber Joe Loya. Loya, who served seven years in prison for multiple bank heists before becoming a writer, explained to me that it was during the getaway that he often had the best chance of thwarting people's spatial expectations. In his case, this meant that what he did immediately after leaving the bank was often the most important decision of all. In robbing twenty-four banks, he had seen that the security guards almost always assumed he had turned left or right after exiting the bank. Further, they had expected to see Loya fleeing in a conspicuous getaway car or running away at top speed. But they almost never checked the cars just sitting outside in the parking lot.

Loya realized that he could jump into his car and wait a few minutes, effectively hiding in plain sight, before calmly driving away. "I'd go straight across the parking lot toward the Rite Aid or the CVS or whatever, where my car was actually parked. I'd literally be thirty-five feet away, looking at them. If they had just looked straight ahead into the parking lot, they would have seen me," he told me. "That's mostly how I got away."

Loya is an architectural enthusiast. In our conversation, he spoke at length about the design of building interiors, including a series of intriguing observations about prison floor plans. Loya described the Metropolitan Detention Center in downtown Los Angeles—the same jail seen on the cover of Mike Davis's *City of Quartz*—as a paragon of architectural disorientation. It is built in the shape of a V angled across its site, which means that as you walk around inside, it can be extremely difficult to maintain a sense of direction or even to know how you are positioned to the larger city outside. Even your official entry into the prison deliberately seems to have misalignment and confusion built in.

"When they first drive you in," Loya began, "you go around in circles underground before you get put into an elevator at the center of the building. When you finally get out of the elevator—and, remember, the building is at an angle to the street—you are so lost!" He laughed as he said this, as if amazed by the spatial ingenuity of the prison's designers. "I'm really good at keeping track of orientation. I'm really good at knowing where I am—north, south—even indoors. But every time I got moved, I was so turned around. It was like my interior compass was just spinning. *Where am I in this building?* But they're designed that way." It's as if the jail's original architect had been aware of burglars' spatial superpowers, Loya suggested, and had sought to disarm them by any means necessary. "It's just another level of anxiety, of you being off your game, of them making it challenging for you to navigate and orient yourself in that space. It's part of the intention of prisons to make you feel incidental. They want to make it as tough as possible. You're not grounded, and you don't know where you are."

For Loya, linguist George Lakoff's book *Metaphors We Live By* took on an unexpected spatial resonance, revealing ways in which the built environment could be read or understood as a series of metaphors or signs. He said that after being released from prison, he spent a lot of time taking long walks around the suburban landscape of Southern California. He began noticing that every twenty-five feet, he would hit a driveway; he'd then walk eight feet across the driveway before hitting another stretch of grass; then another twenty-five feet to the next driveway, and so on, seemingly forever, "and the uniformity of that totally echoed the uniformity of the prison environment," he said to me, "where I had my cell and my seven feet of wall and then a door. And I remember thinking, '*Oh my God, man.*'" He laughed at the utter despair of it all, having gone from one system of containment to another. How would you get away or escape from this?

Urban Escape and Evasion

"You can't get away from the aircraft," LAPD tactical flight officer Cole Burdette explained. The police use helicopters for a reason, he reminded me, and you're not going to outrun them on the ground, whether you're on foot or you're driving a Ford Mustang. The Air Support Division has tracked fleeing suspects halfway to San Francisco, he pointed out, before the drivers simply gave up, whether due to exhaustion or an empty gas tank. There's no realistic outer limit for a chase, he said; you can't just leave Los Angeles and expect Air Support to throw up their hands and turn around at the city border. They'll follow you to Arizona if they have to.

Burdette used this point to launch into a long discussion of how helicopter crews successfully track people who try to get away on foot. Most people don't realize the kinds of trails they leave behind them, he said, let alone the ease with which their probable routes can be deduced from above. He lumped this under the idea that even cops flying around the city in a helicopter need to be street-savvy: they have to be able to think like a perpetrator, to predict what he or she might do next. You have to be able to see what they see and you have to imagine what sorts of decisions they might make—whether they turned left or right at a certain corner, or if they ducked behind a tree or maybe even slipped into another building. Occasionally something altogether new happens. Think of the bank bandits who, while fleeing Los Angeles police back in September 2012, started throwing handfuls of cash out the windows of their SUV, hoping to clog the road behind them with local residents running out to collect free money. That sort of behavior can be hard to predict.

To illustrate his point, Burdette told me the story of a recent night flight. A burglary had been reported; the burglar was last seen standing in someone's driveway. By the time Burdette's helicopter got there, the burglar was nowhere to be found. So where did he go?

Next, in a series of spatial deductions, Burdette had to study the built landscape below and guess what most likely occurred down there. Writer Nate Berg has described L.A. as "a vast landscape of pursuit potential," with getaway routes and police surveillance details all colliding to form complex knots on the ground. Burdette's narration of this from the helicopter's point of view sounded more like someone trying to beat the next level in a computer game, outthinking the terrain from above.

"We could see the driveway," Burdette began, "which was the spot where this guy was last seen. Now, you look at the size of the fences on either side of the house. That's almost like a tunnel for him. It would make no sense for him to try to make it over one of those walls. It would slow him down too much, and it would be too hard. But, now, if you run into the backyard and you're feeling stressed—if you follow that tunnel—what are you going to see? The first thing you'll see is there's a doghouse right there. If you run and hit that doghouse, you could probably make it over that fairly short fence out back. So now you're in the next person's yard. Okay—let's look and see what we have here. Look at that abandoned garage out back, the one that looks like it was on fire a few years ago. It's only got three sides on it; that'd be a pretty good spot for him to go."

As Burdette and his pilot zeroed in on this abandoned garage, based solely on spatial reasoning, the radio buzzed: a nearby homeowner had just called 911, having seen someone slink into a half-burned garage behind their house. Bingo: Burdette had the right place. He turned on the FLIR—the helicopter's forward-looking infrared camera—and sure enough, there was a heat signature, a white blur crouched inside among the wood framing. When a patrol car arrived seconds later and officers were in place to contain the area, the game was up.

It's all about containment, Burdette emphasized: "If we have an aircraft overhead, it really limits their abilities. It doesn't mean that they can't still move or that they won't try to run, but it's much more of a challenge now. We try to shrink down the size of their world. We try to contain it and to control it."

For Christopher Hawthorne, architecture critic at the *Los Angeles Times*, stories such as Burdette's also signal a spatial and conceptual shift in contemporary urban policing. It is moving, Hawthorne explained to me, from the *chase* to the *manhunt*. He meant that while the widely televised arrest of O. J. Simpson had been a chase, albeit conducted at little more than walking speed, the search for LAPD officer Christopher Dorner—or even for the younger of the two Boston Marathon bombers, Dzhokhar Tsarnaev—had been a manhunt. In a chase, the suspect's location is clearly known; the police simply have to stop, intercept, and capture him or her. In a manhunt, however, the suspect could be anywhere; what's required is an intensive search through the landscape, a literal hunt with a human being as its target.

To Hawthorne, the chase and the manhunt are fundamentally different ways of using the landscape. One is the active pursuit of a suspect moving through the environment, usually at high speed but more or less continuously visible to the pursuers; in the other, someone has deliberately made him- or herself invisible to view, hidden somewhere in the city or terrain, leaving the police to deploy advanced forensic expertise and new technologies of visibility to discover them. Getting away in the former case simply means moving through the built environment more effectively than the police; think of the example set by Herman Lamm. In the latter example, getting away means blending in so well that you successfully avoid detection.

The Dorner case provides a particularly chilling example. Christopher Dorner had been fired from the LAPD in what he claimed was racially motivated revenge for his having reported a case of police brutality. After publicly declaring, in a rambling and often incoherent manifesto posted on his Facebook page, "unconventional and asymmetric warfare" against the entire L.A. police department, Dorner ambushed two separate teams of police officers in their patrol cars, killing one of them and murdering two civilians. Then he disappeared. His actions sparked a massive, nationally televised manhunt, including a surveillance drone, stretching nearly from the U.S./Mexico border to the mountains outside Los Angeles. Dorner was eventually located hiding inside a cabin—a structure he had technically burglarized—where, surrounded by SWAT teams, he shot himself in the head. At no point was Dorner really chased, however; instead, it was a manhunt, spatial detective work, an urgent attempt to find one man amid the Rhode Island–size landscape of Greater Los Angeles.

Finding both Dorner and Tsarnaev required the activation of every territorial aspect of urban police authority, from preemptive roadblocks and unmanned aerial vehicles to FLIR-enabled helicopter patrols. One of the most memorable moments in the Tsarnaev manhunt came when the Boston PD released FLIR footage shot by a police helicopter; the heavily zoomed-in shot depicted the strange, flickering white light of Tsarnaev's circulatory system glowing from within his hiding spot beneath a boat cover in the Boston suburb of Watertown. This was as much about police bragging rights as it was an open taunt to anyone else who might try to get away. Its message: if you have a circulatory system, the police can see you.

No sooner does one side develop a new technology or technique, however, than the other side ups its game, in an endless arms race over who controls the built environment. Criminals are quickly developing ways to stay ahead of the game even against FLIR, with a range of DIY techniques of thermal camouflage. Burdette explained some of this to me, focusing on methods he had recently seen (these techniques failed, as Burdette would not otherwise have noticed them): "People are definitely catching on. They'll rub mud all over themselves, like that movie *Predator*, or they'll wrap themselves up in pool covers to mask their heat signature."

I laughed. "Does that work?" I asked, highly skeptical.

I was expecting him to laugh along with me, but after only a slight hesitation, he said, "It does work—except a little bit of light starts to shine out of each end. Once they've been in there for a while, the temperature builds up, like it starts to cook a little. That's how we find them." Remember that when Burdette says "light" here, it is just a metaphor: he is talking about heat generated by someone's circulatory system being given a visual signature by advanced technology. This vision of criminals wrapping themselves up in pool covers like human burritos to avoid police helicopter patrols seemed almost too absurd to be real. But Burdette insisted he had seen this; it was just part of the ongoing cat-and-mouse game between cops and the people who flee from them.

Even the region's flight paths have come to influence how criminals use the city, he explained. The heavily restricted airspace around LAX has made the area near the airport a well-known hiding spot for criminals trying to flee by car. LAPD helicopters cannot always approach LAX due to air-traffic-control safety concerns, Burdette said; it is surrounded by what he called "very challenging airspace." All those planes streaming down into the city, dropping off tourists and air cargo, exert a kind of geometric effect on crimes in the city: their flight patterns limit the effectiveness of police helicopter patrols and thus alter the getaway routes of criminals. Next time you fly into LAX, save a thought for the crimes your flight might be affecting far below.

I had gone into these conversations—with Joe Loya, with Christopher Hawthorne, with the LAPD, even with many of the figures we met earlier in this book, including Jack Dakswin and Special Agent William J. Rehder—expecting to find something like a Top Ten Tips for the Ultimate Getaway waiting for me at the end. But what I learned instead should have been obvious from the beginning: the best getaways are often the Hollywood ones—which are as unrealistic as their fictional context would indicate. In real life, getaways are not so tidy. Different techniques work at different times, for different reasons. Sometimes you have to drive away as fast as possible. Other times you don't need to go anywhere at all; you can just sit in your car until the pressure fades away. You can wrap yourself in a pool cover. You can convince your judge and jury that you never set foot in the building—or even that the type of structure you broke into falls outside your state's burglary laws. You can escape through tunnels or you can jump through bedroom windows; you can get away on foot or by public bus. It varies.

Some successful getaways do leave a trace. Think of an ingenious June 1995 bank heist in Berlin, Germany, where, unbeknownst to the bank's managers or the city's police, burglars had dug an escape tunnel for themselves beneath the target vault; rather than enter the bank through this tunnel, however, they saved it for the getaway. Taking over the bank the old-fashioned way, they locked down the business and held a group of hostages upstairs in the lobby. After the burglars received $3.6 million in ransom money, they headed downstairs into the basement, as if to have a meeting and discuss their next steps—but the hostages began to hear "an odd clamor, like pickaxes chipping at concrete," the *Washington Post* reported. Only moments later, police raided the bank. When the authorities, prepared for a possibly fatal shootout, descended into the basement, they instead found nothing but an empty room with a hole bashed through the floor. "The hole led to a 384-foot tunnel," the *Post* explained. "Running about 10 feet beneath the surface, the tunnel had been shored up with timber and steel plates. It emerged in a garage, where police assume the robbers had a getaway car waiting." Sure enough, they got away.

A similar tactic worked in February 2006 on the other side of the world, in Buenos Aires, Argentina. There, police raided a bank where hostages were being held—only to find a hole chipped through a concrete wall in the basement. An iron plate had been bolted across it from the other side. The burglars had not only prepared this escape route for themselves—a tunnel leading down into the city's storm sewers, then on to a nearby river—but they had sealed it behind them to prevent anyone from following.

However, for the most part, any attempt to track down the perfect getaway is made all the more complex because almost everything we know about burglary—including how they did (or did not) get away—comes from the burglars we've *caught*. As sociologist R. I. Mawby pithily phrases this dilemma, "Known burglars are unrepresentative of burglars in general." Great methodological despair is hidden in such a comment. Studying burglary is thus a strangely Heisenbergian undertaking, riddled with uncertainty and distorted by moving data points. The getaway to end all getaways—the one that leaves us all scratching our heads—to no small extent remains impossible to study.

Rather than just watch more heist films or read another bookshelf of crime thrillers, if I wanted to learn something useful about the art and science of fleeing crime scenes, I would need to take a different approach.

I flew to Las Vegas.

"Urban Escape & Evasion" is a three-day tactical workshop dedicated to training the general public—with an emphasis on international business travelers—on how to avoid being kidnapped, how to escape from captivity if you are unfortunately nabbed, and how to navigate your way through unfamiliar urban terrain. Though it was not explicitly aimed at aspiring burglars, I wanted to see what the course had to say about *getting away*—whether the lessons of escape and evasion might offer new skills for successfully fleeing a crime scene.

We met in a La Quinta hotel on the northernmost outskirts of the city, near the entrance to Nellis Air Force Base. This is far beyond the normal tourist geography of the Las Vegas Strip; gone are the bright lights and ritzy casinos, as a landscape of discount liquor stores and half-empty strip malls trails off into the desert, the towers of downtown Las Vegas barely visible on the horizon. New subdivisions have pushed their way here over the past fifteen years, but they look and feel more like speculative real estate deals still waiting to break even rather than lived-in communities. Unpredictable waves of dust and street litter would whirl up and blow across the hotel parking lot.

The class is run by a company called OnPoint Tactical, which is one guy, Kevin Reeve. He has trained Navy SEALs and police SWAT teams; along with tracker Tom Brown, Jr., Reeve's former mentor, he also helped prepare actor Benicio Del Toro for the role of a former Special Ops soldier gone rogue in the forests of Oregon for a 2003 film called *The Hunted*. Reeve's overall goal with the escape-and-evasion course was to take militarized skills of tracking, camouflage, and evasion, which had previously been seen as more appropriate for wilderness areas, and apply them, instead, to an urban environment. To date, the course has been taught in cities across the United States, including Chicago, Los Angeles, Detroit, Philadelphia, Kansas City, and Salt Lake City, to name only a few.

The specific premise of the workshop is that you are traveling overseas on business. You are in an unfamiliar environment that you can't navigate on your own and where you do not know the local customs. Something goes horribly wrong—you're kidnapped, there's a terrorist attack, or maybe the grid fails, plunging the city into multiple days of darkness—and you have to escape. You have to *bug out*, as it's known in the peculiar lingo of survivalists. We were repeatedly told that this could happen anywhere: in Phoenix or New York, as much as in Baghdad or Mexico City.

On the first day, Reeve and a co-instructor wheeled in a huge plastic bin full of military gear. We were all given lock-picking sets, handcuffs, bobby pins, and various other bits and pieces, including parachute cord—otherwise known as paracord—and plastic zip ties. Most of the workshop consisted of desk learning: we sat indoors and looked at slide shows, flipped through some instructional papers, and discussed building sieges. We learned how to barricade hotel doors from the inside and how to climb our way to safety through windows and over fences using short bamboo poles known as Kali sticks as makeshift ladders. After a brief lunch break, we turned down the lights to watch kidnapping videos on YouTube, allegedly filmed by agents of al-Qaeda.

Reeve, who has a curious tendency to close his eyes, stop talking, put his hand on the bridge of his nose, concentrate for several seconds in silence as if fighting off a headache, and then start speaking again, spent the better part of an hour enumerating all the obstacles we might encounter in an urban environment. Listening to the ensuing discussion, you would have thought most cities in the United States had already gone feral and that we were perhaps only days away from a civilization-ending event. Indeed, an atmosphere of paranoia was cultivated throughout the workshop, stoked as a motivational fire for getting us excited about the ensuing exercises.

Alongside advice for determining the cardinal directions in an unfamiliar city without using a compass, we were told how to blend in, warned about the difficulty of caching things (that is, hiding or burying goods around an environment for later use, something we briefly experimented with in a Walmart parking lot), and advised where to go for medical treatment if we were injured on the run (think veterinarians, not the emergency room). Not all of this would be useful in getting away from a burglary or bank heist, but a range of spatial tips for evading trackers could be directly mapped onto the postcrime getaway. We constructed caltrops, for example, using nothing more than bolt cutters and some chain-link fencing. Caltrops are small spiked stars, like game jacks, that can be dumped out onto a road, ready to pierce and deflate the tires of any cars driving behind you. They are similar to the spike strips deployed by police for shredding the tires of a suspect's car.

Then out came the zip ties. Things became literally hands-on at this point as we learned a variety of methods for breaking out of physical constraints, including police handcuffs, plastic zip ties, paracord, and duct tape. Duct tape was by far the easiest, and Reeve's instructions for defeating the material came with the unexpected benefit of triggering an old memory for another workshop attendee. The only female participant in the group began telling us about an experience from her childhood, in a way that implied all of us had undoubtedly been through the same thing. Her mother, she said, used to duct-tape her and her siblings together into a large knot, then leave them like that for an hour or more at a time. Had the woman known back then how easy it was to escape from duct tape, she said, perhaps she would not have spent so many hours duct-taped to her siblings. Unsure of how to reply, I laughed—then saw the expression on her face and immediately regretted it.

The final stretch of the workshop was an inversion of where we began, looking at how to navigate unfamiliar urban environments and find shelter in abandoned buildings. We learned how to hot-wire cars, how to make improvised weapons out of everyday materials, such as credit cards and hiking socks, and we got down to the brass tacks of how to sneak through a city's streets without being seen (or at least captured). The advice here was interesting, it also rudimentary. Dress like a local, we were told. Keep your head down. Avoid being memorable or visually unique. Blend in. This was called "reducing your signature." Reeve advised us to tune in to different parts of the city—in essence, this boiled down to seeing the urban environment the way George Leonidas Leslie would have seen it, as a welcoming labyrinth of shadows and protective blind spots. Reeve urged us to study maps of future destinations long before arriving. Find "workable hide locations," our coursepack advised, not necessarily by going somewhere alone, but by deliberately infiltrating another group of people. The first rule of a successful getaway is not to look as if you're trying to get away.

By the time I was scheduled to head back into downtown Las Vegas, the sun had set. We had just spent two days sitting indoors with the blinds closed, watching YouTube videos of al-Qaeda kidnappings and sucking down sixteen-ounce energy drinks and chocolate-brownie-flavored Clif Bars. I could escape from handcuffs with my hands behind my back, blindfolded, and I could hide random things in a parking lot so that only I was able to find them the next day. To imply that we all had somehow been transformed into secret agents by this weekend together at a La Quinta would be absurd, yet the urge to double-check all my mirrors for a tail and to engage in gratuitous displays of evasive driving—taking unexpected turns and a much longer, indirect route back to my hotel—was real and hard to resist.

This new sense of power over my surroundings reminded me of a great essay by designer Matt Jones, about pop-culture action hero Jason Bourne. Bourne, Jones explains, moved through a world of densely connected urban environments, cityscapes "that can be hacked and accessed and traversed—not without effort, but with determination, stolen vehicles and the right train timetables." Jones memorably suggests, "Bourne wraps cities, autobahns, ferries, and train terminuses around him as the ultimate body armor." The city itself becomes a weapon, a multitool—or, in Jones's words, "Bourne uses public infrastructure as a superpower. A battered watch and an accurate U-Bahn time-table are all he needs for a perfectly-timed, death-defying evasion of the authorities." Seen this way, Jason Bourne's superpower is simply that he uses cities better than you and I; he is the ultimate urbanist, a low-tech master of the getaway.

Together We'll Go Far

When I arrived back home in New York, I was carrying a new pair of handcuffs, a lock-picking set, some paracord, a handful of bobby pins, and something of an obsession. I was daydreaming about what I might do if the grid went down—if my wife and I had to enact our own urban-scale getaway—but more to the point, I started wondering what would happen if I decided to put all my burglary research to work.

Subtly, imperceptibly, I found myself becoming attuned to the presence of surveillance cameras and security guards, studying even the people ahead of me in line at my local bank branch the way an anthropologist might take field notes in an exotic locale, noting who seemed likely to resist if I announced a takeover robbery or how I'd get out of the bank and, if I managed to, what I'd find out there on the street. I noticed that the traffic light outside was timed, for example, and that someone could use it as a metronome or stopwatch to schedule a burglary; one could flee just as it was about to turn through its next cycle, using Manhattan's in-built traffic patterns and pedestrian rhythms as a screen for a getaway.

One afternoon while taking a break from work, I was standing in line at the ATM when two police officers walked into the bank lobby behind me. I remembered, as soon as I saw them, that I still had my handcuffs, lockpicks, bobby pins, an emergency glass-breaking device, and, on that specific day, a heavily underlined copy of

Confessions of a Master Jewel Thief by Bill Mason stuffed into my backpack. I suddenly felt nervous. What would happen if I was targeted for NYC's infamous "stop and frisk" campaign or, worse, if I reached into my bag to retrieve the checks I was about to deposit and a jumble of handcuffs and lockpicks spilled out onto the marble bank floor? Surely this weird assemblage of tools—I was standing inside a bank!—would constitute "intent"?

It had become so normal to travel with this stuff—to walk around New York with criminals' memoirs and burglars' tools in my bag—that I had forgotten I even had them in my possession. It was so easy to convince myself that everyone else was thinking like this—that every building represented a puzzle to solve or an obstacle course to break free from—that I'd lost sight of the peculiarity of my recent investigations.

Pretending to be looking for something, I pushed the lockpicks aside and shoved my handcuffs farther down in the bag. By the time I was done depositing checks, the police had walked out the door, and I was free to get away however I wanted. I chose the subway.

7

BURGLARY REQUIRES ARCHITECTURE

Suburban Interlude

While I was writing this book, my in-laws were burgled. The small suburban house in which my wife grew up, in the leafy world of culs-de-sac and roundabouts southwest of London, was broken into by what was later determined to be a group of fourteen-year-olds. They were never caught.

The temptation in writing a book like this has been to root for the underdog, to crown an unexpected spatial antihero who, as my evidence would show, had simply been misunderstood all along. The burglar is just a person—no, a genius!—who happens to use his or her talents in a morally troubling way. But we shouldn't hold illegality against them—indeed, we should hold that *for* them, I thought I might argue, because we would never have discovered the true potential of the built environment had it not been for someone willing to break the rules. In fact, we should celebrate the burglar, this new archetype, this devil in the details of the built environment, a mythic figure who shows us what architecture, all along, could really be and, more important, how we should have been using it all along.

But that is too simplistic an inversion, and the upside-down ethics of a position like that quickly become impossible to sustain. Burglars, as we've seen—and as you probably already suspected from the beginning—are not supermen or wonder women, dark lords of architectural analysis. To say otherwise, even with some of the extraordinary stories we've read so far, would be absurd. Burglars are not always stupid—again, think of all we've read, think of all we've learned—but for the most part, if you'll pardon my French, they're assholes. They wreck the lives and security of others for as little as a necklace—often far less—leaving psychological scars no insurance policy can cover.

You hear the same thing, over and over: that being burglarized can destroy any feeling of trust or safety a person might have, replacing it with a crushing, near-omnipresent sense of paranoia about your friends, your family, your next-door neighbors. Those kids up the street. The local FedEx driver. The guy who fixed your refrigerator last week. Your building's new cleaning crew, who have their own keys to the downstairs lobby. That friend of a friend who came around for drinks one night—didn't he specifically comment about the very thing that got stolen? Had he secretly been casing the place? You can't trust anybody—or at least you struggle to try. Irreplaceable family heirlooms are sold for fifty dollars on eBay—a fraction of their value—which is then probably blown on drugs or strippers. On beer and cigarettes. Your hobbies and habits led you out of your house at certain times, until a total stranger—or a dishonest friend—took advantage, slipping into your patterns like Roofman, when the rhythms of vulnerability were just right. These were the inner details of your life: studied, dissected, peeled open, used against you.

What is there to celebrate in this, or to be spatially thrilled by? Something so pointlessly destructive, often done on a whim, for a rush of adrenaline, on the spur of the moment, to sustain some idiot's high? Seductive visions of Cary Grant slinking across rooftops in *To Catch a Thief* are replaced by the sight of underage gang members too stupid to know what your jewelry's really worth. In his canonical work of eighteenth-century legal theory, *Commentaries on the Laws of England*, Sir William Blackstone points out that burglary is considered so invasive, so offensive to the idea of private dignity and public order, that burglars fall outside the sphere of legal protection and deserve death. Burglary, he explains, "has always been looked upon as a very heinous offense; not only because of the abundant terror that it naturally carries with it, but also as it is a forcible invasion and disturbance of that right of habitation which every individual might acquire even in a state of nature; an invasion, which, in such a state, would be sure to be punished with death." Can all those bank tunnels and well-sawn holes in hotel walls, all those annotated floor plans and cool tools, cancel that out, offering something so aesthetically and strategically interesting—everyday life transformed into a thriller, even if you're the victim of the crime—that we're somehow meant to forgive the world's burglars?

Burglary loses any sense of architectural glamour when you call it home invasion or when you witness the violence of a smash and grab. Both the cops and the robbers I spoke to warned me about this; but still, it was all too easy to be seduced by mystic visions of slipping into buildings in ways no architect had ever imagined.

The burglars who hit my in-laws' house thankfully did so when no one was home. They came in through the sliding glass doors at the back of the house—and the embarrassing thing about crime prevention is how predictable it all should have been in the first place, how you should have trusted your gut and made those changes, added those extra locks years ago, not because locks are unpickable but because they might have slowed the burglars down just enough to make them look elsewhere. My in-laws have an underlit backyard that is well fenced and heavily vegetated; it offers perfect cover to a group of burglars. Yet the house is also on a cul-de-sac (usually a deterrent), it backs up onto a frequently traveled road (another deterrent), and it is not located on anything like a grid, but deep in the winding streets of suburban England.

All of that should have canceled out the high hedges and the sliding glass doors. And yet.

Absurdly, because the kids were exactly that—kids—they didn't drive there. It's England, after all, and commuter trains run right to the heart of this neighborhood from any point in London. The train station is also just a short walk from my in-laws' house. I have walked it many times. This was finally it, I ironically realized: the perfect getaway. Not some jacked-up act of urban-scale hacking or a subterranean expedition leading halfway across Greater London: they just got on the train and went home again.

Because of their age, these burglars were also small. Some fourteen-year-olds are strong, of course, but not many want to carry, say, a plasma television or a large piece of framed art for several minutes through the center of town on their way to the nearest train station. Then to get on board the train, holding a bunch of unboxed appliances or a set of silverware, sweating, acting nervous, having to explain to anyone who asks where they got it all from. It might be a short ride back to London, but then you have to get off the train and start walking all over again—or hop on a bus, perhaps hike down a set of stairs or escalators to get on the tube, and it's all too much to handle. It's Kafka's paradox all over again, but replayed with idiot teenagers incapable of figuring out how to bring their stolen goods home.

This means that nothing of real value was stolen from my in-laws—good news—just some random euros unspent from an earlier trip to the Continent and whatever else would fit into a backpack or pocket. But the angering pointlessness of it all doesn't go away: the feeling that these kids—or others—will someday come back, the haunting unease that it might now be come one, come all for the region's burglars. Your house is now a target, once and forever. Because of their age, you could not have done much about it even if you had caught them red-handed inside the house, perhaps just inflicted a few weekends' worth of community service while they laughed and wondered about which house they might hit next.

Burglars, then, far from being interdimensional John McClanes of the built environment sliding through the many unseen topologies of Nakatomi space, are more like human mosquitoes: irritating, seemingly pointless, and unending in number. If only they really were the heroic explorers that this book seems so badly to want them to be. If only they really were Dr. Livingstones of the architectural world, hacking new paths through the dark continent of walls we've watched helplessly accumulate around us.

When Sky Thief Comes

I was not, however, alone in my delusions. Burglars have played a role as trickster figures in the public imagination for millennia, always finding unexpected ways into locked spaces or devilish new uses for objects in our midst. Visions of the ultimate burglar—an omnipotent, nearly supernatural bandit who can break into any building, pick any lock, slip through any barrier using ingenious tools indistinguishable from magic—ultimately serve as a kind of shared global folklore. Pop culture and urban myths around the world are already filled with such characters, as the sheer quantity of films referenced in this book makes clear.

The thirteenth-century German poem "Meier Helmbrecht," for example, is a kind of *Ronin* tale from Old Europe in which corrupt knights form a thieves' brigade—a medieval burglary crew—and amass their ill-gotten gains by conducting raids on foreign homes throughout the countryside. In the poem, we meet a man called Wolfsrüssel, a proto-superhero of Bogotá rakes:

> *Wolfsrüssel, he's a man of skill*
> *Without a key he bursts at will*
> *The neatest-fastened iron box.*
> *Within one year I've seen the locks*
> *Of safes, at least a hundred such,*
> *Spring wide ajar without a touch*
> *At his approach! I can't say how.*

Stranger still, consider the pervasive medieval fear that witches armed with severed hands stolen from corpses— surely the eeriest burglary tool in this book—might try to break into your family's home. As scholar Richard Kieckhefer points out in his history of magic in the Middle Ages, "using the hand of a dead person to break into a house" was seen as a talismanic way of warding off arrest or capture. Kieckhefer points out that entire spells, ceremonies, and ritual incantations were developed specifically for burglars to perform before approaching a house and breaking its close.

For example, the eleventh-century *Book of Stones*, written by Bishop Marbode of Rennes, advises how to use magnetized rocks and hot coals almost as a remote-control device for convincing people to leave their houses. Expose the coals to magnets in just the right way, and your targeted residents will simply abandon their homes in short order; you can walk right in and ransack the place. That Kieckhefer's examples are sometimes a thousand years old—and that, even at the time, Bishop Marbode had suggested he was compiling much older folk traditions— speaks volumes about the enduring presence of burglary in Western society.

Even Kafka, we could say, bucking generations of literary interpretation, was really an author of heist novels. Two of his most famous pieces of writing—"Before the Law," a short parable originally published as a chapter in *The Trial*, and the entirety of his novel *The Castle*—are focused on the specific challenge of obtaining entrance to a work of architecture. They are stories about breaking and entering. Whether this is achieved through long arguments of logic with a gatekeeper in "Before the Law," or through conspiratorially gaining access to the city's main palace in *The Castle*, Kafka's characters are, in a technical sense, failed burglars.

It's as if we cannot imagine a building without also imagining someone who wants to break into it, endlessly speculating on the city's impending misuse. Every new technology comes with an accompanying threat—or perhaps promise—of new crimes. Consider the case of the airplane bandits. In an article published on September 11, 1910, the *New-York Daily Tribune* predicted that silent airplanes would be the next big thing in burglary tools. According to the article, "those who have watched the growth of aviation most closely are speculating upon the probable appearance of the aeroplane burglar, or 'sky pirate,' as he might be called." This is presented matter-of-factly, as if anyone would see an airplane and immediately speculate as to its potential for robbing the city.

The author of the piece rapidly gets carried away, describing a lengthy fictional scenario in which a New York City mansion has been robbed from above by the pilots of a silent aircraft. "The easiest access to a locked house is to be had from overhead," the author writes, "as any city dweller can see for himself if he will go up and look at the door in his own roof." Accordingly, the article suggests that a private corps of "wealthy amateurs" should be formed, volunteering en masse to serve as a new neighborhood watch on the rooftops of Manhattan's fanciest towers and hotels.

The accompanying illustration looks like something out of *Batman*, with a shadowy airplane swooping down over a Gothic roofscape; the pilot's accomplice leaps up from a skylight to grab a rope ladder dangling precariously from the plane's fuselage. The article's subtitle is "When Sky Thief Comes."

As long as we have had houses, we have had burglars on the brain.

Today, even robots are getting in on the act. If we're not scared of silent airplanes, perhaps we'll learn to fear children's toys. A security research team led by Tamara Denning and Tadayoshi Kohno at the University of Washington suggests as much. They have explored the criminal potential of wireless electronic toys being turned into semiautonomous accomplices to burglary.

In a situation as notable for its comedic potential as for its criminal ingenuity, Denning and Kohno suggest that belligerent hackers might take control of your "household robots" before ever stepping inside. Writing back in 2009, they chose toys known as the Rovio, Robosapien, and Spykee, pointing out how these specific products could be used together to obtain private information about your house—things such as room layout, the location of motion sensors, whether you locked the back door before going to bed at night, if anyone is at home in the first place, and, more important, where certain things— jewels, cash, pharmaceuticals, car keys, even a handgun— might be kept.

Interestingly, Denning and Kohno point out that certain combinations of robots could make different types of crime possible. You might own, say, a Rovio and a Robosapien, but only on that fateful day when you come home with a Spykee is their disastrous cabal realized: working together in criminal synchrony, coordinated in ways their manufacturers had never anticipated, this specific combination of robot toys can now act.

From rocks to robots, the tools of burglary surround us: they are adversaries in waiting.

George Leonidas Lazarus

Nineteenth-century superburglar George Leonidas Leslie is buried in Brooklyn's Cypress Hills Cemetery under the name George Howard, one of his many criminal pseudonyms. "George Leonidas Leslie, alias Western George, George Howard, J. G. Allison, George K. Leslie, C. G. Greene, etc., ad infinitum," retired New York City police chief George Washington Walling lists with clear exasperation in his memoir, referring to a man for whom identity was as fluid and easy to pick as a combination lock.

A "large crowd of curious spectators" was on hand to witness Leslie's funeral, *The New York Times* reported back in June 1878, yet Leslie's grave today is unmarked by any headstone. On a cloudy spring afternoon threatening rain, my wife and I drove out to visit the grave with a friend of ours, fellow true-crime enthusiast Jimmy Stamp. Stamp studied architecture at Yale and has worked for firms on both coasts. He and I had talked so many times about true-crime burglary stories, not to mention our mutual love of heist films, that I thought he might get a kick out of seeing where one of the most notorious architectural criminals of American history had been interred.

The grave was not easy to find. We were given a photocopied map at the cemetery's administrative office, as well as a series of ever more specific coordinates—section, division, block, grave number—yet even then I had to use my cell phone to call the superintendent a few times and confirm that we were in the right location. It felt like triangulating ourselves through a supernatural variation on GPS, a macabre manhunt, reading the names off nearby headstones and radioing in for confirmation that Leslie's grave was nearby. It probably took us half an hour to find the grave, and we were probably there for another forty-five minutes, talking about Leslie's life and trading several stories from the strange-but-true world of modern burglary.

Then, perhaps because the afternoon was so relentlessly gray, the temperature so unseasonably chilly, our subject shifted closer to home: What were we doing there? Why had three busy New Yorkers, with plenty of other commitments on their plates, not to mention the plethora of more conventional attractions offered by the city, taken almost an entire afternoon to visit the grave of a dead criminal who made his living stealing things from others?

For Stamp, burglary represented far more than a quest for money, revenge, or newfound wealth. From the instant an architect shapes a space, Stamp argued, people feel compelled to second-guess it, to look for something the architect might have missed or to be the first person to notice a key detail everyone else has overlooked. Heists obsess people because of what they reveal about architecture's peculiar power: the design of new ways of moving through the world. Every heist is thus just a counterdesign—a response to the original architect—and something of a transformative moment in a burglar's relationship to the built environment. It is the moment at which the burglar has gone from a passive consumer of architecture to an active participant in the world's design.

That we constantly line up to see new films about burglary—or that we buy so many crime novels featuring ingenious ways to break into bank vaults and buildings—suggests that something is fundamentally lacking in our own relationship to the city, and that there is something universally compelling about the abstract idea of breaking and entering. Indeed, even as I finish writing this book, a long slew of new heist blockbusters is set to hit the big screen, implying a nearly inexhaustible public interest in seeing people subvert security systems or sneak into locked buildings in unexpected ways. This is precisely where "burglary" becomes a myth, a symbol, a metaphor: it stands in for all the things people *really* want to do with the built environment, what they really want to do to sidestep the obstacles of their lives.

Burglary reveals that every building, all along, has actually been a puzzle, Stamp said, a kind of intellectual game that surrounds us at all times and that any one of us can play—in fact, that each of us *does* play, even if that means just sneaking into a girlfriend's bedroom for a late-night kiss or tiptoeing down the hall to use the bathroom without waking up the rest of the family. In both cases, that means using a building as a burglar would: operating through stealth and silence while sticking to the shadows and blind spots.

For my wife, the appeal was almost more folkloristic:

people are always dreaming about discovering a hidden corridor behind a sliding bookcase, she pointed out, or stumbling onto a previously unknown second bedroom lying in wait behind old clothes in the back of the closet. People are fascinated by secret passages, she said; burglary, in a sense, just makes that fantasy real. Burglary's strange conceptual promise is precisely that the world is riddled with shortcuts and secret passages—we just have to find them. It's a crime, but it also symbolizes that there are ways of navigating the world that we ourselves have yet to discover.

As we stood there at Leslie's grave, New York City's subways, streets, and skyscrapers just over the horizon of a small hill, it became clear that the very idea of the burglar—this mysterious, trespassing figure able to misuse buildings and bend whole cities to his or her will—is the unavoidable flip side of any architectural creation. Burglary, in its very essence, is a crime that cuts down through the outer layers of the world to reveal the invisible grain of things, how cities really work and buildings are meant to function, from quiet side streets to emergency fire stairs and elevator shafts. Burglars are the stowaways of the metropolis, hidden deliberately in the shadows, haunting us like poltergeists, malevolent spirits conjured into existence by the magic of four walls, even if only to reveal those walls' inherent fragility. For every building designed, a theoretical burglar is somewhere scheming to break into it, undermining architecture's implicit sense of security.

We snapped a few more pictures at Leslie's grave before leaving the cemetery behind and heading back into the streets of Brooklyn. It was not hard to wonder when anyone had last come to see Leslie's grave. After all, there had been no evidence of previous visitors. I'd only half-jokingly been expecting to find a set of lockpicks there—or an old skeleton key tucked into the grass as a form of tribute—but there was nothing. Just a twisted, old tree, some heavily worn headstones for people other than Leslie, and the leaden-gray skies that made late spring seem more like the first week of autumn.

In the very definition of what makes a building, in the shadows of our streets, in dark cars roaming our neighborhoods—perhaps even looking down at you now through an air vent, listening to your family's dinner conversation, counting down the hours till you put away the dishes, turn off the lights, and go to sleep—these secret agents of the built environment lie waiting. Burglars are as much a part of architecture as the buildings they hope to break into.

References and Citations

Parts of chapter 2 previously appeared in *Cabinet* magazine; parts of chapter 3 previously appeared in *Icon* magazine; parts of chapters 3 and 6, originally written for the book, previously appeared in a different form on *Gizmodo*; parts of chapter 4 previously appeared on *newyorker.com*; and various parts of this book previously appeared in a different form on my own blog, *BLDGBLOG* (bldgblog.com). Thanks to Sina Najafi at *Cabinet* and to novelist Will Wiles (formerly my editor at *Icon*) for their input.

1: Space Invaders

There is much to read on the life of George Leonidas Leslie. A good place to start is Herbert Asbury's still-fascinating book *The Gangs of New York: An Informal History of the Underworld* (New York: Garden

City Publishing, 1927), where Leslie is introduced as "The King of the Bank Robbers," or George Washington Walling's memoir, *Recollections of a New York Chief of Police* (New York: Caxton Book Concern, 1887). Leslie's life was also the focus of a useful biography by J. North Conway called *King of Heists: The Sensational Bank Robbery of 1878 That Shocked America* (Guilford, CT: Lyons Press, 2009), which describes Leslie's arrival in New York City, the criminals he associated with, and his sophisticated use of duplicate vaults and architectural surrogates for training.

For more on the life of Marm Mandelbaum, Conway's book is also a valuable resource; however, specific details in this chapter, including descriptions of Mandelbaum's fake chimney and her criminal headquarters on Rivington Street in Manhattan, come from "The Life and Crimes of 'Old Mother' Mandelbaum" by Karen Abbott (*Smithsonian .com*, September 6, 2011), and "A Queen Among Thieves: Mother Mandelbaum's Vast Business" (*New York Times*, July 24, 1884).

A great architectural introduction to the Gilded Age in New York City and elsewhere—albeit focusing primarily on the decades after Leslie's death—is *Gilded Mansions: Grand Architecture and High Society* (New York: W. W. Norton, 2008) by Wayne Craven.

Bruce Schneier discusses his idea of the "defector" in *Liars and Outliers: Enabling the Trust That Society Needs to Thrive* (Indianapolis: John Wiley & Sons, 2012).

Tales of burglaries and heists gone wrong are almost too numerous to believe. The specific cases mentioned in this chapter come from the following news stories: "Burglar May Have Used Pet Doors to Break In" (Tony Rizzo, *Kansas City Star*, February 2013); "Mystery at the Monastery Ends as CCTV Reveals 'Chamber of Secrets' Daring Thief" (Paul Webster, *Guardian*, June 2003); "Man Writes Novel Chapter in Annals of Library Thefts" (Laurie Becklund, *Los Angeles Times*, April 1991); "The Doheny Library Book Thief" (USC Digital Folklore Archives, April 2014); "Burglar Squeezes Through Drop-Off Box at Moultrie Business" (Ashton Pellom, WALB ABC News 10, February 2013); "Burglar Breaks Through Wall to Rob Store Again" (Jeff Smith, NBCDFW, March 2013); "Burglar Punches Holes in Apartments to Steal TVs, Electronics" (WBALTV, April 2013); "'Drywall Burglar' Set to Appear in Court" (Jessica Anderson, *Baltimore Sun*, July 2013); "Drawn to Food and Liquor, Burglar

Gains a Stiff Term" (Wendy Ruderman, *New York Times*, September 2012); "Serial Burglar Who Tunneled Through Walls Sentenced to at Least 28 Years in Prison" (New York County District Attorney's Office, September 2012); "The People of the State of New York Against Shawn McAleese" (SCI No. 3586/2012); "Alleged Burglar Found Hiding Inside Building Wall" (Shellie Nelson, WQAD8 Quad Cities, January 2013); "Burglar Caught After Getting Stuck in JCPenney Wall" (Tiffany Choquette, ABC6 Providence, July 2013); "Police: Would-Be RI Thief Found Trapped in Wall" (Associated Press, July 2013); "'Moss Man' Attempts Rock Museum Break-In" (CBS News, October 2010); "Naked Burglar Gets Stuck in Milwaukee Vet Clinic Air Vent" (Ashley Luthern, *Milwaukee Journal Sentinel*, September 2013); "FBI: Bank Robbery Charges Against Man Pulled from Air Duct in Oak Lawn" (Deanese Williams-Harris, *Chicago Tribune*, June 2012); "Burglar's Toe Gives Hiding Spot Away" (Maryanne Twentyman, *Waikato Times*, December 2013); and "Thief Caught After Leaving Ear Print at 80 Robberies" (AFP, May 2013).

The incredible story of Operation Stagehand comes from Ronald Kessler's book *The Secrets of the FBI* (New York: Broadway Paperbacks, 2011). Another useful resource on this topic is the FBI's own collection of "surreptitious entry" files, available online as a thirty-part sequence of PDFs called "Surreptitious Entries (Black Bag Jobs)." The FBI's definition of burglary also comes from the FBI website (fbi.gov).

Retired burglar Jack Dakswin—a pseudonym—told me his story over Skype and, to a certain extent, e-mail.

Witold Rybczynski's question "Where is the front door?" comes from his book *How Architecture Works: A Humanist's Toolkit* (New York: Farrar, Straus and Giroux, 2013).

2: Crime Is Just Another Way to Use the City

The specific flights with the LAPD Air Support Division described in this chapter took place in July 2013 and January 2014; quotations or references to conversations with LAPD pilots and tactical flight officers come from my interviews. The NASA/Jet Propulsion Laboratory study of aerial policing in Los Angeles is called "Effectiveness Analysis of Helicopter Patrols," published in July 1970. The full text can be found on archive.org.

Mike Davis's *City of Quartz: Excavating the Future in Los Angeles* (London: Verso Books, 1990) remains a provocative introduction to L.A.

The anthropological study of CCTV control rooms mentioned in this chapter is called "Behind the Screens: Examining Constructions of Deviance and Informal Practices Among CCTV Control Room Operators in the UK" by Gavin J. D. Smith (*Surveillance & Society* 2, no. 2/3 [2004]).

Grégoire Chamayou's essay "'Every Move Will Be Recorded': A Machinic Police Utopia in the Eighteenth Century" was published online by the Max Planck Institute for the History of Science and is available on the institute's website (mpiwg-berlin.mpg.de).

More information about "stepped frequency continuous wave" radar technology can be found at the website of L-3 CyTerra (cyterracorp.com). The court case involving the man in Wichita, Kansas, was covered extensively in the media; in particular, see "New Police Radars Can 'See' Inside Homes" (Brad Heath, *USA Today*, January 2015) and "Police Home Radar a Possible Amendment Violation" (editorial, *USA Today*, January 2015). *Kyllo v. United States* was argued before the U.S. Supreme Court on February 20, 2001, and decided June 11, 2001.

Tad Friend's article about high-speed car chases in Los Angeles is called "The Pursuit of Happiness" (*New Yorker*, January 23, 2006). The interview with *LA Creek Freak* blogger Jessica Hall was conducted by Judith Lewis ("The Lost Streams of Los Angeles," *LA Weekly*, November 2006).

FBI special agent Brenda Cotton spoke to me as part of a symposium I organized while director of Columbia University's Studio-X NYC, an off-campus event space in Manhattan; the specific event was part of a film festival called "Breaking Out & Breaking In" (April 2012). Cotton appears briefly in the memoir of retired special agent William J. Rehder, written with Gordon Dillow, called *Where the Money Is: True Tales from the Bank Robbery Capital of the World* (New York: W. W. Norton, 2003). Chapter 4, "The Hole in the Ground Gang," was particularly useful for this book, but I recommend the entire book. The June 1986 heist by the Hole in the Ground Gang was not widely covered in the media at the time. However, see "Burglars Dig Tunnel into L.A. Bank, Take $91,000" (Ashley Dunn, *Los Angeles*

Times, August 1987) and "Tunnels to Lucre: Cases of Bank Thefts by 'Sophisticated' Burrowing May Be Linked" (David Freed, *Los Angeles Times*, August 1987); more recently, see "Boring Thieves Had Tunnel Visions" (Steve Harvey, *Los Angeles Times*, December 2009). The lunch with Rehder described in this chapter took place at the Spitfire Grill in Santa Monica, in June 2012. The website for Rehder's new consulting firm run with Douglas Sims, Security Management Resource Group, can be found at bankrobberysecuritysolutions.com.

The story of Albert Spaggiari has been told and retold dozens of times. Although he has since disowned it, novelist Ken Follett's nonfiction book *Under the Streets of Nice: The Bank Heist of the Century*—which is essentially just Follett's revision of a book originally written by René Louis Maurice—is nonetheless interesting. See also "Albert Spaggiari, 57, Mastermind of Notorious Riviera Bank Heist" (Constance L. Hays, *New York Times*, June 1989). In August 2010, a member of Spaggiari's gang, Jacques Cassandri, published a book claiming that he, not Spaggiari, had planned the heist; Cassandri's book, *La vérité sur le casse de Nice* (The truth about the Nice heist) was published in French under the pseudonym Amigo. Sensational headlines notwithstanding, Cassandri's role as the true mastermind has not been confirmed. See "Police Arrest Mastermind of 1976 French *Ocean's Eleven* Bank Heist" (Henry Samuel, *Telegraph*, January 2011). As this book went to press, Cassandri was out on bail.

"Crumbly Berlin sand" refers to Berlin's having seen more than its share of bank tunnel jobs over the decades; a local criminal is even dubbed the Tunnelgangster by German media. See "Berlin Bank Robbers Dug 30-Metre Tunnel into Safe" (Associated Press, January 2013) and "Mystery Bank Heist Is Flashback to Berlin's Murky Underworld" (Joseph de Weck, *Bloomberg Business*, January 2013). Although I refer to this story in the getaway chapter, it is relevant to mention it here: "Berlin Bank Robbers Escape . . . Right Under Cops' Noses" (Rick Atkinson, *Washington Post*, June 1995).

The anecdote about New Songdo City came from an interview with a New York City–based IT consultant who requested anonymity due to the nature of his remarks.

Richard Stark's novel *The Score* (reissued in 2009 by the University of Chicago Press) remains a great read, with a brilliant premise, and should be adapted for the screen. *Breakout* (New York: Mysterious

Press, 2002) is another worthwhile Stark novel, featuring the elaborate heist of a converted armory. Note that "Richard Stark" was a pen name for novelist Donald E. Westlake, whose books *The Hot Rock* (New York: Grand Central Publishing, 1970) and *Thieves' Dozen* (New York: Mysterious Press, 2004) are particularly enjoyable.

3: Your Building Is the Target

Bill Mason's memoir, *Confessions of a Master Jewel Thief* (New York: Villard, 2003), written with Lee Gruenfeld, is a thoroughly enjoyable introduction to the life of a cat burglar. Mason's appearance on CNN was in September 2003; a transcript of the show is available online.

My conversation with Jack Dakswin—a pseudonym—took place over Skype, with some preliminary details shared over e-mail. The book I refer to here, *Local Code: The Constitution of a City at 42 Degrees North Latitude* by architect Michael Sorkin, was published by Princeton Architectural Press in 1996 and appears to be out of print. "Where Have All the Burglars Gone?" was published by *The Economist* in July 2013.

The long section in the middle of this chapter about burglary law, history, and theory relies upon a handful of texts. "'Breaking the Plane' in Burglary Cases" by Nate Nieman appeared on the *Northern Law Blog* in March 2011; there, Nieman specifically discusses an Illinois Supreme Court case called *State v. Beauchamp*. The Illinois State Bar Association also discusses this case in a weekly roundup on their blog; see "Quick Takes from Thursday, Feb. 3, Illinois Supreme Court Opinions" (Chris Bonjean, *Illinois State Bar Association*, February 2011). "Statutory Burglary—the Magic of Four Walls and a Roof" by Minturn T. Wright III was published in the *University of Pennsylvania Law Review* 100, no. 3 (December 1951). The state burglary laws of Nebraska, New York, and California, referenced in this chapter, can all be found online. The Brooklyn Bridge white-flag stunt was well documented by *The New York Times*: see "A Brooklyn Bridge Mystery: Who Raised the White Flags?" (Vivian Yee, *New York Times*, July 2014), "German Artists Say They Put White Flags on Brooklyn Bridge" (Michael Kimmelman, *New York Times*, August 2014), and "Charges Weighed in Flag Swap After 2 Say They Did It" (Joseph Goldstein, *New York Times*, August 2014). The quotation "there is a possibility you could charge burglary" was found in this latter article.

"The Burglar in the Suitcase" by Kristyn K. Wilson and Chris Achong appeared in *Mathematics Teacher* 106, no. 4 (November 2012).

The section of this chapter exploring what burglars look for in the houses they target relies on a core group of books and interviews. *Burglary* by R. I. Mawby (Portland, OR: Willan Publishing, 2001), *Breaking and Entering: Burglars on Burglary* by Paul Cromwell and James N. Olson (Belmont, CA: Wadsworth/Thomson Learning, 2004), and *Burglars on the Job: Streetlife and Residential Break-ins* by Richard T. Wright and Scott Decker (Boston: Northeastern University Press, 1994) were especially useful. A research paper called "Defensible Space: Deterring Crime and Building Community" by Henry G. Cisneros (Washington, DC: U.S. Department of Housing and Urban Development, 1995), as well as *Defensible Space: Crime Prevention Through Urban Design* by Oscar Newman (New York: Collier Books, 1972), were also good reference points. Mark Saunders, crime prevention design adviser with the Surrey Police (U.K.), helped walk me through many of these concepts (author interview, July 2013). Multiple conversations with LAPD detective third grade Chris Casey, recorded from 2013 to 2015, were both fascinating and helpful; I only wish I'd had more space for his stories in this book.

In the U.K., Detective Chief Inspector Dave Stopford of the South Yorkshire Police spoke with me at length about Yorkshire's capture-house program. For media coverage of capture houses, see "'Capture Houses' Trap Burglars" (*Yorkshire Evening Post*, December 2007), "Police 'Capture Houses' Setting CCTV Traps for Leeds Burglars" (*Yorkshire Evening Post*, April 2008), "Capture Houses" (BBC, March 2008), "Police Set Up High-Tech 'Capture House' Filled with Valuables to Catch Teenage Burglars" (Harriet Arkell, *Daily Mail*, March 2013), and "Police Set Up Burglar Traps Disguised as Houses in Dudley" (*Birmingham Mail*, June 2012), to name but a few.

The Chinese burglary study mentioned in this chapter is called "Assessing Temporal and Weather Influences on Property Crime in Beijing, China" by Chen Peng, Shu Xueming, Yuan Hongyong, and Li Dengsheng, published in *Crime, Law and Social Change* 55, no. 1 (February 2011).

Harry Houdini's book *The Right Way to Do Wrong*, originally published in 1906, was reissued by Brooklyn's Melville House in 2012.

For more on PleaseRobMe, see "Please Rob Me: A Foursquare/Twitter Crime-Spree in the Making" (Martin Bryant, *Next Web*, February 2010). PleaseRobMe is still online at pleaserobme.com.

The use of social media by burglars for choosing their targets will only increase. For now, see "Sheriff: Alleged Burglar Admits to Using Facebook to Pick Her Targets" (Kara Mattingly, 14News, September 2013), "Hunterdon County 'Facebook Burglar' Who Paddled Kayak to Canada Found Guilty of Jumping Bail" (Mike Deak, *Daily Record*, March 2014), "Overland Park Burglary Victim Thinks Thieves Used GPS" (Tony Rizzo and Robert A. Cronkleton, *Kansas City Star*, April 2013), and "Dating App Used to Snare Heist Victims" (Kara Coleman, *Daily Herald*, August 2014). To the best of my knowledge, the case described by Kara Coleman was still pending as this book went to press.

Other stories in this chapter include "Bold Burglar Takes a Shower, Steals a Quad" (Z107.7 News, February 2014), "Police: Easton Intruder Helps Self to Fried Chicken and Beer" (Pamela Lehman, *Morning Call*, January 2010), "Wireless Meters Tell Snoopers When You Are Not Home" (Jim Giles, *New Scientist*, October 2012), my own article for *New Scientist*, "The Ghosts That Keep Your House Safe" (February 2015), "The Emptons: Estates Forsaken as Hamptonites Flee for European Shores" (Richard Kirshenbaum, *Observer*, July 2013), and "Bradbury—a Quiet, Private Haven for the Horsey Set" (Sue Avery, *Los Angeles Times*, March 1988).

I spoke with Jerry Toner in August 2013 on the advice of a mutual colleague, Professor Mary Beard at the University of Cambridge.

4: Tools of the Trade

The Brooklyn Bridge "love picking" event took place on Saturday, September 7, 2013. TOOOL's list of state lock-picking laws can be found on their website, toool.us. New York City Administrative Code 20-301 is available online; it is part of New York City Administrative Code, Title 20: Consumer Affairs, Chapter 2: Licenses, Subchapter 15: Locksmiths.

The John M. Mossman Lock Collection can be found online at generalsociety.org and, in the real world, at 20 West Forty-Fourth Street in Manhattan. *The Lure of the Lock* by Albert A. Hopkins was first published in 1928 and is available for purchase at the General Society. Schuyler Towne maintains a website at schuylertowne.com, where he describes himself as a "security anthropologist." On June 4, 2015, @DavidJBianco tweeted that Towne "is a machine for turning locks into anthropology." Towne and I visited the Mossman Lock Collection in September 2013.

Pumping Station: One (PS:One) is located at 3519 N. Elston Avenue in Chicago, Illinois. The scene described here took place on June 5, 2013. John "Jack" Benigno is a sergeant with the Chicago Police Department, but spoke to me in an unofficial capacity, as a civilian locksport enthusiast. We spoke in person at the event at PS:One, but much more extensively over Skype and e-mail. Michel Foucault's *Discipline and Punish: The Birth of the Prison* (New York: Vintage Books, 1995, translated by Alan Sheridan) has become a classic in the field of security studies.

The story of the Antwerp diamond heist is told in the book *Flawless: Inside the Largest Diamond Heist in History* by Scott Andrew Selby and Greg Campbell (New York: Sterling, 2010). A version of the Antwerp diamond heist was more famously published in *Wired* under the title "The Untold Story of the World's Biggest Diamond Heist" (Joshua Davis, April 2009). It's worth noting, however, that Selby and Campbell convincingly explain that the narrative presented by the *Wired* story is incorrect at best—or worse, that *Wired* was duped by Antwerp diamond thief Leonardo Notarbartolo.

Phil Christopher's story is told in *Superthief: A Master Burglar, the Mafia, and the Biggest Bank Heist in U.S. History* by Rick Porrello (Novelty, OH: Next Hat Press, 2006). Although I do not refer to it in this book, *The Art of the Heist: Confessions of a Master Thief* by Myles J. Connor Jr. with Jenny Siler (New York: Harper, 2009) is also an interesting and relevant read.

The "keys to the city" described in this chapter are documented in "Key Set Available for $150 on eBay Provides an All-Access Pass to NYC" (Brad Hamilton, *New York Post*, September 2012) and "Lock Away These NYC Keys!" (Susan Edelman, *New York Post*, October 2012). Schuyler Towne discussed how to duplicate keys using high-resolution photographs in a Quora post in November 2013 called "If You Took a Picture of a Car or House Key, Could You Use That Picture to Get a Copy Made?" Since that time, companies such as KeyMe ("a secure and convenient way to copy, share and personalize keys") and Keys Duplicated ("Copy keys online using your phone") have been launched, turning a similar method into a business model.

For more on Marc Weber Tobias, see "The Ultimate Lock Picker Hacks Pentagon, Beats Corporate Security for Fun and Profit" (Charles Graeber, *Wired*, May 2009), as well as Tobias's own two-volume set, *Locks, Safes, and Security: An International Police Reference*, 2nd ed. (Springfield, IL: Charles C. Thomas Publisher, 2000).

I met ATF special agent Kenneth Crotty as part of a workshop organized by the Writers Guild of America East in May 2014. Tactical Energetic Entry Systems can be found online (energeticentry .com), as well as breaching-tool firms such as Broco-Rankin (broco -rankin.com/tactical) and Gerber Tactical (gerbergear.com/tactical). Many retail stores sell these products, as well, including Atlantic Tactical (atlantictactical.com).

As this book goes to press, Karl Alizade is considering a move to Nevada with his firm, CitySafe; for now, CitySafe can be visited online (citysafe.com and modulxstrongroom.com), where many videos and diagrams are available for view. U.S. Patent No. 6,848,372 B2 (Modular Security Safe with Offset Security Bolt Box Having Expandable Characteristics and Method of Manufacturing Same), filed by Alizade, is also worth viewing. Alizade was interviewed in *The New York Times* for an article called "Secret Hideouts for the Rich and Scared; in Homes and Apartments, Safe Rooms Can Withstand Small Rockets" (Hope Reeves, April 2002). See also "New Ways to Fight Crime" (Miles Z. Epstein, *JCK*, June 1999) and "Barbarians at the Gate" (Patricia Leigh Brown, *Chicago Tribune*, October 1997). I also covered Alizade's work in the September 2015 issue of *Dwell* magazine (dwell.com). All quotations from Alizade come from various conversations from 2012 to 2015.

For more on artist Gordon Matta-Clark, see *Gordon Matta-Clark* by Corinne Diserens (London: Phaidon, 2006).

5: Inside Job

My telling of the story of Jeffery Manchester, aka Roofman, is based on an interview in December 2014 with his arresting officer, Sergeant Katherine Scheimreif of the Charlotte-Mecklenburg Police Department. Additional references came from the following articles: "'Roofman' Gets the Blame for 38 Robberies in 9 States" (John M. Glionna, *Los Angeles Times*, April 2000), "Escaped Convict Lived Inside a Wall" (Shawn Flynn, News 14 Carolina, January 2005), "Escapee Attended Church, Gave Toys" (Associated Press, January 2005), and "Escaped Robber Returns to Annals of Weird Crime / Cops Say 'Roofman' Lived Large in Store" (Demian Bulwa and Charles Burress, *San Francisco Chronicle*, January 2005). Thanks to Anthony Carfello for first introducing me to Roofman's story.

Bernard Tschumi and I spoke in August 2013. *The Manhattan Transcripts* and many other important early texts can be found in Tschumi's monograph *Architecture Concepts: Red Is Not a Color* (New York: Rizzoli, 2012).

The story of the Kunsthal heist was widely covered in the global media at the time. For more on the alleged vulnerabilities presented by the museum's architectural design, see "OMA's Gallery Design Blamed for Rotterdam Art Heist" (*Dezeen*, October 2012) and "The Art of Stealing: The Tragic Fate of the Masterpieces Stolen from Rotterdam" (Lex Boon, NRC.nl). The Museum Security Network can be found online at museum-security.org.

Alphaville by Michael Codella with Bruce Bennett (New York: Thomas Dunne Books, 2010) is an interesting introduction to the genre of the urban police memoir. Although I do not refer to them in this book, I also read and recommend *Blue Blood* by Edward Conlon (New York: Riverhead Books, 2004), the excellent *Homicide Special: A Year with the L.A.P.D.'s Elite Detective Unit* by Miles Corwin (New York: Owl Books, 2003), and *Vice: One Cop's Story of Patrolling America's Most Dangerous City* by Sergeant John R. Baker with Stephen J. Rivele (New York: St. Martin's Griffin, 2011).

Jason England spoke to me from his home in Las Vegas in June and July of 2013. My conversation with Darrell Clifton from Circus Circus in Reno took place in July 2013. Jes Stewart from the Nevada Museum of Art spoke to me in May 2013 by phone, then gave me a security tour of the museum in June 2013. For more on trifoliate orange, see "Marine Corps Using Living Fence to Boost Security" (Associated Press, September 1988) and "No-Tech Terrorist Control: 'Rambo Bush' Defends Its Turf with Foliage, Vicious Thorns" (Mike Klingaman, *Milwaukee Journal*, February 1989).

I spoke with Janice Kerbel in September 2013. Thank you to Tim Maly for lending me his copy of *15 Lombard St.* (London: Book Works, 1998) while I worked on this book.

Randy Smith spoke to me in August 2013 from his home in Texas. Andy Schatz spoke to me in June 2013 from his home in San Diego.

The phrase *voluntary prisoners of architecture* refers to a project called *Exodus, or the Voluntary Prisoners of Architecture* by Rem Koolhaas, Elia Zenghelis, Madelon Vriesendorp, and Zoe Zenghelis (1972). It is in the permanent collection of the Museum of Modern Art.

"Lethal Theory" by Eyal Weizman was originally published in *Log* 7 (Winter/Spring 2006) and can be found online. The paper was expanded and partially rewritten for his later book *Hollow Land: Israel's Architecture of Occupation* (London: Verso Books, 2007).

The story of my wife's great-aunt, archaeologist Joan Harding, and the practice of deliberately omitting certain key architectural details from publicly available British estate floor plans, comes from conversations with my in-laws.

6: A Crime Is Nothing If You Can't Get Away

Franz Kafka's "A Message from the Emperor" was originally published in 1919; a new translation by Mark Harman was published in July 2011 by *The New York Review of Books* and is available online.

For more about the teenager in Łodz, Poland, see "Hacking Polish Trams" (Bruce Schneier, *Schneier on Security*, January 2008) and "Polish Teen Derails Tram After Hacking Train Network" (John Leyden, *Register*, January 2008). Cesar Cerrudo's traffic-hacking work is documented in "Hacking U.S. (and UK, Australia, France, etc.) Traffic Control Systems" (Cesar Cerrudo, IOActive, April 2014) and "Traffic Light Hackers Could Cause Jams Across the U.S." (Hal Hodson, *New Scientist*, August 2014). The example of faking gridlock on

Waze was first reported in "Waze Under Attack: Israeli Students Fake Traffic Jam on Popular Map App" (Ido Efrati, *Haaretz*, March 2014). These stories also appear in Marc Goodman's excellent book, *Future Crimes* (New York: Doubleday, 2015), which I refer to here for its discussion of GPS spoofing. For more about GPS jamming and spoofing, see "Car Thieves Using GPS 'Jammers'" (Charles Arthur, *Guardian*, February 2010), "Organised Crime 'Routinely Jamming GPS'" (Matt Warman, *Telegraph*, February 2012), "The Threat of GPS Jamming: The Risk to an Information Utility" (Jeff Coffed, white paper for Exelis, February 2014), and, of course, Marc Goodman's *Future Crimes*.

Evgeny Morozov's op-ed appeared under the title "The Rise of Data and the Death of Politics" (Evgeny Morozov, *Observer*, July 2014). The "Haussmannization" of Paris has been exhaustively covered by other writers; for an explicitly architectural focus, see *Rubble: Unearthing the History of Demolition* by Jeff Byles (New York: Three Rivers Press, 2005) or even *The Kill*, a great novel by Émile Zola set during Haussmann's demolitions, originally published in serial form in 1871 (New York: Modern Library, 2005, translated by Arthur Goldhammer). In his book *The Insurgent Barricade* (Berkeley: University of California Press, 2010), historian Mark Traugott disputes the notion that Haussmann's renovations were explicitly directed at preventing street barricades, claiming that their counterrevolutionary effects simply came from pushing the working class out of central Paris. For more on the history of urban lighting programs, see A. Roger Ekirch, *At Day's Close: Night in Times Past* (New York: W. W. Norton, 2005). For more on predictive policing, see, among other articles, "Predicting Crime, L.A.P.D.-Style" (Nate Berg, *Guardian*, June 2014).

The "Lamm technique" seems to be a favorite topic of crime writers; references to it are legion. I found *Herman "Baron" Lamm, the Father of Modern Bank Robbery* by Walter Mittelstaedt (Jefferson, NC: McFarland, 2012) and *This Here's a Stick-Up: The Big Bad Book of American Bank Robbery* by Duane Swierczynski (New York: Alpha Books, 2002) particularly useful. The Lamm technique is recommended as a business management strategy in *The Talent Code* by Daniel Coyle (New York: Bantam Books, 2009).

For more on the story of Anthony Curcio, see "Out of Prison, Real-Life Thomas Crown Looks Back on Almost-Perfect Heist" (Brooke Stangeland, ABC News, June 2013), "Tip Leads to Arrest in

'Inner-Tube' Robbery" (Christine Clarridge, *Seattle Times*, November 2008), and "Former High School Star Athlete Sentenced to Prison for Armored Car Robbery" (U.S. District Attorney's Office, Western District of Washington, July 2009).

Reformed bank robber Joe Loya spoke to me from his home in the East Bay in August 2013. While in prison, Loya began writing a memoir that was subsequently published upon his release as *The Man Who Outgrew His Prison Cell: Confessions of a Bank Robber* (New York: Rayo, 2004).

The story of Los Angeles bank bandits throwing cash out of their getaway car comes from "Bank Robbery Suspects Throw Cash out the Window During Car Chase Through Downtown LA" (Anna Almendrala, *Huffington Post*, September 2012).

The phrase "a vast landscape of pursuit potential" comes from an article called "Anatomy of an L.A. Police Pursuit" (Nate Berg, *CityLab*, September 2012). Christopher Hawthorne first described his idea of the chase versus the manhunt to me in May 2013. For more on Christopher Dorner, see "The Manhunt for Christopher Dorner," a special illustrated series by the *Los Angeles Times* published in December 2013. Grégoire Chamayou, whose essay " 'Every Move Will Be Recorded': A Machinic Police Utopia in the Eighteenth Century" was referred to in chapter 2, has an interesting book on the history of the manhunt, called *Manhunts: A Philosophical History* (New York: Princeton University Press, 2012, translated by Steven Rendall).

For more on the Berlin bank-tunnel getaway, see "Berlin Bank Robbers Escape . . . Right Under Cops' Noses" (Rick Atkinson, *Washington Post*, June 1995), as well as "Swede Held for Dramatic 1995 German Bank Robbery" (*Local*, June 2008). For more on the Buenos Aires tunnel getaway, see "S. America's Big Dig: Bank Robbers Tunnel Their Way to Millions" (Monte Reel, *Washington Post*, February 2006).

"Urban Escape & Evasion" is a course offered by OnPoint Tactical; a schedule of upcoming instruction dates is available on the company's website (onpointtactical.com).

Matt Jones's essay on Jason Bourne's use of cities first appeared on his blog, *Magical Nihilism*, in December 2008 under the title "The Bourne Infrastructure."

7: Burglary Requires Architecture

Thank you to my in-laws for discussing the burglary of their home in suburban London, and for sharing with me details of the ensuing police investigation. I can only hope that the break-in was not some strange karmic payback for my writing a book called *A Burglar's Guide to the City*.

The poem "Meier Helmbrecht" has been published in a variety of translations over the years; for this book, I relied on *Peasant Life in Old German Epics: "Meier Helmbrecht" and "Der Arme Heinrich"* (New York: Columbia University Press, 1931, translated by Clair Hayden Bell).

The tactic of "using the hand of a dead person" to commit burglary comes from *Magic in the Middle Ages* by Richard Kieckhefer (Cambridge: Cambridge University Press, 1989).

Franz Kafka's parable "Before the Law" is probably best read in the context of his novel *The Trial* (New York: Schocken Books, 1998, translated by Breon Mitchell). See also *The Castle* (New York: Schocken Books, 1998, translated by Mark Harman).

No author is given for the article "When Burglars Learn to Handle the Aeroplane with Precision and Silence" (*New-York Daily Tribune*, September 1910). Its subtitle? "Our artist takes a look into the future and foresees the time when roofs must be secured as carefully as any other part of the home." In many ways, it is more accurate to describe this piece as a work of speculative crime fiction, not an article.

The security research of Tamara Denning and Tadayoshi Kohno can be found online, primarily through Denning's own website (note that Denning is now an assistant professor at the University of Utah: cs.utah.edu/~tdenning). A ninety-four-page PDF from November 2009, called "The Future of Household Robots: Ensuring the Safety and Privacy of Users," presents perhaps the most straightforward explanation of their research. For more, see "A Spotlight on Security and Privacy Risks with Future Household Robots: Attacks and Lessons" by Tamara Denning, Cynthia Matuszek, Karl Koscher, Joshua R. Smith, and Tadayoshi Kohno (Ubicomp 2009) or "Computer Security and the Modern Home" by Tamara Denning, Tadayoshi Kohno, and Henry M. Levy (*Communications of the ACM*, January 2013).

Jimmy Stamp's writings on architecture and the city can be

found online at his website (jamestamp.com) as well as on his blog (lifewithoutbuildings.net).

George Leonidas Leslie was buried in Brooklyn's Cypress Hills Cemetery under the name George Howard on June 9, 1878. *The New York Times* covered his funeral in a small column called "The Yonkers Murder" on June 10, 1878. With not inconsiderable effort, Leslie's unmarked grave can be found in Cypress Hills Cemetery, Division No. 1, Old Locust Grove Subdivision, Block 35, Grave 7534.

Acknowledgments

Like any other book, A *Burglar's Guide to the City* was not written in isolation. Crucially, it could never have been written without a core group of people whose insights and willingness to speak—often at great length—about the architecture of crime kept everything from coming apart. Those people include retired FBI special agent William J. Rehder, LAPD tactical flight officer Cole Burdette, Karl Alizade of CitySafe, Sergeant Katherine Scheimreif of the Charlotte-Mecklenburg Police Department, Jes Stewart of the Nevada Museum of Art, Darrell Clifton, Jerry Toner (and Mary Beard, for introducing us), Chief Inspector Dave Stopford of the South Yorkshire Police, "Jack Dakswin," Joe Loya, Janice Kerbel, Tamara Denning, Schuyler Towne, Eric Michaud, Deviant Ollam, Victoria Dengel, Jason England, Bernard Tschumi, Christopher Hawthorne, Andy Schatz, Randy Smith, Lana Corbi, and Tom Gaffney. Thanks again.

The Los Angeles Police Department deserves particular commendation for being uniquely accessible and open to my queries throughout my research. In particular, I am indebted to Tactical Flight Officers Cole Burdette and Mark Burdine; Detective Chris Casey, Commercial Crimes Division; Lieutenant Rob Edgar, who at the time of our meeting was head of the LAPD's Burglary Special Section; and Detectives Don Hrycyk and John Clark. Based on my experience, the LAPD exhibited an openness and approachability that other police departments in the United States would be wise to emulate.

At the FBI, retired special agent William J. Rehder was notably generous with his time, insights, and willingness to discuss so many of the old cases detailed in his book, *Where the Money Is*. Retired FBI special agent Thomas McShane and Special Agent Brenda Cotton in New York City also spared time to speak at an event I organized at Columbia University in April 2012 about the architecture of burglary, bank crime, and museum heists.

In Chicago, I owe special thanks to Sergeant Jack Benigno of the Chicago Police Department, and to Patrick Thomas of the Chicago chapter of TOOOL.

In San Francisco, I had a useful and good-humored

rooftop conversation with Robert Nagle of *The San Francisco Examiner* about crime in the Bay Area, and with Eric Michaud about the nature of lock-picking, technical innovation, and security research.

In England, I owe thanks to Chief Inspector David Stopford of the South Yorkshire Police; Mark Saunders, Surrey Police crime prevention design adviser in the Woking Borough; and my own in-laws, Steve and Valerie Twilley, whose unfortunate first-person experience with suburban burglary while I was working on the book nonetheless did not affect their encouragement for my writing it.

I also benefit from having incredibly interesting and supportive friends and colleagues. Architect and fellow true-crime enthusiast Jimmy Stamp was integral in helping develop some of the early ideas that formed this book; game designer Jim Rossignol served as an ideal matchmaker for putting me in touch with exactly the right people at the right time in the gaming world; art historian Michael Lewis from Williams College gave me a fascinating introduction to the role of fortification in early modern American domestic architecture; architect Minsuk Cho set up—and translated—a great conversation with Korean film director Choi Donghun about heists, capers, and crime that unfortunately did not make it into this book; and Christopher Hawthorne, Scott Macauley, Matt Jones, Ilona Gaynor, and Jason Grote all offered input during various phases of the book. Sean McDonald at FSG gave *Burglar's Guide* its ultimate coherence and form.

Finally, trying to impress my wife, Nicola Twilley, remains my life's central motivation; her generosity while I worked on this project, in time, support, editorial feedback, and so much more, was unparalleled. This book is for her.